The Mood of Information

The Mood of Information
A Critique of Online
Behavioural Advertising

Andrew McStay

continuum

2011

The Continuum International Publishing Group
80 Maiden Lane, Suite 704, New York, NY 10038
The Tower Building, 11 York Road, London SE1 7NX

www.continuumbooks.com

Library of Congress Cataloging-in-Publication Data
McStay, Andrew, 1975-
The mood of information: online behavioural advertising / by Andrew McStay. – 1st ed.
    p. cm.
Includes bibliographical references and index.
ISBN-13: 978-1-4411-7614-1 (hardcover: alk. paper)
ISBN-10: 1-4411-7614-4 (hardcover: alk. paper)
1. Internet advertising. 2. Consumer behavior. I. Title.

HF6146.I58M39 2011
659.14'4–dc22   2010035950

ISBN: HB: 978-1-4411-7614-1

Typeset by Newgen Imaging Systems Pvt Ltd, Chennai, India
Printed and bound in the United States of America

Contents

Chapter 1

Introduction: Setting the Scene

The business of advertising is undergoing seismic activity as it asserts its role in a twenty-first century defined by networks and digital devices. Online advertising now jostles with television as the medium of choice among advertisers and superseded print and radio some time ago. The advent of online and wider digital media has presented today's Mad Men with headaches and challenges, as well as opportunities. As highlighted in my first book, *Digital Advertising*, there is a dizzying array of means to reach and engage consumers via the internet. These include display advertising, locative targeting, geo-tagging, augmented reality, viral formats, metaverses, social media campaigns, classifieds, search, the humble sponsored link and a range of other platforms in between with trends emerging at a rate difficult for even the keenest watchers to keep up with or make sense of. This book investigates online behavioural advertising and takes up Raymond Williams' challenge in 'Advertising: The Magic System', which posits that the real business of the historian of advertising is

to trace the development from processes of specific attention and information to an institutionalized system of commercial information and persuasion; to relate this to changes in society and in the economy; and to trace changes in method in the context of changing organizations and intentions. (2005 [1980], p. 170)

What he is calling for is, in essence, the employment of political economy to study advertising. This book then has little interest in advertising texts, instead, preferring to concentrate on form over content; the manner in which advertising is circulated; the means by which users' actions are accounted for over a period of time; coupling and complexity; and factors having to do with the ways in which subjectivity is engaged by behavioural advertising systems and mined for information. To understand this palpable transformation in the reach of the market requires awareness of cognate advertising businesses, institutions, law and regulation, the social construction of privacy, techniques of handling information, profiling, technocultural antecedents of behavioural control systems and related factors accounted for here that give rise to the contemporary means of buying, selling and circulating the output of attention and the mining of behaviour.

This book then is about online behavioural advertising and the nature of the relationship it establishes with users of the internet. It seeks to better understand the changing nature of advertising and the techno-cultural, legal and political environment it operates within. Given its relatively recent emergence, many may be unfamiliar with the term 'online behavioural advertising', while remaining subject to its practices. Generally, online behavioural advertising involves tracking users' browsing activity over a period of time for the purposes of serving advertising tailored to what organizations working on behalf of advertisers assume are users' interests. It is a form of commercial solicitation that is intrinsically reliant on data both wittingly and unwittingly provided by users and is made up of two different forms: one involving the delivery of advertising based on assessment of users' web-based movements; the second involving the examination of communication and information as it passes through the gateways of internet service providers (ISPs). My argument here is that the relationship established between behavioural advertising systems and users is highly unique and marks a departure from traditional relationships between advertising and consumers. Such a personalized technique of advertising represents significant revenue for all businesses involved: these being comprised of advertisers, advertising networks, advertising agencies and online content producers and web publishers. Given that advertising remains a key determinant of online media content, culture and economy, behavioural advertising represents an important phenomenon for examination.

Although online behavioural advertising is a highly specific subject, it is one that teases out well the make-up and orientation of a digital economy defined by a tendency towards informational transparency, at least in regards to terms and conditions of use. This arises in a milieu of informational abundance where services and content are often 'free', at least in the sense that money does not change hands between the giver and receiver of information. Perhaps most conspicuous is the will-to-quantification and that although the need to define audiences has long been understood, the vigour with which they are pursued and parsed is of a substantially different order today. As such this book sits within a wider domain of contexts, technologies and techniques where in regards to mediatised experience we now see the intensification of discourses of personalization, customer relationship management, recommendation, co-production, constructivism and the pre-empting of intent. Such omnipresence has led critics to query the extent to which these systems will structure and determine our lives, mediate our identities and affect social and power relationships. This book then represents a departure from the more familiar interrogation of visual components of advertising to one based on structure, systems and relationships between people and advertising systems. Although systems that circulate data and facilitate the delivery of advertising are less discernable than visual manifestations of advertising production, the impact of online behavioural advertising is no less as profiling machines are integrated into day-to-day life. The path we are on is a constructivist one where through personal media technologies, applications and feedback we facilitate and create a tailored perspective of how we see and experience the digital environment. Such user-centricism is heterogeneous in nature and through data mining and the inferring of preferences, wishes, desires and orientations we strike relationships with advertising systems that reflect ways of being, or moods of information.

Beyond the Bubble

Some background is required to set the context from which this book departs. Online behavioural advertising developed out of web advertising that first made its appearance on webpages in 1994 when banner advertising was placed on HotWired's website[1]. Advertisers and the wider advertising industry quickly recognized the potential for measurability, accountability, quantifiable effectiveness and 'return on investment', although there rightly existed significant scepticism as to the reach and scope of online media. Along with other dot.com businesses the online advertising industry went through the inception, bubble and burst cycle so common to the technology sector. In spite of this, as Perez (2002) in discussion of technological revolutions describes, although bubbles deflate, new infrastructures are left in place and this is no different for online advertising. The overall growth of online advertising has been exponential, even considering the blip in upward trajectory that was the dot.com crash between Q1 2001 and Q1 2002 when the bubble fell in on itself. Assessed overall, the downturn in online advertising was minor and the direction of growth soon resumed. The industry subsequently grew in confidence and solidified itself as a mainstream media option for advertisers and has since become a vital source of revenue for content and media service providers. As recent changes in advertisers' media spending also shows, growth in digital and behavioural advertising reflects users' new media habits and how they interact with advertising and online marketing communications. At the time of writing, development and growth in behavioural and wider online advertising are occurring against a backdrop of enormous loss in media revenue in the traditional advertising media sector that is reeling from economic gloom and the fallout from the credit crunch as companies cut marketing budgets. The Internet Advertising Bureau (IAB, 2010) report on online advertising spending by advertisers for 2009 indicates a struggle with television for the most popular medium with advertisers, although this is heavily skewed by search-based advertising and marketing that comprises slightly over 60 per cent of money spent on online advertising (the other two dominant formats being display and classified). Undoubtedly Google makes up by far the largest portion of advertising and marketing predicated on search engines.

Use of behavioural advertising by advertisers

Behaviourally targeted advertising that utilizes longitudinal profiling techniques has been in operation since around the late 1990s. Specific statistics are unavailable but although online behavioural advertising is increasing in use, at the time of writing it is not the default option for online advertisers. For example, the president of the IAB Europe, Alain Heureux, observed that the practice is an increasingly important trend, but is cautious about over-emphasizing its current position in the online advertising landscape (Marshall, 2009a). A report commissioned by AudienceScience and conducted by Forrester finds that use of behavioural advertising in the United States has been higher than in the United Kingdom or Europe where privacy is a more significant factor. In addition, language barriers and the localization of brands in Europe cause more complex media market-by-market purchasing. Regulatory scrutiny has also played a factor with many advertisers choosing to avoid advanced targeting altogether after the negative attention received by advertising networks such as Phorm and NebuAd who utilize deep-packet inspection (DPI) techniques (Marshall, 2010). Although this book focuses on behavioural targeting that involves profiling over a period of time, there are a variety of online targeting methods including traditional approaches such as those based on demographic information such as age, gender and income. Another familiar approach is time-based targeting where advertisements may only be shown on certain days of the week or times of the day (AudienceScience, 2010). More novel are conversational, geographic, contextual as well as behavioural methods. Conversational analysis is one of the more recent developments where analysts measure the flow of conversation across different websites in order to target their advertising accordingly. BuzzLogic, for example, a social media marketing company, targets advertisements to particular sites by focusing on social activity that suits a particular advertising campaign. This is done through the tracking of comments on blogs and other social media. Such a strategy intends to capitalize on word-of-mouth referrals. Geographic targeting, using both internet and mobile/locative protocols, refers to advertising by location to deliver geo-specific and potentially augmented reality-based content. Contextual advertising works by scanning key words and delivering advertising based on the content being displayed to the user. As the IAB (2009d) describes, contextual targeting involves the positioning of advertising adjacent to related content such as editorial or written matter, user generated content, online video or in search results.

As highlighted in McStay (2011), behavioural advertising is made up of web-based and internet-based formats, although both use past behaviour to determine advertising content. These consist of first-party web-based behavioural advertising where a web publisher (or a company working on its behalf) collects users' browsing data from its own web domain and serves advertisements accordingly across a site (IAB, 2009b). Far more widespread and richer in targeting potential is third-party web-based behavioural advertising that involves an additional party in the form of advertising networks. Advertising networks are companies that connect web publishers and media owners with relevant advertisers, or agencies working on their behalf. Advertising networks' success stems from the number of web publishers they have signed up to their services. They collect and use information when an internet user visits one of a number of websites participating in that particular network. If the network is a search engine, they also will be able to utilize and include information about searches a user has made (IAB, 2009c). To put the current effectiveness of behavioural advertising into context a 2010 report from the US self-regulatory trade group, Network Advertising Initiative (NAI), found that the average cost for reaching a thousand people using behaviourally targeted advertising was 2.7 times higher than standard online formats at $4.12 per thousand impressions versus $1.98. However, behaviourally targeted advertising also obtained a much higher conversion rate at 6.8 per cent versus 2.8 for standard advertisements (Beales, 2010). Lastly, there is third-party internet-based behavioural advertising that although not currently in use in the United Kingdom (or the United States) is the most controversial as it uses internet traffic that passes through the gateway of an ISP. At the time of writing, these techniques were not fully rolled out anywhere in the world. As accounted for more fully in Chapter 2, third-party internet-based behavioural advertising is where an advertising provider teams with an ISP and via a process called DPI scans packets of data that pass through an ISP's bottleneck where traffic flows to and from the internet and marries suitable data with relevant advertising.

Unlike contextually targeted advertising where advertising refers to the content or editorial immediately adjacent, all types of behavioural advertising track user movement across publishers' sites and pages that are registered with a particular advertising network. The modus operandi of behavioural advertising is to display advertisements according to who is looking at a particular webpage, rather than according to the content of the page itself. It uses previous online user activity (having to do with pages visited, content viewed, searches, clicks and purchases) so as to generate a segment or cluster that is employed to match a user with a relevant advertisement. For example a user on obtaining a new job in a different town decides to rent a flat and reads through local estate agents' offerings. On leaving the website to browse entirely unrelated content, he or she might find that they receive not only advertisements for estate agents and flats, but property targeted by district, price bracket and the amount of bedrooms required. Similarly, we may buy an item from a given retailer and then find that as we peruse the web we are exposed to an unusually large amount of advertisements for related products. For instance, our user could buy a train ticket so to inspect a property through a rail ticket retailer's website and might be shown a travel-related advertisement when he or she later visits a local takeaway's website or logs onto their social networking account. Advertising, then, may have nothing to do with a page's content and everything to do with the person looking at the screen based on their prior behaviour. These methods of tracking users across the web so as to display more relevant advertising have created polar perspectives of surveillance and efficiency. For instance the IAB, the trade representative of the internet advertising industry (whose remit is to represent the interests of those involved with online and mobile advertising), describes online behavioural advertising as

a way of serving advertisements on the websites you visit and making them more relevant to you and your interests. Shared interests are grouped together based upon previous web browsing activity and web users are then served advertising which matches their shared interests. In this way, advertising can be made as relevant and useful as possible. (IAB, 2009a)

In contrast the World Privacy Forum (2009) is more specific, defining behavioural tracking as 'the practice of collecting and compiling a record of individual consumers' activities, interests, preferences, and/or communications over time' and behavioural targeting as 'when behavioral tracking is used as a basis to serve advertisements and/or otherwise market goods or services to a consumer based on his or her behavioral record'. Whereas the former definition frames behavioural advertising in terms of a service, the latter recognizes behavioural advertising as a means of engaging the subjectivity of computer users.

Web-based behavioural advertising

It is worth clarifying how web-based and internet-based DPI-facilitated advertising works. A web-based behavioural advertising system collects information from users' cookie-enabled web browsers (for example Mozilla's Firefox, Microsoft's Internet Explorer or Google's Chrome), including types of sites visited and pages viewed to offer more highly targeted advertising. A cookie is a small text file stored on a user's computer by a web browser and stores identifiers (IDs) that recognize each session between a browser and a server (the computer that a browser 'talks' with to receive information). To see cookies that are in operation on any given web page, type: javascript:alert(document.cookie) into the search bar of a web browser. Similarly, a look at my Google Ads preferences where I may manage my Google AdSense cookie indicates that I am interested in cycling and contains the following string of text: id=224cd73 8fe0000be|879418/745194/14680|t=1267735670|et=730|cs=6kfhnkrk. Cookies are used to monitor the activity of a user over a period of time, with some having a validity of 30 years (Benoist, 2008), although Google's cookies now expire after 2 years (unless renewed for another 2 years by visiting Google) following complaints from users and privacy advocates. They are harmless in that they contain no executable code, meaning that the cookie cannot cause a computer to carry out any tasks. Most websites identify visitors by assigning a unique identifying cookie to each and every visitor to the site thereby allowing them to be tracked throughout their web journey. The content however on most webpages does not come from one source but is assembled from a variety of sources. These include the advertisements, potentially along with other images and objects on a page. Advertisements are then served by a third party, that is, not arriving from the address of the server a user has typed into their web browser. While the advertisements are being retrieved from the third-party (the advertising network), a cookie will be set on the user's computer unless explicitly blocked so as to more effectively target advertising. The advertising net-work then makes a rules-based decision about what content to serve by clustering users into highly refined interest groups. As that cookie ID moves between sites registered with a given advertising network, a richer profile is developed as more information is gathered about a browser's interaction with advertising and enlisted sites. Notably, many sites will not work if a user's browser is set not to accept cookies. As discussed more extensively in Chapters 2 and 3, there is significant campaigning and lobbying being undertaken by industry representatives to ensure that web-based online behavioural advertising remains an opt-out system where users have to extract themselves from the system. In contrast, an opt-in system would mean that people would express an active preference for more relevant advertising derived from web profiling. Although Google represents a significant portion of the behavioural advertising market, there are a number of other key networks that work with web publishers, agencies and advertisers. In addition to search engines (additional players unsurprisingly include Yahoo and Microsoft's Bing), other behavioural advertising networks include adknowledge, AudienceScience, Burst Media, Claria, Specific Media, Tacoda, ValueClick and many more busi-nesses[2] who sell inventory (or advertising space) to advertisers and deliver advertising across a range of publishers of content online. As discussed in more depth in Chapter 4, although these companies are largely invisible, use of Ghostery[3], an add-on to the Firefox web browser, is highly illuminat-ing and allows users to see which data miners and advertising networks are gathering information on any given webpage.

Internet-based behavioural advertising - DPI

As more fully accounted for in Chapter 2, the second form of beha-vioural advertising that forms the focus of this book involves ISPs and advertising networks such as Phorm who wish to serve advertising at the gateway of internet access. This is a point through which all of a user's traffic must flow. Bearing in mind that the internet represents a network of computers and devices predicated on internet protocol (IP), and that the web is a means of sharing information over the internet, behavioural advertising that uses DPI involves the use of software and hardware installed in ISPs' networks to intercept webpage requests generated by subscribers as they peruse the internet. This is the more novel version of the two behavioural techniques, and certainly the most controversial. Although Phorm in the United Kingdom, and the now defunct NebuAd in the United States, have received attention from regulators and privacy groups alike, they represent only the visible surface of a range of companies interested in access to network infrastructure as a means of delivering advertising. It is this form of behavioural advertising that has received the most severe criticism and negative public relations since the realizable potential for advertising at ISP-level emerged. Concern revolves around the quasi-public nature and gatekeeper-type role of ISPs. For example, if telephone exchanges were monitored for the purposes of identifying consumer behaviour and serving advertising, this may be considered an abuse of the exchange–owner's position. Similarly, many campaigners against the employment of DPI for advertising have argued that internet gateways should be off-limits to those seeking audience attention and interaction

Structure of the Book

Feedback is central to behavioural advertising techniques. By definition, systems cannot operate without information about users. Conversely, the more feedback they receive, the more effectively behavioural advertising systems may operate. The aim of this book then, is to better understand the role, nature and implications of feedback relationships in online behavioural advertising. In addressing these recent developments in advertising, this book has two broad areas of investigation with Chapters 2, 3 and 4 being somewhat more practical in orientation, while Chapters 5 and 6 are more theoretical and technocultural in exposition.

The aim of Chapter 2 is to provide shape, flesh and case substance to help elucidate more speculative material in the later chapters. It takes as its case study online behavioural advertising and, in particular, the advertising network Phorm, which ignited controversy among interested consumers, privacy activists, technologists, regulatory authorities and both technology and mainstream media outlets. Against the background of Digital Britain, the re-brand of the UK's information society, this chapter offers an exposition of Phorm and the legal, political and public relations storm they generated between 2006 and 2010. As a case study, Phorm denotes particularly well the concerns regarding network neutrality and advertising in that use of behavioural techniques facilitated by DPI to monitor users' traffic at network bottlenecks portends undue influence and control over data flows across the networks. Chapter 3 explores in more depth the relationship between behavioural advertising and political economy. This involves discussion about affiliation between businesses and governments, and the extent to which principles of network neutrality should be applied to management of quasi-public networks. Further, this chapter inquires into the status of the consumer as conceptualized within neo-liberal logic and teleonomic understanding, discourses of rationality, and self-interest and user-centred responsibility. In addition to critiquing classic economic perspectives, it also draws attention to the setting of parameters for behavioural advertising, and antagonism between self-regulatory approaches and legal enforcement through law. Whereas Chapter 3 addresses wider concerns about relationships between the state, online behavioural advertising businesses and citizens, Chapter 4 examines more closely conceptualizations of privacy and the blurring of our private and public selves in a period increasingly deemed to be characterized by transparency. As information about web users becomes progressively relied upon as the fuel for the digital economy, traditional conceptions of privacy are under question. Debate over privacy is far from straightforward or one-sided. At an individual level, as Acquisti and Grossklags (2007) describe, feelings over privacy may be torn. We feel privacy as an inalienable right, yet freely trade it away for rewards and convenience so to make our digital lives run more smoothly. Moreover, we worry about encroachments that are of little consequence yet ignore or fail to see those of significant consequence. There is therefore contradiction, confusion and inconsistency in user behaviour regarding decision-making and privacy. The aim of Chapter 4 is then to offer a range of conceptualizations and understandings of privacy, particularly in relation to notions of responsibility and self-determination.

The second half of this book drills down further into some of the implications of behavioural advertising practices and how we may best theorize and understand them. This is achieved through a thorough exposition of the role of feedback and coupling. Feedback relationships in advertising are not especially novel as consumers have always interacted with advertisements and responded through a variety of behaviours and practices, for example, buying goods, finding out more about products and offering brand approval through wearing and displaying logos, in addition to reactions gathered by audience research organizations, advertisers and research conducted by advertising agencies. Advertiser/consumer feedback relations have traditionally received much less interest from critical theorists with textual analysis and accounts of consumer societies often privileged. Whereas critical studies of advertising, and the wider enterprise of Debordian (1992 [1967]) and Barthesian (1972) inspired visual culture, have conventionally focused on semiotic understandings of texts and signs (Williamson, 1978; Jhally, 1990; Odih, 2007), this is only a minor concern here. The approach presented here involves a shift from consideration of the spectacular found in mass and niche manufacturing societies to one where new communication structures facilitate greater personalization and localized experience. In relation to online and behavioural strategies a need exists to understand these nascent forms of advertising and the implications for lives mediated through the web. A post-representational understanding of commercial solicitation that examines advertising from within is required so as to better grasp structure, data relations and users' subjectivities imbricated within these relationships, particularly when the primacy and logic of visual culture is being re-organized through novel forms of feedback management.

The title of this book and that of Chapter 5 derive from Mark Poster's book, *The Mode of Information*. Partially updating Marx's (1973 [1939]) mid-nineteenth-century arguments over the mode of production that centre on the relationship between productive forces (land, resources and technology) and the relations of production (the social relations people enter into when they acquire and use the means of production), Poster (1990) traces developments in late capitalism and the shift from the mode of production to that of information. Here the subject is produced through databases and whereas language in the past was a vehicle for us to depict reality, language or information becomes the means by which we find ourselves electronically mediated and constituted.

The mode of information is thus a means of understanding constructions of the self through our data traces. This involves a poststructuralist reading of information cultures. Poster argues that

> the mode of information enacts a radical reconfiguration of language, one which constitutes subjects outside the pattern of the rational, autonomous individual. This familiar modern subject is displaced by the mode of information in favor of one that is multiplied, disseminated and decentered, continuously interpellated as an unstable identity. (1995, p. 57)

This thesis of the linguistic construction of the subject, otherwise expressed in terms of modulation and informational commodification is observable on a practical basis, particularly in regards to the creation of digital advertising subjects. Rather than critique then, this book updates, explores and opens up new avenues of theoretical pursuit. What is presented here is a requirement that we better understand *The Mood of Information*, as a means of conceiving of online behavioural advertising and the meta-discourse of the information economy it sits within. Chapter 5 is a multifaceted and extended chapter that begins with an account of techno-historical and cultural antecedents of control-based technologies and techniques in reference to bureaucracy, cybernetics and profiling to render the context for the present milieu. The need for feedback and control among advertisers and other marketing managers has a distinct lineage, in particular in the business and writings of Daniel Starch (1914) and Claude Hopkins (1998 [1923]) who hawked 'scientific advertising' as characterized by the laws of automation and feedback. More recently as advertising and marketing media continue to fold into digital, the lure of accountability, informatization and precision targeting often leaves creative concerns behind in exchange for relevance expressed through the orientation of the user, time and location. As exemplified by the logic of behavioural targeting, many advertisers are gravitating and returning to control-based advertising. Whereas Hopkins' understanding was a Newtonian one of mechanism, cause and effect, more recent advances in advertising and management of feedback relationships have taken on qualities readily articulated in biological and evolutionary terms, particularly in the case of co-productive behavioural advertising systems. Exploring conceptions and models of feedback Chapter 5 argues for an autopoietic understanding of behavioural advertising, having to do with recursive systems and the ways in which components of behavioural advertising participate in processes of production that in a loop-like fashion results in production of more of the same. Moreover, through collaboration and immanence that involves us being fully present, we are active in its construction as we negotiate, create, search and deal with information and progressively couple with behavioural advertising systems. Indeed, Poster (2006) in *Information Please* makes a passing reference to autopoiesis as accounted for by Maturana and Varela (1980) also noting an 'inextricable mixing of consciousness with information machines' (Poster, 2006, p. 114). However, whereas Poster's remit was a much wider sweep of new media technologies and critical theory, mine is an internal investigation into online behavioural advertising as a means of understanding contemporary and nascent relations with coupling-based systems. In what are increasingly heterogeneous relations, data-flow has personality, character and is of a more personal nature. Probing further into the connection between behavioural systems and users' lifeworlds, this chapter articulates these relationships by exploring links between phenomenology and behavioural advertising technologies by examining Bergson's concept of *durée* (having to do with difficulties in capturing moments), mobility, and his recognition that mathematics and science need not be predicated on analysis that renders continuity immobile. This chapter thus posits that it is only a matter of time before behavioural technologies offer a passing off of understanding of duration and that which is perceived through intuition.

Chapter 6 expands upon interest in feedback relations within online advertising comprehended in terms of autopoiesis and phenomenological experience through a biopolitical account of contemporary co-productive audiences. Picking up the historical slack on audience-as-commodity arguments (Smythe, 1977; Curran, 1981) this chapter unpacks these approaches to advertising in relation to configuring consumers in terms of standing-reserve, biopower, neo-vitalist conceptions of mobility, the means of processing of behaviour, relationships with inorganic systems and politics of code. In a behavioural context then, users are immanent commodities in that they are constituted by, and aid in constituting, the cycle of feedback and commodity production in real-time. The practice of behavioural and predictive targeting as constituted by users' moods, habits and ultimately information flows signifies a new stage of advertising represented through aggregation and disaggregation. Reaffirming the need for a reconceptualization of cyborgs as a blending of the organic and the technical created in a particular time-frame and cultural practice (Muri, 2007), this chapter articulates more clearly the relations between humans and technological systems by highlighting that the relationship between people and machines, and subjects and objects is not one of estrangement – certainly not for the clever animal, as described by Heidegger.

Chapter 7 concludes this book by reflecting on the trajectory of behavioural advertising and the relationship between people and profiling machines ultimately arguing that as our subjectivity and phenomenal selves determine the mood of information, greater care and value should be given to our private selves.

Chapter 2

Exploring the Controversy over DPI and Phorm

Given that behavioural advertising is a somewhat niche topic of interest, the aim of this chapter is to provide a tangible snapshot of the furore that accompanied the launch of behavioural advertising facilitated by DPI in the United Kingdom. In particular, it highlights the inter-relationships among interested citizens, privacy campaigners, Phorm, the European Commission, the UK government and the strategic and political interaction between these groups.

Debates in London, Brussels, Washington and other legislative bodies over the use of behavioural advertising and how it should be regulated have intensified in recent years and many of the decisions made post-2010 within regional and cross-border assemblies will affect how advertising is delivered across digital platforms for many years to come. A particularly illuminating case study of the controversy surrounding online behavioural advertising is that of Phorm, the DPI–based behavioural advertising company that in 2008 and 2009 raised much ire among privacy campaigners and interested citizens in the United Kingdom. Intense campaigning, particularly from the Open Rights Group (ORG) and NoDPI, also managed to rouse the major broadcast news agencies with favourable coverage of campaigners' concerns. Specifically, three of the United Kingdom's largest ISPs (BT, Virgin Media and Carphone Warehouse's TalkTalk who account for around 70% of the broadband market) were to sell users' browsing history to an advertising broker called Phorm so as to build up a profile of subscribers' interests and deliver advertising targeted by users' behaviour over a period of time. British Telecom (BT) was first to pull out in 2009 due to consumer resistance despite over 2 years of experimentation with Phorm's systems. As a means of justifying earlier involvement as well as navigating away from Phorm's PR crisis, BT publicly stated they had to prioritize their investment in next-generation broadband services. BT did however comment that they would be monitoring Phorm and the wider interest-based (behavioural) advertising market. Other ISPs withdrew from the behavioural advertising market fearing controversy and being disinclined to take the lead in what became a privacy minefield. Charles Dunstone, head of Carphone Warehouse, commented: 'We were only going to do it if BT did it and if the whole industry was doing it. We were not interested enough to do it on our own' (Judge, 2009). Virgin also chose not to go ahead with trials or rollout, although as of July 2010 their customer help pages do not rule out the possibility of trials in the future[1]. The case drew to a close in Europe in late 2009 as Phorm was effectively blocked from operating in the United Kingdom, although at the time of writing there is potential that legal action may be taken against BT and Phorm for allegedly breaking the Regulation of Investigatory Powers Act 2000 (RIPA) due to the carrying out of secret tests of DPI–facilitated advertising systems in 2006 and 2007 and intercepting communications without user consent.

The case has drawn attention and interest from significant web luminaries, not least Tim Berners-Lee who is recognized as its inventor. An exchange between Berners-Lee and Kent Ertugrul, Chief Executive Officer (CEO) of Phorm, during a debate on 11th March 2009 at the Houses of Parliament best sums up the ideological positions of Phorm's critics and supporters. Berners-Lee (2009) argued that the internet, in general, has and deserves the same protection as paper-based mail and telephone, and that the data revealed by such 'snooping' would give information on highly private matters about how we conduct our lives. He also argued that despite claims that this would increase ISP revenue and therefore user services, many users and sites might switch to using Secure Sockets Layer (SSL) encryption that would involve a slowing down of the internet. In published notes prepared for the discussion, Berners-Lee (2009) contends: 'The act of reading, like the act of writing, is a pure, fundamental, human act. It must be available without interference or spying'. At the discussion itself, he argued that 'Targeted advertising is an improvement, but there's so many ways of doing it without messing up [the internet]' (Williams, 2009a). To this end he continues to argue that advertising using DPI, if ever implemented, should be heavily regulated and require an explicit opt-in model. Ertugrul, in response, claimed that opposition to Phorm's systems represented 'neo-Luddite retrenchment' (ibid.).

The Context of Digital Britain

Interest in DPI–based behavioural advertising should be considered against the wish and perhaps need to develop faster and more efficient networks and services. We should also then take into account ISPs' endeavours to monetize what in the past have been considered 'dumb pipes'. The future of UK's telecommunications systems was articulated in a report titled Digital Britain released in June 2009, delivered by Lord Stephen Carter (first Minister for Communications, Technology and Broadcasting). This describes what the next generation of communications in Britain will look like and what the plan of action is for tackling infrastructural concerns and foreseeable challenges. In August 2009 Stephen Timms took charge of implementing these changes and was briefed in his new role to report to Lord Peter Mandelson and Culture Secretary Ben Bradshaw. The Labour government that ended in 2010 stated that it was committed to providing all homes in the United Kingdom with speeds of at least 2 Mbps by 2012 in the transition from analogue to digital. The subsequent Conservative–Liberal Democrat coalition government (2010–) promised the fastest broadband network in Europe describing 2 Mbps as unambitious. Research commissioned by the Labour government highlighted that many areas are below this level of 2 Mbps, including many in suburban districts and streets in major UK towns with the coalition government that followed pledging that rural and urban areas would be treated equally. According to a 2009 survey carried out by the Communications Consumer Panel, 73 per cent of the British population sampled consider a high-speed broadband connection as important. The Chair of the Communications Consumer Panel, Anna Bradley, also highlighted comparisons by consumers to gas and electricity – 'things which they think we all ought to have access to, almost as a right' (Cellan-Jones, 2009). The Digital Britain report sees Britain as being in a transformational period and that a successful Britain requires high-speed networks so as to facilitate a high-tech economy. The 2009 UK budget states that delivery of this vision could be met in part by funds saved through a smoother than expected transition from analogue to digital television and radio[2] (HM Treasury, 2009). It further declares:

It will allow virtually everyone to experience the benefits of broadband, including the increasing delivery of public services online. It will also offer advantages to UK businesses, both those located in areas that will benefit from the network upgrade and those that make use of online channels to engage with their customers. (ibid., 4.40, p. 81)

Other costs are to be met by public funds and through private money and revenue generation schemes alike. Digital Britain is the latest in a series of visions of the United Kingdom as an information society. For example, in the 1980s, as Lyon describes, the 'information sector' was hailed as 'the harbinger of the new age' with the British government publishing a booklet entitled *Information Technology: The Age of Electronic Information* that, for example, asserted that 65 per cent of employed Britons will earn their living through what were classified as information occupations (1988, p. 53). The more recent version, Digital Britain, states that the UK's digital economy accounts for around 8 per cent of gross domestic product (GDP) and that the digital and communication sectors are worth over £52 billion a year. It notes that Britain has the highest proportion of internet advertising of any developed economy and that by 2012, £1 in every £5 of all new commerce in this country will be online. Much of this is predicated on the need for a robust broadband service as computing becomes even more firmly embedded in everyday life. Moreover it declares that the state plays a supporting role to 'complement and assist the private sector in delivering the effective modern communications infrastructure' (Department for Culture, Media and Sport, and Department for Business and Enterprise and Regulatory Reform, 2009a, p. 1). The report also highlights the need for competitiveness and that the United Kingdom has slipped to 12th place in the European Commission's global league table of digital adoption, skills and use, despite the United Kingdom having been in the top 7 earlier in the decade. Globally the United Kingdom is placed twenty-fifth out of 66 countries in terms of the quality and reach of its networks (BBC, 2009d). Perhaps worryingly for privacy campaigners, the Labour government demonstrated its aim to support industry, stating:

We need to plan now, identify the market failures that are standing in the way of a full roll out of digital infrastructure in the UK, and act swiftly in Government to help the market in the timely delivery of the high-capability infrastructure we will need. This industrial activism from government will be critical to ensuring that the UK gets the most out of the digital economy. (Department for Culture, Media and Sport, and Department for Business and Enterprise and Regulatory Reform, 2009a, p. 4)

The incoming Conservative–Liberal Democrat government of 2010 offers a similar neoliberal sentiment highlighting plans in their technology manifesto to open up network infrastructure, ease planning rules and boost competition. Although few will question the role of market forces and capital in helping to deliver this vision, more questionable is what the nature of this assistance may be, particularly in the face of lobbying by private interests. The Register (a UK information technology news and opinion website known for satire, criticism of corporations and whom Phorm considers as the media mouthpiece for privacy activists) highlights that Kip Meek, a member of Phorm's board, also worked on the Digital Britain report, although a spokeswoman for the Department for Business, Enterprise and Regulatory Reform (BERR) maintained there is no conflict and that 'Kip Meek is not working on delivering universal broadband', and is instead working on the division of the radio spectrum among mobile phone operators (Williams, 2009b). The Register also reported that Lord Stephen Carter had limited his direct public pronouncements on Phorm to describing it as an 'interesting and innovative business' to a parliamentary committee in March 2009. However, prior to becoming a peer, via a period leading the Number 10 strategy unit, Stephen Carter was chief executive of PR and lobbying group Brunswick, whose clients in 2009 included Phorm (ibid.). He also returned to the private sector after delivering the report. Both the interim and final Digital Britain reports (delivered in January and June 2009 respectively) recognize the centrality of advertising to the digital economy in that as digital outlets and platforms have increased, so have the methods of delivering advertising. The interim report states: 'The challenge is to demonstrate value to consumers while ensuring that there is no risk of abusing personal data, for example by developing mechanisms to ensure transparency, and at this stage the industry has yet to bridge that gap'. It also adds that

In developing a digitally engaged community in the UK, and allowing the development of new businesses to generate economic growth and innovation, the Government of course needs to uphold protection of privacy and the principle of transparency. This will always remain a guiding principle. But we also need to ensure that apparent concerns are properly assessed and understood, and that artificial barriers do not spring up. (Department for Culture, Media and Sport, and Department for Business and Enterprise and Regulatory Reform, 2009b, p. 201)

As explored in Chapter 4, the idea of artificial barriers is very much open to interpretation. Although definitions of data protection exist in law, social conceptions of privacy are currently being redefined as pressure is applied by a myriad of companies seeking to offer their own articulation of where the line between private and public should be drawn. Although there are a wide range of companies and practices interested in the reorganization of this distinction, the activities of the advertising network Phorm whose business is based on DPI informs this chapter and book.

Case history: Phorm

Until 2007 Phorm was known as 121Media, a company dealing in what for many was the dubious yet highly profitable practice of adware that involves gathering information about internet users' interests by bundling advertisement-serving software with other free applications, for example, free file-sharing applications such as those offered by Kazaa. 121Media's software then monitored users' surfing habits and used the resulting data to serve pop-up advertisements. Although such practices are vaguely legal in many countries (there is debate around the nature of consent) adware businesses became pariahs, irrevocably tarnishing the reputation of the digital advertising industry through seeding widespread distrust as adware is difficult to remove from PCs. Adware is problematic to uninstall because it assumes administrator-level control that allows it to hide files, directories, registry keys and processes, and when files and registry keys have been hidden, no user-mode process is permitted to access them. At least two security companies, Symantec and F-Secure, blacklisted 121Media's practices with F-Secure stating that 121Media's 'PeopleOnPage' 'collects browsing habits and system information and sends it back to ContextPlus servers' (F-Secure, 2009). Symantec notes that this form of spyware monitors browser activity and periodically contacts a remote server for instructions. It may also: download and execute a program; reconfigure itself to contact a different remote server; adjust the interval between updates and send information to the remote server (Symantec, 2009). 121Media in 2007 rebranded as Phorm, moved into the behavioural advertising market and solicited interest from UK ISPs, most notably BT with whom they conducted undisclosed tests on BT's customers in 2006 and 2007, and an announced opt-in test in 2008.

The tests

The first test, performed while Phorm was still known as 121Media, involved a contextually based advertising system called PageSense aimed at delivering per-user profiled and individualized advertising. The UK tests involved a user-base of approximately 18,000 customers with the principal phase of the trial taking place over 14 days (23 September to 6 October 2006). BT customers were unaware of the tests and had not actively given consent. These tests were 'established by BT to characterize the system's usability, availability, integrity, resilience, performance, and compatibility and to gauge the reaction of end-users to the system [. . .]' (BT Retail Technology, 2007, p. 4). Furthermore, according to the leaked document, the 'customers who participated in the trial were not made aware of this fact as one of the aims of the validation was not to affect their experience' (ibid.). In addition, the BT report states that 'the current opt-out method is cookie-based to preserve the user's anonymity. This will cause a user to become opted-in again if they erase their cookies' (ibid., p. 13). Similarly the report states that users opt-out by navigating to a website to download an opt-out cookie, and

Should they subsequently clear their browsers' cached data, they will be silently opted back-in [. . .] The current opt-out method does not actually avoid the system entirely. A user who has opted-out will still have their web-pages tagged and partial JavaScript execution will occur on every page browsed, although no data collection of any kind will occur. (ibid., p. 18)

The legality of this is highly dubious, particularly given that RIPA makes intercepting internet traffic without a warrant or consent an offence (see Chapter 3 for a more in-depth legal account). Regulation 6 of the Privacy and Electronic Communications Regulations 2003 (PECR) also states that 'clear and comprehensive information' should be given to subscribers or users. The UK's Information Commissioner's Office (ICO) that was set up to uphold information rights in the public interest did not pursue this matter; the ICO, which is tasked with enforcing PECR, stated: 'Our view is that, whether or not there was a technical breach of the Regulation, there is no evidence that the trials generally involved significant detriment to individuals involved' (NoDPI, 2008), although the rules are explicit regarding the need for consent and that users be informed. According to pressure group NoDPI (2009c) and the

European Commission, the United Kingdom and the ICO have displayed a lack of commitment to enforcing privacy directives. It is on the basis of this test and the next conducted in 2007 that the European Commission launched privacy directive infringement proceedings against the United Kingdom. The 2007 test that BT and Phorm carried out was for a trial for a new advertising platform based on DPI. This again was without the consent of users. As Williams (2008a) writing for *The Register* describes, the minimum for such a test would have been 38,000 people and potentially as high as 108,000. Phorm said the 2007 trial was actually performed on tens of thousands of broadband lines (ibid.). Evidence that BT may have acted unlawfully in 2006 and 2007 was collated and presented to the City of London Police on 16 July 2008. On 22 September 2008 the City of London Police stated that they would not open a criminal investigation into the BT trials because there was no criminal intent on behalf of BT and Phorm in relation to the tests, and there would have been a level of implied consent from BT's customers. NoDPI claims that the case was handed to someone who 'confessed to knowing nothing about computers and illustrated he also knew nothing about RIPA when he claimed it only applied to Public Bodies and not private companies' (NoDPI, 2009e). The police suggested that rectification could be sought from the Office of Surveillance Commissioners (OSC), even though this organization only has jurisdiction over surveillance carried out by public authorities whereas BT is not a public authority (Inphormationdesk, 2009)[3]. In response to the City of London Police' decision, Nicholas Bohm, general counsel at the Foundation for Information Policy Research (FIPR) and NoDPI campaigner, stated:

> The City of London Police's response expresses massive disinterest in what occurred. Saying that BT customers gave implied consent is absurd. There was never any behaviour by BT customers that could be interpreted as implied consent because they were deliberately kept in the dark. (Williams, 2008b)

BT admitted it had tested the technology in 2006 and 2007 without informing the customers involved in the trial. This led to protests from privacy campaigners and several complaints to the European Commission that resulted in talks with the ICO. The ICO and the UK government subsequently cleared the DPI-based advertising technology, providing consumers are required to opt-in to it. BT also denied that the trials breached privacy laws, stating that no customers' IP addresses were divulged and it had no way of knowing who was taking part in the trials in 2006 and 2007. The third test was on an opt-in basis, conducted between the 30th September and 10th December 2008, where selected BT subscribers numbering 10,000 received unavoidable pages (interstitials) inviting them to take part in the trials. This opt-in basis was won through campaigner pressure applied against the UK ICO who eventually advised that Phorm's system must not be opt-out. Operating through the Webwise brand, BT customers were presented with a webpage that highlighted provision of additional safety against suspected fraudulent or 'phishing' websites. It was only in the second bullet-pointed paragraph describing Webwise that targeted advertising was mentioned. Such a presentation is at best disingenuous.

Interception and Specifics of Phorm's System

In March 2008, Richard Clayton, a security specialist from Cambridge University (UK), member of ORG, and treasurer for the FIPR, inspected Phorm's systems and subsequently published online what all parties recognize as an accurate technical analysis of Phorm's technology. In relation to RIPA and the issue of interception, Clayton said:

> Phorm have accepted the accuracy of my detailed write-up of the way their system works. Examining the detail makes it crystal clear that our earlier letter [addressed to the ICO expressing concern over Phorm's system] came to the right conclusion. Website data is being intercepted. The law of the land forbids this. (Clayton in FIPR, 2008a)

However, in regards to the interpretation of the system, Phorm argued that user consent is always obtained and there is no interception issue. They also maintained that there remains the possibility of misinterpretation of RIPA and that they consulted the Home Office for advice (Phorm, 2008b). As Marsden (2010) also describes, the Home Office and Phorm together built a case for the legality of the interception arguing that consent was given through users signing up to the ISP's terms and conditions. Concerns over opting in and opting out have also been recorded by the UK's House of Commons Home Affairs Committee who state that Phorm has been criticized on the grounds of consent and privacy, and the interception of communications. However, the House of Commons Home Affairs Committee (2008) records that Phorm gave assurances that its systems are configured so that the company does not have a record of the actual sites visited or the search terms used by the user. Moreover, advertising categories exclude certain sensitive terms and are widely drawn so that the profiles it holds of certain users will not inadvertently reveal the identity of a user or return advertising of a sensitive nature. Furthermore, the ISP does not hold or have access to either the advertising categories users have been matched against or the user ID and does not keep a lasting record of internet traffic for any other reason than it would have originally. Phorm also passed legal tests by the Information Commissioner in early 2008 that stated that Phorm had not breached guidelines on the use of personal data or the methods it used to monitor those enrolled in the system, although Phorm would have to operate on an opt-in basis to use ISP traffic data. However, the ICO only covers consent (PECR 2003) and use of data (Data Protection Act 1998), as well as the Freedom of Information Act 2000 and Environmental Information Regulations 2004. This means they do not enforce RIPA whose main powers address: the interception of communications (the most pertinent here); the acquisition of communications data (e.g. billing data); intrusive surveillance (on residential premises/in private vehicles); covert surveillance in the course of specific operations; the use of covert human intelligence sources (agents, informants, undercover officers); or access to encrypted data. The Chief Surveillance Commissioner who leads the OSC instead handles this. Privacy organizations such as NoDPI argue that interception 'is a more fundamental issue than consent, and is specific to DPI-based behavioural targeted advertising, interest-based advertising or any other "ISP value added service" based on DPI technology' (NoDPI, 2009d).

Phorm is adamant that users are stored as a 'unique random number' rather than a name, and that it does not gather personally identifiable information or store IP addresses. Security expert Richard Clayton, who visited Phorm to see how its systems worked, observes that at the core of Phorm's initiative is a plan to take a copy of the data that passes between an end-user and a website. This allows its systems 'to inspect what requests were made to the website and to determine what content came back from that website. An understanding of the types of websites visited is used to target adverts at particular users' (Clayton, 2008a, p. 2). He states that overall, 'I learnt nothing about the Phorm system that caused me to change my view that the system performs illegal interception as defined by s1 [section one] of the Regulation of Investigatory Powers Act 2000' (Clayton, 2008b). In describing how Phorm's systems work, Clayton

(2008a) notes that Phorm's systems only inspect traffic through port 80[4], the port used for Hypertext Transfer Protocol (HTTP) that underpins web communication; traffic through other ports such as those used in banking and email are not inspected. In addition, only text-based (text/html) content is processed and other content extensions such as images are ignored. Individual pages are broken into words and useless words such as and/but/the/or/a/etc. are excluded, as are those words only stated once. Words are then ranked by frequency and form the basis of what the page is about. This is done by a machine at the ISP called a 'Profiler' that is aware of a user's IP address. It also picks out the UID (the unique identifier through which Phorm processes data) that identifies the user from the cookie on a user's computer that accompanies a webpage request. A record of the URL that was visited, the search terms (if any), the top 10 words and the UID are passed to a machine called the 'Anonymiser'. This passes the data on to another machine called the 'Channel Server'. Although running software provided by Phorm, the ISP controls the Profiler and the Anonymiser; Phorm controls the Channel Server. This takes the URL, search terms, UID and words-based records and processes this against a database to determine all of the 'channels' that match and connect advertisers with users (in the form of their UID). Having established matches between words on webpages and words that define a channel, the channel, UID and date-stamp are saved to a disk to be called up when an advertiser makes a request for a particular audience. These records (channel, UID and datestamp) are discarded within 6 months as this the maximum amount of time permitted for targeting. Further, words are vetted so as to not identify individuals and advertising is not served until it matches 5000 UIDs so as to reduce possibility for identification. HTML tags containing advertisements are served by the Phorm Webwise system and fetched by a user's browser, for example, img src="http://webwise.net/advert". This is similar to how other online advertising systems render advertising. The request from the browser is sent to the Anonymiser that forwards the UID to the Channel Server so as to protect the IP address from being passed onto Phorm. The Channel Server then determines which advertisers are seeking to advertise to that specific type of user. A real-time auction among advertisers is then held so as to determine which advertiser's advertising is displayed to the user. The most profitable for Phorm is chosen and displayed to the user[5]. Certain websites, such as those involving adult material, alcohol, tobacco, gambling, medical or political content are excluded from the system, at least, in that data is not stored nor are advertisements served. Sites where people can read and compose email are also excluded, as are details in web forms (that may contain personal data, although the webpage itself will be processed). Clayton confirms that the system does not permit them to identify individuals and that they meet and exceed all necessary Data Protection Act (DPA) 1998 regulations, thus agreeing with Phorm's repeated claims that it has produced a system that in certain regards is an improvement on other advertising platforms based on cookies and the tracking of IP addresses.

Pinning Down DPI

Before we proceed further, it is worth clarifying precisely how DPI works. Anderson (2007) writing for *Ars Technica*, a technology website known and respected for its extended and detailed articles, describes that DPI boxes allow ISPs to block, shape, monitor and prioritize that traffic in any direction. It is thus a traffic management tool. Lending a degree of credibility to Phorm and their system Webwise, DPI can also root out viruses passing through a network and identify attacks on websites that seek to make resources unavailable to its intended users through denial of service (DoS) attacks and distributed denial of service (DDoS), and apply rules to those packets. Before it can shape that traffic, the system must know what is travelling through it. Procera, for example, a DPI box retailer, is able to detect more than 300 application protocol signatures (the means by which computers communicate with each other across a network), including BitTorrent, HTTP, FTP, SMTP, and SSH, and markets itself as being highly sensitive to users' location within the network. Promotional material for Procera also observes that this granularity 'enables you not only to see the Xbox Live traffic, but rather the Xbox Live users who are playing Halo 3' (Procera, 2008a). It facilitates classifications for 'interactive', 'streaming', 'random-looking' and 'bulky' data. All data is available to view in real-time. Although shallow inspection will tell a system where a packet came from, the IP addresses of where it is heading, and the port the packet is directed towards; shallow inspection is of little use for modern applications designed to get past firewalls. These include telephony applications such as Skype, as well as many peer-to-peer (P2P) applications. DPI in contrast lets network managers know more about the content of packets so rather than simply understanding the destination, it allows them to know that web-browser HTTP traffic (port 80) is actually video or YouTube streams, that arguably make up 80 per cent of all web traffic and potentially downgrade their priority through the piping. As broached in Chapter 3, this has resulted in action from network neutrality supporters who argue for open access and the non-discrimination of packets in the same way that when we use the electric grid we can plug in a wide suite of appliances without one domestic apparatus being privileged over another. In the United Kingdom, in late 2009, concern over DPI was widespread as Virgin Media, via Detica's DPI product CView, announced later retracted plans to profile 40 per cent of their consumers for the purposes of determining whether packets containing music data are licensed or unlicensed, based on data provided by the record industry. Detica, the company that Virgin employed to carry out the tests, was keen to distance itself from Phorm stating that its system (CView) is not reliant on a user's IP address to work, although like the Phorm tests, customers whose traffic would have been examined were not to be informed. Detica media accounts director, Dan Klein, noted that the practice of determining packet content is currently anonymised and while non-anonymised monitoring of web users is technically feasible, such measures would probably not be popular with UK citizens (Espiner, 2009). In 2010 Privacy International (with Alexander Hanff, head of ethical networks) asked the European Commission to assess the legality of software being used to analyze file sharing in the United Kingdom.

What DPI represents then is the ability to scan all Open System Interconnection (OSI) Reference Mode layers. Comprised of seven layers they are split into two stacks. Four of these are the transport set (layers 1 to 4) and three are the application set (5 to7). The transport layers involve: (1) *physical properties* of the network (such as voltage); (2) *data* and the type of physical protocol that needs assigning to the data; (3) *network* and the manner in which the data will be sent to the recipient device and (4) *transport* where flow control of data is managed, errors are checked for, and data is examined to see if it is coming from more than one application so as to integrate each application's data into a single stream for the physical network. Whereas both shallow packet inspection and DPI scan the first four layers, DPI goes further and analyses the three layers that tell more about the content of the packets and the type of destination. These are: (5) *session* that maintains and ends communication with the receiving device; (6) *presentation* that takes information from the application layer (the next) and converts this into a form that all the layers below can understand. Last then is: (7) *application* which interacts with the operating system, or an application brought into play when a user wishes to transfer files, read messages or perform any other network activity (also see Blank, 2000; Erickson, 2003). Privacy concerns have been raised due to the potential for DPI equipment provided by companies such as Ellacoya, Procera and Narus to look inside all of these packets and put them together them to form a legible record of emails, web browsing, phone numbers, log-in accounts, VoIP calls and passwords (Narus, 2009). As Narus describes on its website, it is able to tailor its profiling machines to monitor each packet on the network link and analyze it against a target list input by given providers or law enforcement agencies. Procera (2008b) somewhat unfortunately compares its own PacketLogic profiling systems to listening in on a conversation that in DPI terms involves the conversation between a user's client and a server. Whereas other more shallow data harvesting methods may miss key phrases, context, or relevant detail leading to potential misinterpretation as to what a discussion is about, Procera's system gives an exact representation of conversation or communication flow.

Packet inspection

Packets are a means of breaking down large blocks of information into formatted units of data so as to efficiently and speedily send and receive data across networks. The idea of packet routing has to do with message-switching as originally used to handle telegraphic messages and is in part intended to handle traffic congestion and reduce queuing time/delay for data movement (Davies, 1972). Packets of data are sent across networks in a non-linear manner. This means that rather than going directly from sender to receiver they may instead take a number of routes to arrive at their destination to be recompiled into information a user requires. Paul Baran (1964), the inventor of packet switching in the 1960s (also see Kleinrock, 1961), and a key contributor to the ARPANET (the first packet-switching network), describes packet switching networks as having two features: messages are broken down into equally sized packets carrying information about the sender's and receiver's addresses and the position of the packet within the overall message; secondly, they are dispatched on their own to find the best possible way of travelling from node to node to reach their destination. The header of a packet includes the address of where it is to be sent and also contains information about the form of the content in the packet of data. Whereas shallow packet inspection only checks the header part of the packet of data, DPI analyses both the header or address, and the payload or content, of the packet of information. Pressure groups such as NoDPI have highlighted potential comparisons between internet packets and offline packets of information where we may expect a letter or parcel to be to delivered on the basis of address, weight and size, and for the postman to not open the parcel. Thus another way of imagining DPI is to think of packets as pieces of mail you would put in a regular post box. Indeed, long before DPI was invented, Baran describes the internet switching process as 'The Postman Analogy', stating that the 'switching process in any store-and-forward system is analogous to a postman sorting mail' (1964, p. 25). He further explains that

> each standardized message block contains a 'to' address, a 'from' address, a handover number tag, and error detecting bits together with other housekeeping data. The message block is analogous to a letter. The 'from' address is equivalent to the return address of the letter. (ibid., p. 26)

The header represents information on the front of a letter and DPI is the process of opening the envelope and analyzing the data inside. Inspection carried out as packets pass inspection points at ISP sorting offices enable observers to collect statistics, or search for viruses, security threats, data leaks, intruders and spam, and allows inspectors to search for controversial content and illegally downloaded or copyright-protected material. In addition to these, it also contains the minutiae of daily life lived out through web requests across the internet. Perhaps unsurprisingly, Phorm rejects the Post Office analogy stating that this is a

> deliberately alarmist and inaccurate statement which suggests that our system is not anonymous. The 'Post Office' tag is also designed to give the impression that consumers will not be offered a clear choice and that our system stores personal information and reads email. Neither of these assertions are true [. . .]. (Phorm, 2009b)

Phorm claims that the analogy of mail being opened and read by prying eyes is inflammatory and unfair as it cannot manually scan traffic, although the language and analogy is concurrent with early conceptualizations of data packets. In regards to choice, the more substantive point remains in that Phorm sought an opt-out system that involved packet interception without active consent.

A Way of Funding the Internet

At the beginning of June 2009, Phorm launched a consumer-facing content recommendation engine designed to provide users with personalized web content called 'Webwise Discover' to support their advertising system. This assesses content viewed and collates relevant material from elsewhere on the web presented as a homepage offered by a user's ISP or within a widget. Like their advertising system, this also uses behavioural targeting and offers users content based on sites they visit, and search terms they use. The main purpose of this is to encourage consumers to opt-in to their advertising system. Phorm and other behavioural advertising companies globally claim users will welcome DPI-based advertising as it will provide content that is more relevant and useful. *The Economist* (2008b) records Kent Ertugrul, CEO of Phorm saying 'This idea that we don't provide a service by doing this is as far from the truth as it's possible to be', and that 'It creates a situation where there's less rubbish bombarding you.' Furthermore, Ertugrul maintains that behavioural targeting is a way of funding the internet that will allow ISPs to start making money from online advertising, which they can then spend on upgrading their networks, without raising prices for subscribers. Phorm's homepage states that the personalization/privacy dyad reflects 'established thinking' and that they have created a system 'that turns that thinking on its head, and some of the world's leading privacy advocates in the UK and worldwide agree with us' (Phorm, 2009a). Their homepage similarly embraces the notion of a 'privacy revolution' in tandem with an 'online advertising revolution'. Phorm's 2009 interim report describes that 'careful choices have been made to ensure that the collection of personal data in the Phorm system itself is eliminated' (80/20, 2009, p. 7). It further states that 'Phorm is engaged in a war of perceptions based on conflicting core beliefs' (ibid.), and that users will be able to opt-out through a variety of methods including the blocking of cookies and a network-level opt-out where the user informs his or her ISP.

Phorm's business performance

The privacy storm within which Phorm found itself had a significant impact on Phorm's cash reserves and its ability to fund its UK interests. By the end of June 2009 it had lost $15m (just over £9m) although managing to raise $24.2 million (£14.8 million) in funds. Neate (2009) writing for the Telegraph.co.uk notes that Phorm made a pre-tax loss of

$48m in the previous financial year. In trying to cut costs it reduced outgoings per month to $1.8 million (£1.1 million). As of 31st August 2009, it had cash of $30.1 million (£18.5 million), reflecting equity fundraising and substantial reduction in monthly cash expenses. As a zero-profit company since its inception in 2007, funds were derived from shareholders (Guardian.co.uk, 2009a). Such controversy led to investor concern over Phorm's stocks. Prior to ISPs' withdrawal, Investors Chronicle (2009) highlighted that key positive points for potential investors to note were the agreements Phorm had with three major UK ISPs (BT, Carphone Warehouse and Virgin Media) and the overall growth in the online advertising sector. However, its list of downsides highlighted the significant privacy concerns facing the company, the formidable competition from web-based behavioural advertising companies such as Google, and that it was not forecast to make a profit until 2010 (by mid-2010 this had not happened). Moreover, the concern for investors, as well as privacy campaigners, is the nature of opt-in and opt-out, with investors recognizing that an opt-in system was unlikely to win many customers. As such, for many, they were perceived as an unstable proposition. Share prices fell from a high of 3500 pence in February 2008 to less than 500 in July 2009 (Guardian.co.uk, 2009b). As noted, Phorm is not the only company operating in the behavioural advertising sector, bearing in mind distinctions between behavioural advertising that uses DPI and web-based formats. In addition to technical differences, there are of course also regulatory differences with DPI now being opt-in and web-based formats remaining opt-out. To highlight the scale and competition of web-based behavioural advertising, in 2007 Google spent $3bn on advertising server Doubleclick, AOL spent $275m acquiring behavioural advertising specialist Tacoda, and Yahoo bought the behavioural targeting company Blue Lithium for $300m (McStay, 2009a). For many of the other DPI-based behavioural advertising businesses, Phorm was seen as taking the fall by bringing privacy debates centre stage and into the public sphere while they were able to look on from the sidelines. However, for Phorm, this was offset by being first on the scene and managing to obtain deals with larger ISPs (Investors Chronicle, 2009). Moreover, although possessing contracts with large ISPs Phorm's early success left them exposed as a takeover target and while Phorm is an interesting company in an area with significant potential, for investors it was an unstable proposition (ibid.). However, although down it is not out, and by 2010 Phorm had signed deals to profile five of Brazil's leading ISPs having also successfully completed two trials in Korea in late 2009.

Not Just Users and Investors Opting Out

On 22 March 2009 ORG sent an open letter to Chief Privacy Officers or their equivalent at Microsoft, Google/YouTube, Facebook, AOL/Bebo, Yahoo!, Amazon and eBay asking these firms to block Phorm's attempts to profile their sites and to opt-out of Phorm's Webwise system so as to thwart Phorm's profiling operation. Live Journal and Amazon were among the first companies to opt-out of Phorm's systems, the latter excluding Phorm from all of their domains. This represented a serious blow to a company already in the middle of a tussle between the European Commission and the UK government over the inconsistencies between the requirements of European directives and the UK's implementation of them. Viviane Reding, the EU telecoms commissioner remarked:

> Do you want to turn the internet into a jungle? This could happen if we cannot control the use of our information online, . . . There is an undeniable risk that privacy is being lost to the brave new world of intrusive technologies. (Wray, 2009)

With pressure and awareness building a number of other companies and organizations followed suit, for example, Wikimedia who handles all Wikipedia domains. They stated that 'we consider the scanning and profiling of our visitors' behavior by a third party to be an infringement on their privacy' (Wikimedia, 2009). Other organizations to have opted out include, Netmums[6] and mySociety[7]. The UK government is also understood to have opted-out its domain names, such as www.direct.gov.uk, from Webwise amid concerns about privacy despite seeing such businesses as a means of winning back revenue from Google. Interestingly, publicly, the BBC has maintained an ambivalent position. Seetha Kumar, controller of bbc.co.uk, writes on her blog that 'for those for whom the internet feels like alien territory, anxieties around issues such as safety, security and privacy can stand in the way of making the most of what the web has to offer'. She also adds: 'These concerns are real. Our public service ethos acts as a powerful motivator: we want to provide a safe environment within which people can enjoy our offer' (Kumar, 2009). However, as a Freedom of Information request made by NoDPI (2009a) regarding whether or not the BBC intended to opt-out of Phorm's Webwise highlights, internally the BBC considered Phorm's systems as morally wrong. Bill Thompson (a technology journalist for the BBC), for example, comments in an email to a colleague that the systems are reprehensible, but not illegal. However, by getting into this situation as an anti-Phorm player and making a public stand would have resulted in action from the Trust that manages the BBC. He also argued Phorm's use of the website goes beyond normal terms and conditions as it makes revenue from audiences of the BBC in a way that is not acceptable for a publicly funded service. In addition, concern was expressed in email form that the BBC already use web-based behavioural targeting provided by AudienceScience for their Worldwide services. Anthony Rose (Head of Digital Media Technology for the BBC) also stated that he did not see Phorm surviving and that undue attention need not be paid to it, although Phorm would have successors with variants on its business model.

By Monday, 6th July 2009, the MediaGuardian was the first to report that BT had no immediate plans to implement Phorm's technologies, stating that it was focusing on other priorities such as speedier networks. A spokesman for BT, Mike Jarvis, stated that they were not completely closing the door on Phorm's Webwise service: 'We're interested in this area but for now we have no immediate plans' and

> It's more a case that we have other stuff to work on – Project Canvas, rolling out the fibre network and so forth – so we've taken a step out of Phorm and will see how it develops. [Our decision has] nothing to do with cost or privacy, it's about resources and priority. (BBC, 2009c)

As a result Phorm's shares on the Alternative Investment Market (AIM), operated by London Stock Exchange for smaller companies, lost 40 per cent of their value before markets closed that Monday. Also by the end of that day, Carphone Warehouse's TalkTalk terminated its agreement with Phorm stating it was only interested if BT and the wider industry were going to use DPI-based behavioural advertising. Virgin's comments were reported less widely but a spokesperson for the company said that it had not ruled out behavioural advertising, or Phorm, but that it was looking at other suppliers (Kobie, 2009). With no published plan of business in the United Kingdom, Nick Barnett, Phorm's UK managing director, left the company with no clear replacement in sight.

Parliament, Government, DPI and Phorm

Parliamentary perspectives on the use of DPI to provide online behavioural advertising are mixed. Lord Stephen Carter (who delivered the aforementioned Digital Britain report) of the incumbent Labour government in 2009 is a fan of behaviourally targeted advertising seeing this as an opportunity to increase revenue in a period of low economic overall growth and transition to digital media. Peter Luff, the Conservative chairman of the Business and Enterprise Committee of MPs, argued that Phorm could provide struggling traditional media businesses – such as local newspapers – with a crucial revenue stream along with reducing the influence that Google has over the online advertising market. The BBC and ORG respectively reported and accused the government of colluding with Phorm and offering advice on the legal status of Phorm's services (BBC, 2009b). The BBC obtained emails between the Home Office and Phorm released under a Freedom of Information Act request made by a member of the public who sent the emails to the BBC. They reveal that the Home Office asked Phorm for comments and changes to a document it was drawing up in order to ascertain the company's legal status. Specifically, in January 2008, the Home Office having had their documentation reviewed by Phorm asked: 'If we agree this, and this becomes our position do you think your clients and their prospective partners will be comforted' (ibid.). Commenting on the legality of interception, Simon Watkin, senior policy advisor at the Home Office, in regards to RIPA and interception, posits that behaviourally targeted advertising is lawful when consent has been given for interception and/or interception is for purposes connected with the operation of the telecommunications service. He also states that

> targeted online advertising can be regarded as being provided in connection with the telecommunication service provided by the ISP in the same way as the provision of services that examine e-mails for the purposes of filtering or blocking spam or filtering web pages to provide a specifically tailored content service. (Cryptome, 2009)

This assessment of the legality of interception describes that interception should be provided with the explicit consent of ISPs' users *or* by the acceptance of the ISP terms and conditions, and that ISPs and those contracting services and making them available to their users, 'should then – to the extent interception is at issue – be able to argue that the end user has consented to the interception (or that there are reasonable grounds for so believing)' (ibid.). Such lack of will to regulate interception processes led to the initiation of EU legal action against the British government regarding the 'UK's implementation of EU ePrivacy and personal data protection rules, under which EU countries must ensure, among

other things, the confidentiality of communications by prohibiting interception and surveillance without the user's consent' (EUROPA, 2009a).
Legal action took the form of facing prosecution in the European Court
of Justice, after the Government failed three times to explain to the European Commission's satisfaction why the relevant European Communication Privacy Directives had not been implemented in the United Kingdom.
The EU directive on privacy and electronic communications requires
member states to ensure confidentiality of the communications and
related traffic data by prohibiting unlawful interception and surveillance
unless the users concerned have consented, while the EU data protection
directive specifies that user consent must be 'freely given, specific and
informed'. Specifically, the EU Commission press release states that

> Technologies like internet behavioural advertising can be useful for
> businesses and consumers but they must be used in a way that complies
> with EU rules. These rules are there to protect the privacy of citizens
> and must be rigorously enforced by all Member States, said EU Tele-
> coms Commissioner Viviane Reding. We have been following the
> Phorm case for some time and have concluded that there are problems
> in the way the UK has implemented parts of EU rules on the confiden-
> tiality of communications. I call on the UK authorities to change their
> national laws and ensure that national authorities are duly empowered
> and have proper sanctions at their disposal to enforce EU legislation
> on the confidentiality of communications. This should allow the UK to
> respond more vigorously to new challenges to ePrivacy and personal
> data protection such as those that have arisen in the Phorm case.
> It should also help reassure UK consumers about their privacy and data
> protection while surfing the internet. (EUROPA, 2009a)

The Commission's concern revolves around the nature of consent and
the nature of intention, and the way the United Kingdom has implemented EU rules ensuring the confidentiality of communications. The
EU has taken the view that there are structural problems in the way
the United Kingdom has applied these. UK law states it is an offence
to unlawfully intercept communications. However, this is only applied to
intentional interception, whereas EU law requires members states to
prohibit and to ensure sanctions against any unlawful interception
regardless of whether committed intentionally or not. In addition,
according to UK law, interception is also considered to be lawful when
the interceptor has reasonable grounds for believing that consent to

interception has been given. These UK law provisions also do not comply with EU rules defining consent as freely given specific and informed indication of a person's wishes. The Commission is also concerned that the United Kingdom does not have an independent national supervisory authority dealing with such interceptions, in particular to hear complaints regarding interception of communications. As noted earlier, there are two agencies that address surveillance, but cannot enforce the RIPA, which covers interception. These are the OSC, which oversees conduct of covert surveillance, but only looks after public authorities, while the ICO only addresses issues such as data protection (and not RIPA or interception). In 2009 Phorm responded to criticism of illegal interception by stating that 'Phorm's technology is fully compliant with U.K. legislation and relevant E.U. directives. This has been confirmed by BERR and by the U.K. regulatory authorities.' The company added, 'We do not envisage the Commission's proceedings will have any impact on the company's plans going forwards,' (Marshall, 2009b). Moreover, Justin Griffiths from Phorm also said the company felt it was being made an example in a broader regulatory struggle between Britain and the Commission. By February 2010, the UK's Crown Prosecution Service (CPS) said it was considering legal action against BT due to the breaching of RIPA, with The Register among others reporting that although the CPS is politically independent, criminal prosecution may be viewed as useful in persuading the European Commission that current legislation is adequate to protect internet users.

The privacy groups

As is becoming clear, pressure groups play a key role in a healthy democracy bringing about public debate and drawing attention to issues that may be overlooked by the general public and media organizations. They are a means by which civil society can engage in political discourse and attempt to influence policy. As Melucci (1996) highlights, these movements force powers that might like to remain hidden out into the open for public scrutiny, give their objects of attention both form and face, and act as key sources of information, albeit often with limited funds. With the Phorm case there are a number of actors with membership crossing into each other's groups. Of varying degrees of influence among policy makers and the media, they include: AntiPhorm, Anti Phorm League, BadPhorm – When Good ISPs Go Bad!, Deny Phorm Blog, Dephormation, InPhormationDesk, NoDPI, ORG, Phorm Watch, in addition to a range of groups created on social networks. Of these, NoDPI and ORG have most successfully engaged policy makers. As Rossiter (2006) describes in discussion of Williams' *Marxism and Literature* (1975), such organizations are building 'structures of feeling' against their common enemies. In regards to online campaigning, Kavada (2010) also observes the propensity for tight clusters of websites to be organized as affective alliances and networks that enjoy the capacity for multimodal communication. These may include synchronous, asynchronous, mass or interpersonal communication that may be disseminated both locally and globally. The capacity to harness a wide array of communication modes facilitates not only the information exchange between parties but also makes possible coordination and decision making, along with the creation and cementing of trust and a sense of collective identity. In addition, websites provide a means of leaking information that may otherwise be suppressed, perhaps most notably Wikileaks and Cryptome (where BT/ Phorm documents were posted). Although not employed extensively in the Phorm case, video sharing sites, social media and microblogging are commonly used in activism and campaigning. Likewise, in regards to clusters of alliance and cross-fertilization, solidarity and collective identity is generated through the noting and commemoration of landmark events, the creation of timelines, statements of mission intent, the detailing of alliances, and the naming and shaming of opponents.

Such positioning between combatants results in a struggle of ideology, of articulation, and, in our case, the means by which behavioural advertising is conceived and privacy is represented in the wider media-sphere. In addition to competing interpretations of law, debate over behavioural advertising is subject to competing world views to frame a particular issue. Stewart et al. (2006) cite Schön and Rein explaining the frequently transparent nature of frames in the following terms:

> We see policy controversies as disputes in which contending parties hold conflicting frames. Such disputes are resistant to resolution by appeal to facts or reasoned argumentation because the parties' conflicting frames determine what counts as a fact and what arguments are taken to be relevant and compelling. Moreover, the frames that shape policy positions and underlie controversy are usually tacit, which means that they are exempt from conscious attention and reasoning. (1994, p. 23)

Without pockets as deep as their corporate counterparts, guerrilla tactics (or pirate tactics, as Phorm would have it) were employed to manipulate and lobby both the blogosphere and traditional media channels. In such fights, combatants do not tackle each other head-on but rather seek to redefine the objects, phenomena and processes at stake – in this case, having to do with people's understanding of behavioural advertising and privacy via a range of rhetorical devices. The terrain is of a symbolic nature and all interested parties will seek to weave truth and falsehood as a means of conveying their legitimacy and to frame a particular ideology or world view. As Melucci (1996) highlights, one of the most fundamental strategies in wars of articulation is making evident the illegitimacy of the adversary and the negative nature of their position in the eyes of nonaligned observers and prospective supporters. What is sought is the power to name, define and appropriate. When the boundary between what is real and what is represented blurs, as is often the case with privacy matters, there is a rush to fill the semiotic territory with codes and language that best reflect the agenda of a given combatant. This is of course also the remit of the public relations industry and although campaigners do not employ PR agencies, the successful ones tend to be masterly in applying their techniques. Given the emotively charged nature of privacy debates there were a number of discursive appeals or tactics employed by both parties. These can be seen through the prism of Aristotle's conceptions of rhetoric that include logos and appeals to reason, pathos to audience emotion, and ethos that has to do with the character of the speaker (Bakir, 2007). In addition, we may also add kairos, the rhetorical expression for 'opportune moment' and the 'right occasion' (Poulakos, 2002, p. 89) as a means of persuading the public to a particular articulation. Thus in addition to reason, emotion and gravitas, we may also add situation-oriented timeliness. To this end, like other media-aware organizations with strong moral appeal such as Greenpeace, NoDPI and ORG have been successful in influencing the media agenda and affecting policy action at a European level.

Phorm strikes back

Phorm for some time has sought advice from a range of PR agencies and advisors. For example, in 2008 Phorm utilized PR support from Freuds, Citigate Dewe Rogerson and ex-House of Commons media adviser John Stonborough (O'Connor, 2008). However, in late April 2009 Phorm surprised PR and advertising commentators, bloggers and privacy campaigners alike by launching a highly aggressive publicity campaign that sought to smear members of organizations including NoDPI and

ORG. Titled 'stopphoulplay' it lambasted key campaigners through the caricature of 'Privacy Pirates'. These include: Alexander Hanff (a driving figure behind the campaign against Phorm) as the 'Angry Activist', also describing The Register as 'The Media Mouthpiece'. The offensive came under advisement of Patrick Robertson of World PR. As the industry-focused magazine and website PR Week highlights, Patrick Robertson is no stranger to controversy having been called in to turn around perceptions of General Pinochet in October 1998 (Darby, 1998). As campaigners had professionalized their activities by taking advantage of the power of networks as a means of promoting their cause, such social and technological tactics was used as the basis of a PR attack by Phorm who wrote on the stopphoulplay website:

> Beware anyone who dares to disagree. Journalists who write balanced stories, advertising and web publisher representatives who lift the veil on the pirates' tactics, or even unfortunate fellow bloggers who refuse to tow the party line – they are all swarmed by 'letter-writers' and odd-balls who intimidate and bully the poor unfortunate. (Phorm, 2009a)

This resort to slurs and ad hominem arguments to discredit privacy campaigners' contentions represented a strange reaction from Phorm and appeared both an unprofessional and dubious tactical PR move. Alexander Hanff writing for NoDPI (2009b) describes a range of libellous inaccuracies in Phorm's account and states that Phorm's accusation intends to 'make me look bullish and intimidating, which I believe is defamatory'. Although Phorm invited consumers to 'get the facts', it struck a highly aggressive and personalized tone that engaged combatants rather than attempted to reassure the public and, in footballing terms, it went for the player and not the ball. In a bizarre arrangement of events Peter Bazalgette, a key figure behind Big Brother and its creators Endemol, put his considerable influence behind Phorm. In November 2008, he wrote an essay for *Prospect,* a magazine known for quality essays from prominent thinkers and those involved in politics and current affairs. He describes that 'many people seem to feel that targeted advertising based on Google use is acceptable, while unsolicited adverts from Phorm are beyond the pale' (Bazalgette, 2008). In defence of its DPI-based systems, Bazalgette, on behalf of Phorm, cites Google's Gmail where data and communication is analyzed for the purpose of showing advertisements and blocking spam. He argues that this system is illegal under the interpretation of the law made by the FIPR. NoDPI retorts that by using Google you are agreeing to its terms, and if a user does not agree to the terms, then he does not have to use its products or services. Unsurprisingly Google has put significant distance between itself and behavioural advertisers that utilize DPI and is perhaps keen not to draw overt attention to its own web-based behavioural advertising systems (or 'interest-based advertising' as Google refer to it) that began in March 2009. In the article, Bazalgette goes on to argue that media innovation must be funded, proposing that behavioural advertising should be opt-out, with companies ensuring that names, addresses and ISP addresses be protected. Those who choose to opt-out 'become a sort of "digital vegetarian," giving up some benefits for the sake of their principles' (ibid.). In its endeavour to convince the public of its point of view Phorm held many open consultations, more than many other companies engaging in contentious fields. On 20 March 2008, Phorm CEO, Kent Ertugrul, and Phorm Senior Vice President (SVP) of Technology, Marc Burgess, held a web chat inviting and answering questions from the broad to the specific on spying and the nature of information storage and access. In transcribed responses to questions on spying, Kent Ertugrul comments:

> People are losing privacy today because there is no place which serves advertisers' purpose of maximizing relevance whilst at the same time handing consumers a clear on/off switch. And which does this without storing any browsing history. This is what this does and this is why Webwise in fact represents the best defense which consumers have AGAINST spying. (Webwise, 2008)

He also added in response to another question that 'anybody who objects to the system will feel that it is safe once they have understand how it works [sic], and that until then they will freely exercise their ability to opt out and not take part' (ibid.).

A Note on the International Situation

With the expressed hope of bypassing the controversy encountered in the United Kingdom, in 2009 Phorm also launched two trials of its technology with South Korea's largest ISP, Korea Telecom (KT). According to the Organisation for Economic Co-operation and Development (OECD) this is a lucrative market with South Korea being one of the world's most advanced broadband markets possessing 15 million broadband customers, household penetration of about 90 per cent and an advertising market worth $1.6 billion (£1.1 billion) (paidContent: UK, 2009). In 2010 Phorm also launched in Brazil with five ISPs including Estadão, iG, Oi, Terra, and Universo OnLine (UOL) with a significant amount of pre-booked advertising revenue from local advertisers to the value of around $5.6 million (£3.7 million). Beyond Phorm, the United States also has long experience with DPI-facilitated behavioural advertising and has many organizations campaigning against it. These include the Consumers Union, Electronic Frontier Foundation, Privacy Lives, Privacy Rights Clearinghouse, US Public Interest Research Group, World Privacy Forum, Privacy Times and the Consumer Federation of America. As elaborated in Chapter 3, the US Congress are in the process of drafting a Bill to outlaw the use of DPI for behavioural advertising unless it is strictly implemented on an opt-in basis. This arises in response to NebuAd's tests carried out in the United States between 2007 and 2008 without consumers' explicit prior consent. There are distinct similarities between the UK and US cases where CableOne, a US ISP that NebuAd teamed with, argued that its tests were consistent with CableOne's Acceptable Use Policy (AUP) governing use of service. In response to a letter questioning their position from the Committee on Energy and Commerce of the US House of Representatives, CableOne asserted that opt-in was gained through agreement with these policies that state CableOne 'reserves the right to monitor bandwidth, usage, and content from time to time to operate the Services' and that 'Cable One may collect customer traffic pattern usage through the use of traffic management software' (CableOne, 2009). Other companies to have worked with NebuAd include: Broadstripe, CenturyLink (formerly Embarq/CenturyTel), Charter, Metro Provider and WOW!

Conclusion

The Phorm case study represents a highly important milestone in the expansion of behavioural advertising. This is due to both the premise of utilizing ISP gateways and also the intensity of the backlash against those seeking to employ this method of serving advertising. The intention of this chapter has thus been to give an empirical sense of the development of behavioural advertising in the United Kingdom and the controversy in which behavioural advertising providers, ISPs, advertising agencies, advertisers, trade associations, regulators and legislators, the UK government, pressure groups, and citizens all found themselves embroiled. The jostling between these actors has been further enlivened by UK governmental plans to implement Digital Britain. This is driven by an impetus to improve broadband infrastructure so to deliver both more core public and private services over digitally enabled networks, to open up new markets and to draw further revenue from existing ones. Such initiatives involve a quasi-public status for broadband infrastructures augmented by private investment, and a sometimes-uncomfortable relationship between the state and corporations in regards to privacy practices and the manner in which data may be appropriated as a source of revenue generation. While the focus here has been on the United Kingdom and to a much lesser extent the United States, South Korea and Brazil, similar technological, political and social developments are taking place in countries globally.

Chapter 3

Self-interest, Rationality and Regulation

Whereas the previous chapter accounted for technologies, techniques and strategic interests of key actors within the theatre of behavioural advertising and Digital Britain, this chapter examines more closely the informational, cultural and regulatory contours that shape behavioural advertising practice. It proceeds on the premise that to understand the role of any technology in society we should be able to comprehend the economic, political, legal and jurisprudential imperatives that they are informed and shaped by. In addition to how technologies are conceived through regulations and market forces, this chapter also enquires into how individuals as users are configured within this milieu of political economy. By addressing the role of the user, it more clearly establishes expectations of data responsibilities and how this might impact on the regulatory balance between legislation and industry-policed self-regulation.

Profiling the Liberal Self

Rotzoll et al., in their account of ethics and advertising, invoke Adam Smith by stating that 'the individual who did not seek monetarily selfish ends would be doing a disservice to herself or himself, and society' (1996, p. 27). According to proponents of the free market, although not particularly virtuous, self-interest provides impetus or energy in the field of trade. The sovereign consumer is thus the beneficiary from the market as the variety of goods continues to increase. Traditionally, self-interested businesses engage in marketing activities that include advertising, while self-interested consumers sort through the array of advertising messages to arrive at the best choice for themselves. As crystallized in reason-why approaches to advertising, ultimately the consumer is conceived of as rational, sovereign and able to reject, ignore or accept advertising messages. Rebutting critiques of advertising, Rotzoll et al. argue that: no advertiser can make us buy something we do not want; advertising does not make things cost more as competition spurred by advertising makes the efficiencies of mass production possible; advertising does not help bad products sell as consumers may try an item of merchandise once but not twice if they do not like it and, lastly, that advertising is not a waste of money as it provides information and fosters competition. Also, businesses and consumers alike benefit as advertising introduces individuals to products suited to their self-interests. These arguments form the basis of advertisers' outwardly presented conceptualizations about the nature of audiences. Advertising, according to this logic, thus represents a satisfying of mutual interests between two voluntary parties. Viewed from this perspective, the endurance of behavioural advertising is a fait accompli in that it engenders more opportunities for consumers and minimizes hindrances. Such a notion involves a bottom-up approach to economics by beginning at the level of the atomized individual decision-maker who maximizes his or her individual satisfaction. This downplays or ignores social norms and values, and the crystallization or naturalization of cultural attitudes that may guide a particular decision. It represents a classical liberalist position that is egoistic, and characterized by self-interest and rationality, where the relationship between businesses and audiences contributes to a market that is famously a self-correcting force guided by 'an invisible hand' whereby the maximization of individual wealth and revenue maximizes the total revenue of society as a whole (Smith, 1993 [1776]). This then involves a power immanent within the system and that 'the capability to employ opposing, uncooperative forces to establish and maintain equilibrium is a characteristic of self-regulating or – in cybernetic jargon – feedback systems' (Mayr, 1986, p. 175). This 'invisible hand' can also be seen as an example of teleonomy (as opposed to teleology or design), and the idea that goal directedness is attributable to the operation of programs leaving out the need to attribute consciousness, planning, purpose or any other anthropomorphic quality to aggregating systems. Instead of seeking metaphysical reasoning, we instead look for explanations based on immanence where order emerges from within itself.

However, where Smith's teleonomic 'invisible hand' invokes the internal logic of the market with the mass of assemblages, interests and programs at work, Alfred Chandler's (1977) 'visible hand' wrought a new form of managerialism. In this view, modern business enterprise took over the place of market mechanisms in coordinating the activities of the economy and allocating its resources. This was facilitated by the growth of information processing systems and control technologies, and intensification and innovation in management and organizational strategy. In addition, practices of trademarking and branding also enabled producers' greater longevity and control in and over more disparate markets. Rather than facilitating teleonomy, many critics of advertising suggest that advertising destroys the rational and competitive nature of the free market (Leiss, et al., 2005). Being teleological it has more to do with design than evolution. Critics such as Marcuse (1964) saw such one-dimensional developments as the end of individualism along with the erosion of cultural standards to the lowest common denominator. He even went as far to argue that an individual would be cast into a traumatic void if advertising, along with indoctrinating forms of entertainment and information, was to disappear as the individual questions his or her self, along with the nature of society itself. Poster (1995) following Baudrillard (1998 [1970]) through his account of the consumer society similarly argues that advertising does not stimulate rational choice but rather attachment between producer and audience formed at a supra-linguistic level generated through simulation. What is certain is that advertising dissolves clear distinctions between wants and needs, and assumes an anti-rational character in that the 'desire advertising constantly stimulates bypasses all rational criteria (material, moral, aesthetic, political) by which it might be assessed' (Wernick, 1991, p. 35). Accordingly, the meta-message of advertising is thus one that normalizes consumption through both soft-selling (as well as the hard sell) and the fostering of consumption as a modus operandi or way of being. In addition to branding as a means of short-circuiting illusions of rationality, digital mediation engenders its own complexities. Online consumers and users of behavioural advertising are unable or unwilling to make rational decisions and are instead guided by heuristics. Acquisti and Grossklags (2005; 2007) argue that decisions taken by users in their online negotiations negate the rational actor thesis and that another must be posited. This is one that recognizes heuristics and behavioural biases and examines more closely: the role of behaviour; the notion of bounded rationality whereby the rationality of users is limited by the information they have; cognitive limitations along with the amount of time users have to make decisions in any given situation. Therefore, to view individuals as rational economic agents who go about deciding how to protect or divulge their personal information is highly misguided on a number of levels.

Tracing Informational Neoliberalism

To better understand the context that behavioural advertising sits within, we may also trace grand-scale informational initiatives such as the discursive construction of Digital Britain (outlined in Chapter 2). There have been various attempts to brand the information economy with different titles but the economist Fritz Machlup (1962) was arguably the first to coin the idea of an 'information society', although as Thrift (2005) in discussion of Mokyr (2001) highlights, there have been permutations of the knowledge economy since at least the eighteenth century, particularly in regards to the sharing of management techniques and knowledge. Machlup maintained that sectors of the US economy were associated with the production and distribution of knowledge. Among other areas of inquiry, he highlights the role of market research and that increased effort in this may lower costs and raise revenues for firms. In his vision of an 'information society', this is one where 'disclosure, dissemination, transmission, and communication become parts of a wider concept of "production of knowledge"' (1962, p. 7). In contrast to the heavy technologies of iron and steel, information societies see a privileging of the immaterial and represent technical, social and political arrangements whose labour force is engaged in informational activities and whose wealth comes from informational goods and services (Beniger, 1986). Neuman (1991) posits a number of benchmarks that would fulfil the criteria of a post-industrial or information society. These are made up of: the expansion and increasing importance of the service sector of the economy relative to manufacturing and agriculture; the growth in the numbers of managerial, professional and technical occupations within all sectors; the increasingly central position of education, theoretical knowledge, research, and the manipulation and communication of information in society; new postmaterialist values that increasingly emphasize individual self-actualization, rather than the accumulation of material goods, as a measure of status and achievement; continuing economic affluence and material productivity through automation, especially new forms of automation based on computer-aided information processing and artificial intelligence's new flexibility and computer-controlled manufacturing, allowing for more customization and responsiveness to individualized consumer needs. As early as the 1970s the convergence of mass media, telecommunications and computing was foretold and it was at this time that the word 'telematics' was introduced by Nora and Mine (1978) as a portmanteau of 'telecommunications' and 'informatics', or systems that sense, store, process and communicate information. For Castells (2001) components of the information society are also to be found in the 1970s through the emergence and convergence of three key technologies: microelectronics, computers and telecommunications. Lyon (2001) describes early Japanese conceptions of an information society and the French 'l'informatisation' in the 1970s. The French Minitel system for example, a forerunner to the popular adoption of the internet, was a key example of this. By means of this system launched in 1982 users could purchase goods online, make train reservations, check stock prices, search the telephone directory and chat in a comparable way to that made possible over the internet. Other information societies include North America's 'information superhighway', as espoused by Al Gore and promoted by Wired in the 1990s, or Malaysia's 'Multi-media Super Corridor' project, conceptualized in 1996 and rolled out over more recent years. The vision of Digital Britain explained in Chapter 2 is the most recent vision of a techno-modernity predicated on information technologies. Such a vision of the United Kingdom reflects the logic of network society and a version of capitalism that is global in orientation, which prides itself on discourses of 'innovation', and requires flexibility and adaptability from its workers. It also involves the further reduction of the role of the state to one where it acts as a node within network society, albeit a very important one. The UK government then, is only one actor in the theatre of Digital Britain and the field of interactions between citizens, civil society, the state and national and international businesses. As with all communication infrastructure developments, industry and the state are the primary forces of development and their relationship is mutually constitutive. Such courting of the private sector and need for investment has implications for the construction of regulation and the very act of public governance that should act as a check on corporate power. To comprehend the nature of the modern state, we should look to see which organizations they align themselves with, and what social interests and values they reflect. Castells (2003) sees the role of the state as something that both dominates and legitimates. It legitimizes itself through representing the interests of its subjects, yet also dominates through ensuring the domination of key interests expressed by the free market, principles of capitalism, neo-liberalism and also the 'Third Way' that claims to transcend left-wing and right-wing politics (Giddens, 2000). Mosco (2009) similarly describes four patterns of government restructuring, involving: *commercialization,* that establishes state functions such as telecommunications along business and revenue-generating models; *privatization*, that takes this a step further by turning these units into private businesses; *liberalization*, that sees the state opening up sectors to markets and wider competition and *internationalization*, that links the state to other states thus shifting economic power and authority to wider geo-political areas. This is not to suggest that regional or sovereign interests do not play a part, particularly as governments are able to create favourable market conditions and argue for sympathetic transnational regulation. Governments may also potentially be at the behest of companies bringing lucrative contracts or much needed infrastructural expertise into any given region. In regards to Digital Britain and methods of generating money within the digital economy, governmental actors are potentially caught in a bind. Like the much older networks of trading routes where major cities perform as key nodes or centres of financial and informational exchange, the state must reflect the overall interests of digital networks, services carried across these and global economic interests before its constituency (Castells, 2003). This means it must respect the domination of key powerful actors who, although not individually more powerful than states, cumulatively represent protocols and switchers of information vital for a state's participation in the global network state (like many rules, there are exceptions, for example, communist China and its tussle with Google over censorship beginning in 2009). Ironically, the best way to offer protection for national interests is to internationalize, through transnational regulation for example, and as Castells more recently stresses, 'nation-states, despite their multidimensional crises, do not disappear; they transform themselves to adapt to the new context' (2009, p. 39). Flexibility and the sharing of responsibility between previously separate states characterize this new context, although values, willingness to regulate and strategic wants do not always coincide. As described in the previous chapter, Phorm's business and privacy practices within the United Kingdom have revealed and caused a jarring of legal systems and local implementation of European directives resulting in the EU in 2009 launching infringement proceedings against the UK government over lack of compliance with privacy laws.

ISP revenue generation

ISPs face a range of challenges in the contemporary era of deregulated communication oligopolies and shift away from single-service telecommunications providers. Van Dijk (2006) argues that these kinds of services do not benefit from competition as well as other markets and that in relation to broadband and integrated networks, developments carried out by different companies will only be partly interconnected and that it remains to be seen whether their owners will compete with one another. In addition, they all have an interest in passing these costs on to their consumers. Van Dijk offers a number of examples from all over Europe, including digitalized and broadened fibre-optic public telephone networks extended with mobile telephony, cable networks and satellite and mobile communication networks. In regards to DPI, ISPs are placed in a difficult position. As web publishers, search engines and a panoply of internet-based businesses have grown wealthy and expanded their range of business services largely through advertising, ISPs rely on a subscription model that does not generate a great deal of profit per head. To facilitate greater income – measured in terms of average revenue per user (ARPU's) – DPI represents potential not only to target advertising but more broadly to take control of the gateways through entertainment, tiered services and the bringing of 'intelligence' into the equation. Whereas previously ISPs have been conduits, they now seek greater knowledge of their traffic, particularly as online activities become increasingly rich and data intensive. It is then at least understandable that they look to television networks and web giants with some resentment or envy, although concerns over opt-out processes and interception take priority. The potential for ISPs using DPI technology for the purposes of advertising to extract further revenue represents a seismic change in their role within network society and has deep implications for any conception of network neutrality. Whereas in the past ISPs have been more-or-less passive conduits, they are now adopting a much more active approach. The potential use of DPI by ISPs represent an exerting of control over networks and communication, and a deviation from dumb intermediary status given the imperative of knowledge of the audience that advertising carries.

Network neutrality

Stewart et al. (2006) argue that the United States has traditionally led the way in deregulation in regards to policy on telecommunications. This is on the basis that market-led approaches lead to rapid innovation and create the most advanced telecommunications systems. They describe that a direct consequence of this stance is that 'every activity is dealt with as a market, and the government's role is limited to promoting deregulation and redefining its own services as another independent economic agent' (2006, p. 733). This premise was disrupted by the Federal Communications Commission's (FCC) and President Obama's support of net neutrality principles; that is, the idea that the internet works best if it is not tampered with, that all packets are routed with the same priority, and that certain traffic is not prioritized over other traffic. This involves treating internet access as a telecommunications service rather than as an information service, which means that providers cannot discriminate among customers or traffic. Falling under 'common carriage' concerns, there are a number of historical justifications for this. Speta (2002) explains that English common law imposed special duties on certain lines of work and businesses to serve all who sought service on just and reasonable terms without discrimination. Common carrier status has more recently been applied to train networks or railroads and telephone and telegraphy services, but finds its inception arguably as far back as 1441 through innkeeping where due to scarcity and monopoly, an innkeeper was charged with a responsibility to serve the public with reasonable care. As this common law made its way into the sixteenth and seventeenth centuries, areas such as transportation where monopolies may arise came under particular scrutiny and subject to English and American common carrier statutes. In 1887 common carrier duties were levied on the railroads via the Interstate Commerce Act (ICA) of 1887 that required operators to interconnect their services and supply services at just and reasonable prices, and without discrimination. By 1910, US Congress had partially extended the common carrier regulation of railroads to telephone and telegraph companies, pronouncing that the carriage of electronic intelligence should be regulated in the same manner as the carriage of goods and passengers in terms of reasonable rates and non-discrimination requirements. By 1934 the Communications Act was enacted and involved the creation of the FCC to govern communications carriers and radio transmissions, and the imposition of a fuller set of common carrier duties on communications carriers. The last update was the Telecommunications Act of 1996, although in 2010 the US Senate Committee on Commerce, Science and Transportation announced they are to start a process to develop proposals to update the Communications Act for the broadband era. The internet similarly falls under the same common carrier mandate in that ISPs generally make their services available to the public who are willing to abide by established criteria of service. Speta argues that although the internet is not subject to the full implications of the US Telecommunications Act 1934 and the rules of carriage, internet carriers are 'simply the most recent form of carrier, following the great tradition of steamships, railroads and telephones; and all of their predecessors have been subject to some form of common carrier regulation' (2002, p. 271). Moreover, notions of common carriage are not unique to the United States or United Kingdom (where common carriers are also known as public carriers) as most developed countries have granted some form of common carriage arrangement for broadband access. Net neutrality is thus an endeavour to keep the internet open, accessible and 'neutral' to all users, application providers and network carriers[1]. The concern for many heavyweight content providers is the potential of being charged a fee for sending material over broadband lines, users being asked to pay more than once for internet access (as with pay-per-view formats) and that ISPs may favour one content provider over another in terms of which content to delay and which to permit travel (Hahn and Wallsten, 2006). Although net neutrality debates have received significantly more coverage in the United States, throttling has occurred in the United Kingdom where, in 2010, Ofcom began investigating claims from the BBC that BT are curbing traffic due to networks being overburdened with video traffic from the BBC's iPlayer catch-up TV platform. Such capacity to manage traffic is another property of DPI. Incurring ire from the telecommunications industries, the FCC approved open rules so as to continue to generate innovation in the technology sector and by late 2009 the FCC chairman, Julius Genachowski, insisted on open access and net neutrality principles for wired and wireless services (Genachowski, 2009). The campaign for net neutrality has been ongoing for some time. For example on net neutrality, and discussion of public policy and the web, Tim Berners-Lee (2006) wrote on his blog that in the United States, existing principles of neutrality were under threat from companies interested in short-term gain noting that the US House of Representatives was wavering under pressure from interested parties. Listing companies such as Google, Yahoo, eBay and Amazon, as well as technical innovations such as blogging and VoIP, Vint Cerf, speaking on behalf of Google, similarly argues that a neutral network has supported a vast array of innovation that might never have occurred if central control of the network had been required by design (Cerf, 2006). Through this he refers to the end-to-end structure where control lay with users at the ends of the network, rather than at a centre. He offers the example of security where users choose: the level of security; what browsers to employ or what Voice over Internet Protocol (VoIP) system to assemble audio communications with. This contrasts with traditional telephony and cable television networks where decisions are centralized, rather than with users. Moreover, he continues to make the case that IP was designed to be an open standard that allows for the separation of the network, and the applications and services that run through it.

Although questions over throttling and differentiation of packets are significant, of greater importance to this book is net neutrality conceived in relation to the undue use of network gateways for the purposes of control where different stakeholder interests exist and overlap. Online behavioural advertising is part of a meta-suite of processes to monetize internet gateways, which also includes the capacity to deliver entertainment. In the United Kingdom, concern has been expressed over the widening powers of the media regulator Ofcom. Part of the Digital Britain initiatives was to address 'piracy' and to this end new powers were given to Ofcom in 2010 that required ISPs to potentially disconnect some of their customers and deal with copyright infringement claims. The ORG criticized the proposed blurring of Ofcom's role, supposedly to protect competition and the public interest, to one of 'altering market access and conditions in favour of incumbent players' (Open Rights Group, 2009b). In 2010 this was achieved through the controversial birth of the Digital Economy Act 2010 that was delivered with less than usual scrutiny as it was rushed through in the 'wash-up' that involves sorting unfinished business in the few days before Parliament dissolves for general election in the United Kingdom. Among other effects of the Act, it amends the Communications Act 2003 requiring ISPs, on production of sufficient evidence, to disclose details of customers who repeatedly infringe copyright, with a possible fine of £250,000 for non-compliance. Prior to its inception, the Bill (the status of a proposed Act before it is passed by both the Houses of Lords and Commons) ignited protest among consumers and digital rights groups with one of the key first responses being the creation of a petition on the Number10.gov.uk website. Started by Andrew Heaney, TalkTalk's head of strategy and development, it called for the abolition of the proposal to disconnect illegal filesharers. Stephen Fry[2] also used his considerable presence on Twitter to tweet: 'Dear Mandy, splendid fellow in many ways, but he is SO WRONG about copyright. Please sign and RT' (Fry, 2009). Fry's tweet also linked to the petition and resulted in a vast increase of signatures (in the region of 17,000) 2 days later from the original tweet on the 22nd of November 2009. Editorial for *The Guardian* (2009) highlighted that the Digital Economy Bill was 'less about creating the digital businesses of the twenty-first century than protecting the particular twentieth-century business models used in music and film'. Unsurprisingly, there was heavy lobbying from the music and movie industries. The Digital Economy Act aims to reduce illicit filesharing by 70 per cent through the suspension of internet connections for repeat offenders and allows politicians to block pirate websites without primary legislation. It also allows copyright holders to be able to apply for a court order to gain access to the names and addresses of serious infringers and take action against them after three letters have been sent to the ISP's subscriber. It crystallized in legislation a vision of Digital Britain, although elements were both added and subtracted from the original Digital Britain report. Google, Facebook, eBay and Yahoo! also expressed concern that the Digital Economy Bill risks stifling innovation, and by extension damaging the Government's vision for a Digital Britain and also the reputation of the United Kingdom globally as a place to do online business. The Bill also drew criticism for requiring organizations providing internet access to be liable for the actions of their customers. Such activity marks a paradigm shift in the role of ISPs. Previously ISPs have rallied against the offering up of user data to public and private agencies, but now there is greater willingness to harness information passing through their gateways. Within the ISP community however, divergent views exist. For example, Nicholas Lansman, Secretary General of the Internet Services Providers' Association (ISPA), the UK trade association for providers of internet services, has complained that 'ISPs are being asked to police content but this isn't about serious crime but to protect one particular set of rights holders' (Wakefield, 2009). Moreover, in regards to the Digital Economy Bill itself, the 'legal, technical and practical issues have simply not been debated in nearly enough depth. For a policy of such gravity, this is negligent' (ISPA, 2010).

Legal Dimensions

In exploring the political economy of online behavioural advertising it is pertinent to examine privacy laws and other means of regulating industry. There are varying types of privacy protection, including national legislation, international legislation and treaties, self-regulation, codes of conduct and professional codes. Privacy is addressed in most national constitutions, although subject to both different forms of jurisprudence and working legal practice. There are also opposing philosophies in that there is an argument for direct government legislation that increases consumer confidence, and arguably therefore commerce; those supporting less regulation argue that regulations interfere with the working of the free market, causing inefficiency. Protection of some sort is required as the general conclusion is that clear rules where consumers do not have to think about protecting themselves results in better market conditions for all (Ang, 2001). The debate rather has to do with the nature, extent and severity of regulation, and where the balance between legislation and self-regulation should lie. There are problems with the use of legislation alone: Van Dijk (2006) makes the case that law and justice have always lagged behind technological innovation and continue to do so in an intensified manner, although key parts of European legislation have been left technologically neutral so as to account for future developments. However, and less obviously, van Dijk asserts that in civil society this lag is necessarily so. Individuals in civil society initially act freely, and the law reacts and makes corrections. This, in part, is so as not to stifle free initiative. Likewise, legal coverage of technical development is also subject to jurisprudence or notions of law that have more to do with philosophy than conventional legal materials (Posner, 1990). This allows a greater degree of latitude, interpretation and discretion in judging law and novel technological cases. Rather than the laying down of strict deterministic laws, the system, through processes of feedback, manages and regulates itself. Nevertheless, van Dijk (2006) argues that there are seven reasons why network-based technologies challenge legislation and the law. These involve: (1) the intangible, geography-free and continuously changing character of information and communication in networks; (2) the difficulty in implementing law due to lack of obvious national frontiers, perpetrators being difficult to trace, evidence being destroyed or hidden in networks, and problems of national jurisprudence (although cross-boundary agreements do exist in some cases, for example the Safe Harbor agreement between the EU and the United States that bridges opposing views on privacy policy); (3) the fact that networks become international very quickly whereas laws in the main are national; (4) recognition that existing legislation is still bound to the material reality of the industrial revolution and the first communications revolution, or even pre-industrial trade and craft which has led to difficulty in defining what constitutes 'data', 'information', 'program', 'electronic communication', 'information service', 'owner', 'editor', 'controller' or 'processor' of (personal data). Furthermore (5), existing legislation is still tied to preceding phases in economic development: again, this has to do with the problems of boundaries, but also the nature of freedom of competition, monopolies and decentralization; (6) technological boundaries and network technology ends division between tele-, data and mass communications and as such future legislation such should have less to do with material differences but rather more abstract ones. Lastly, (7) are fragmented adjustments to law when legal developments tend to be incremental with tweaks rather than wholesale changes. As such jurisprudence can be contradictory and lack consistency. In addition, detailed alterations may be made over technical definitions only to quickly become obsolete. Van Dijk also posits that the prevailing principle of applying law to networks is that what goes offline, should also be applied to online, although this may fall foul of his criticism that existing legislation reflects an earlier conception of communication and media. In regards to DPI, such a proposition returns us to Baran's (1964) Postman Analogy and requires us to ask: How comfortable are we about the insertion of advertisements into our into our data-packets, even if the mail in question is not deemed personal correspondence? If such a proposition were raised in regards to sending letters and parcels, there would probably be more complaints and media coverage than there has been for DPI. There are however, significant differences between the material and the virtual: despite the literal connection of data being sent in packets, the internet in many ways is a mass medium used for information in the form of entertainment as well as communication. In regards to jurisprudence over what constitutes private communication through port 80, this becomes more contestable.

Communication or information?

Communication is under threat of morphing into information that as a valuable commodity leaves user data exposed to the whims of the market and less protected by regulation. Like knowledge, communication is representative of human freedom in that it has a meaning and value deemed to be intrinsic to it. Information, by contrast, has extrinsically determined meaning and value. The mutation of communication into information thus involves the commodification of communication. It leaves open human interaction and resultant traces to processes and discourses of excavation, aggregation, disaggregation, market value, exchange and generalized equivalence. Classical Marxist accounts of commodification involve transforming use values into exchange values. This definition operates on the understanding that commodities are the form that products take when their production is mainly organized through the process of exchange, as opposed to the satisfaction of human needs (use value). Marx (1976 [1848]) saw this as the initiation of a procedure where the process of production gains mastery over people. In the communications industry, 1980s liberalization and privatization meant that communications were given over to private enterprise. Although UK governments have provided catalysts for such investment, it is for market forces to largely determine and shape the future of the UK's network society. Whereas earlier, capitalist enterprise has relied on sovereignty and the structures it put in place, these structures may, and often do, obstruct the flow of capital. Hardt and Negri (2000) in their book, *Empire*, argue that the entire history of modernity may be seen as this unfolding and a resolving of the contradiction between capital logic and the once transcendental power of state and/or regional sovereignty. They argue that we are witnessing the decline of civil society along with the nation–state and that in addition to global markets and the subsumption of global society to capital, we see the emergence of a world order of control based on deterritorialization. Stiegler (2009) maintains the same, describing that whereas political institutions were based on territorialization and sovereignty, information technologies pervade societies through capillarity. These are the means by which telematics and technics affect political and economic arrangements, knowledge systems and memory (in the sense of how a culture conceives, mediates, represents itself and uses such information as a commodity). Stiegler also argues that, due both to the loss of state control over the monopoly of telecommunications and the power of 'techno-logical' enterprise that is not bound by territorial limitations, the fate of sovereign powers is sealed and 'the state no longer has any guarantee of being its own master' (2009, p. 107). Such a complex and fluid state of affairs requires that states adapt and co-evolve in relation to networks that transform the space beyond each state (Urry, 2005a). Although there is much that is valid in regard to descriptions of the effacement of state and ambition of capital, the situation is demonstrably not one-dimensional and as shown in Chapter 2, both Europe and the United States have rudely thwarted ambitions to commercially harness data travelling along pipes. States and their regulatory powers represent key nodes in the global network and may act in defiance of other states and those who wish to harness the scalability of networks, this consequentially affecting the wider system itself (the European/US Safe Harbor Agreement that bridges differing privacy policy is again a useful example). Also, as Poster (2006) draws attention to, Hardt and Negri (2000) are not clear on technological issues and the nature of technologically empowered business, instead preferring expressions such as 'virtual' and 'high tech' over the materiality of a detailed case study as offered here. They are not alone in preferring the panoramic over the specific as other commentators on capitalism and contemporary techno-logy have argued for a break away from microempiricist approaches in favour of general perspectives and broad conceptual constructs (Suarez-Villa, 2009). The substantive is however to be found in the detail, as Foucault (1972; 1977; 1990 [1979]) demonstrated many times over. Moreover, although generalized critique seeks to inspire, by dint of turn-ing away from the specific it disavows those active campaigners seeking to affect policy, law and other means of regulating the behaviour of busi-nesses within society. Also, when we look to specifics of the relations between capital and technology we find not homogeneity but contradic-tion and opposing business agendas, as is the case with net neutrality issues. Further, in regards to sovereignty, as accounted for in Chapter 2, the European Union has shown greater resolve in the face of lobbying and pressure from industry. As has already been seen in the United Kingdom in the case of Phorm and the UK government, this has already caused ire and conflict with European directives that offer stricter regula-tion than those existing in the US.

Delving into Specifics: Phorm and Legislation

A more inductive approach to understanding the relationship between capital, data and regulation is preferred. Looking at the particulars of the Phorm case study we may draw attention to a number of key pieces of legislation. These consist of EU directives to be enforced at a UK national level that impact on the operations of behavioural advertisers. In the United Kingdom, there is no specific right to privacy although the Human Rights Act 1998 (HRA) has effectively created a statutory right to privacy (Klang and Murray, 2005). It offers local enforcement of Article 8 (that covers privacy) of the European Convention on Human Rights that sets the context of laws on data sharing and ensures that UK compan-ies and other bodies act in accordance with European law. In lieu of no specific right to privacy in English common law, the Data Protection Act 1998 offers privacy protection comparable to privacy laws elsewhere with this Act transposing the 1995 European Data Protection Directive 95/46/EC into UK law. It does not provide individuals with substantive rights to be enforced through the courts but instead individuals who feel their data rights have been breached should make a complaint to the ICO who in addition to enforcing the Data Protection Act 1998 is also responsible for Privacy and Electronic Communications (EC Directive) Regulations 2003, the Freedom of Information Act 2000 and the Environmental Information Regulations 2004. As Thomas and Walport (2008) highlight, the principles of the Data Protection Act are intended to provide a technology-neutral framework for balancing an organization's need to make the best use of the personal details it holds while protecting that information and showing consideration for individuals' private lives. It also requires data controllers to notify the Information Commissioner of their data-processing activities. In addition to the Human Rights Act 1998 and the Data Protection Act 1998, another piece of legislation that applies to the Phorm case, online behavioural advertising and the negotiation of privacy-oriented legislation is the Tort of Breach of Confidence. This protects private information conveyed in confidence and where the information is later used in an unauthorized way. Tort involves an area of law that looks at situations where one person may be liable to another for a civil wrong when the parties are not in a contractual relationship. It examines legal grievance and the circumstances where a party may be held responsible for legal injury. This specific tort gives protection to individuals' private interests and deals with unauthorized use or disclosure of certain types of confidential information and may protect such information on the basis of actual or deemed agreement to keep such information secret (Home Office, 2003). Citing Lord Hoffman of the House of Lords, Elliot and Quinn note that the tort now involves 'the right to control the dissemination of information about one's private life and the right to esteem and respect of other people' (2005, p. 242).

As broached in the previous chapter, the most relevant piece of UK legislation to the Phorm furore is RIPA[3]. This is the piece of legislation that became Phorm's bête-noire. NoDPI along with other groups lambasted Phorm for breaking this law and brought it to the attention of European Commissioners. Campaigners also provided the UK CPS with a file of evidence highlighting abuse of RIPA (at the time of writing, the CPS have not begun prosecution but insist they are still reviewing evidence). RIPA replaced the Interception of Communications Act 1985 when it received royal assent in 2000. The opening section of the Act states that if there is no criminal liability involved on behalf of the person whose data is in question, it is an offence in the United Kingdom for a person intentionally and without lawful authority to intercept any communication in the course of its transmission by means of a public postal service or a public telecommunication system (Office of Public Sector Information, 2008). The Act is wide-ranging[4], but to summarize relevant sections (2 and 3) it means that communications should not be intercepted in the course of their transmission; telecommunications systems should not be modified so as to enable interception, and neither should communications be made available to a person other than the sender or intended recipient of the communication. Of key importance then is the issue of *interception*. Also of paramount importance is *consent*. With regards to consent Phorm have argued that interception is authorized because the law may be read as granting consent by dint of use of that telecommunications system. The law states that data interception and collection is actionable through 'implied consent' (section 1, clause 6b). Much of Phorm's argument hinges on this understanding of consent and this remains a controversial point not only in the United Kingdom with regards to Phorm, but also in the United States with the NebuAd case. Section 3 of RIPA, that details situations when lawful interception without an interception warrant may occur, specifies that communications may only be intercepted if both the sender and receiver have agreed to have their communications intercepted. However, in section 3 potential space for ambiguity arises when the interception of communications is authorized or conducted by or on behalf of a person who provides a postal service or a telecommunications service and 'it takes place for purposes connected with the provision or operation of that service or with the enforcement, in relation to that service, of any enactment relating to the use of postal services or telecommunications services' (clause 3b, ibid., p. 6; also see Marsden, 2010). Section 4 (clause 3) also maintains that communication may not be intercepted 'except in the course of its transmission using apparatus or services provided by or to the person carrying on the business for use wholly or partly in connection with that business' (ibid., p. 7). Phorm's Privacy Impact Assessment carried out by 80/20 Thinking, a UK based global privacy consultancy, whose CEO, Simon Davies, is also founder and director of Privacy International, notes that 'The Home Office concluded that Phorm's system is consistent with the Regulation of Investigatory Powers Act and does not intercept communications' (80/20, p. 15). The report states that the Home Office compares targeted online advertising with email/ spam filtering. This is similar to the argument pursued by Google in its Gmail advertising service where the content of messages is already being processed (or 'intercepted') by ISPs to assess whether they are spam, therefore analyzing content for advertising purposes is no different.

The report also remarks and cautions that, according to unnamed privacy experts, there is quite a difference between processing communication to remove inconveniences such as spam and processing communications to categorize individuals and serve advertising. When the EU launched infringement proceedings against the United Kingdom, the Commission identified three gaps in the existing UK rules governing the confidentiality of electronic communications:

1. There is no independent national authority to supervise interception of communications, although the establishment of such authority is required under the ePrivacy and Data Protection Directives, in particular to hear complaints regarding interception of communications.
2. The current UK law – the Regulation of Investigatory Powers Act 2000 (RIPA) – authorises interception of communications not only where the persons concerned have consented to interception but also when the person intercepting the communications has 'reasonable grounds for believing' that consent to do so has been given. These UK law provisions do not comply with EU rules defining consent as freely given specific and informed indication of a person's wishes.
3. The RIPA provisions prohibiting and providing sanctions in case of unlawful interception are limited to 'intentional' interception only, whereas the EU law requires Members States to prohibit and to ensure sanctions against any unlawful interception regardless of whether committed intentionally or not (EUROPA, 2009b).

Concern regarding the difference between inferred consent and that freely given on an informed basis is set against the background of the EU Directive on Privacy and Electronic Communications. This requires EU member states to ensure confidentiality of the communications and related traffic data by prohibiting unlawful interception and surveillance unless the users concerned have consented to this, as stated in Article 5(1) of Directive 2002/58/EC. The EU Data Protection Directive also specifies that user consent must be 'freely given specific and informed' (Article 2(h) of Directive 95/46/EC). In addition, Article 24 of the Data Protection Directive requires member states to establish appropriate sanctions in case of infringements with Article 28 adding that independent authorities must be charged with supervising implementation. These provisions of the Data Protection Directive also apply in the area of confidentiality of communications (EUROPA, 2009b). Alexander Hanff of the pressure group NoDPI having had direct discussion with members of the EU Commission remarks that on the subject of consent, the 'Commission responded very strongly on this stating that EU law, in contrast to UK law, does not recognise implied consent and that consent must be explicit and informed and that all such services must be Opt-In' (NoDPI, 2009c). In addition to the argument over consent, there are also potential loopholes over whether websites are broadcast for general reception, which RIPA does not cover (see section 4 clause 3). NoDPI (2009c) also records that the Commission have been vocal in insisting that web transactions are communications rather than broadcasts, particularly as web-based services are increasingly predicated on delivering personalized content to users.

A Case For Self-regulation?

Although the US historically has led the way with self-regulatory models and methods, this does not necessarily mean their citizens are in favour of it. For example, in a study on privacy and decision-making carried out by Acquisti and Grossklags, the authors find that

> while respondents' actual knowledge about law and legislative recommendations was weak, many favored governmental legislation and intervention as a means for privacy protection (53.7 percent). Our test population also supported group protection through behavioral norms (30.6 percent) and self-protection through technology (14.9 percent). Nobody favored the absence of any kind of protection; only one subject suggested self-regulation by the private sector. This is a striking result, contrasting the traditional assumption that US citizens are skeptical toward government intervention and favor industry-led solutions. (2005, p. 10)

However, arguing for greater acknowledgement of the potential of self-regulation, Charlesworth (2006) maintains that EU privacy directives are increasingly difficult to adhere to due to the development of data sets that are disaggregated or dispersed and do not conform to the command and control model of data management. Although currently workable, they run a serious risk of being rendered dysfunctional in the future in the face of ongoing shifts in technological and societal practices online. Moreover, in discussion of regulation versus self-regulation Charlesworth draws attention to a perception amongst businesses that the objectives of privacy directives be designed in such a fashion as to render them inflexible, opaque and difficult to comply with. As such they lack legitimacy in the eyes of both data controllers and data subjects,

> with the former because of the difficulty in developing and maintaining effective compliance regimes, and with the latter because of the cumbersome mechanisms provided for individuals to assess whether data controllers are in fact acting in compliance. (ibid., p. 48)

In regards to all forms of behavioural advertising (both web-based and DPI) trade bodies were busy during 2009–2010 announcing new self-regulatory guidelines on how their members use and collect online data so as to fend off stringent regulation[5]. For example in the United States, advertising industry coalitions (comprised of the Interactive Advertising Bureau, the Direct Marketing Association, the American Association of Advertising Agencies, and Association of National Advertisers – overseen by the Better Business Bureau's advertising review body) have created new systems and structures so as to be able to distinguish behaviourally-targeted advertising from other forms. These highlight the entities serving those advertisements, identify collection of behavioural data, give the option to opt-out of future targeting by those companies and determine whether consumer opt-outs from behavioural tracking and targeting are safeguarded[6]. The coalition's principles also call for all organizations collecting and using data for behavioural targeting to disclose the practice in a 'clear, prominent, and conveniently located' manner at the time of data collection. Debates over opting-in and opting-out invoke questions of responsibility and who ultimately should protect an individual's privacy online. For example the NAI, the US pro-behavioural advertising lobbyist, are upfront in their statement arguing that it is the responsibility of users to make informed decisions about what they receive and share online and have developed a Firefox add-on that allows consumers to opt-out from behavioural targeting[7]. Following the logic of rational choice (Phelps, 1985) this position makes the case that individuals will evaluate the degree of gain involved and can take action to delete or reject third-party cookies, or opt-out of behavioural advertising systems. This leaves open glaring questions regarding the extent to which users are able to manage these systems and the asymmetry of knowledge and power in information flows. For example, how can users realistically be expected to know the size, scope and fiscal value of their data? In the context of information management, users will always be at an informational loss suffering from incomplete and asymmetric information (Acquisti and

Grossklags, 2007). Although data subjects may have an idea of what happens to their data in processing, knowing the specifics about data holders and who their affiliates are is unlikely and information in many cases will be inaccessible. Moreover, the lifecycle of data is long and in these early stages of accelerated data mining, we are unfamiliar with the intensity of use and consequences of its processing. The debate over responsibility and regulation involves recognizing that digital life involves a combination of technological developments, regulatory interests, social usage and perhaps most influentially, social perceptions of technological development. The speed of technological development and its integration into cultures has potentially proved faster and more wide-ranging than corresponding citizen and public awareness. For companies who make their money from data extraction, it is not unreasonable to argue that they are happy to go along with this milieu on the basis that behavioural advertising remains opt-out. However, at the highpoint of the Phorm case when ISPs were pulling back from Phorm's systems and an opt-in requirement loomed, this led Nick Stringer, head of regulatory affairs at the IAB and chair of the Behavioural Targeting Council, to highlight the importance of widespread 'consumer education' (Bearne, 2009). Facing critique from legislative bodies, trade associations have been keen to launch educational programmes and codes of self-regulation. The IAB in the United States also launched a non-behaviourally targeted advertising campaign of their own to combat what they see as overly dystopian perceptions of both DPI and web-based behavioural advertising using the headlines 'Advertising is creepy' and 'This banner ad can tell where you live'. On rolling over the advertisement a disembodied arm pulls down a screen with more copy that describes online behavioural targeting as not identifying people individually and invites the user to find out more on IAB's website. It was created by Schematic, one of WPP's interactive advertising agencies. Companies including Disney Interactive, AOL, Microsoft, Google (through YouTube), Yahoo! and CBS Interactive all contributed media space (Rodgers, 2009b).

Self-regulatory Principles

On behalf of the UK digital advertising industry in March 2009 the IAB established a set of principles to guide advertisers and associated data-mining companies with the declared purpose being to win consumer trust. These are based on three principles described as *notice, user choice* and *information,* along with an agreement not to target children under the age of 13 (IAB, 2009b). This means that users should receive clear notification about what types of information advertisers are collecting, how this data is to be used and what users can do to opt-out; it also involves signed-up members providing approved means for users to decline to accept behavioural advertising. The IAB stipulated that information should be prominent and easy to access. It also requires members who have signed-up to the IAB's principles to offer users easy-to-understand information about behavioural advertising. In 2010 the IAB's efforts paid-off when the UK's Office of Fair Trading (OFT) gave its backing for a self-regulatory approach through the online advertising trade association, although the OFT stated it seeks to strengthen regulation should self-regulatory approaches prove insufficient. The IAB (2009b) argue their principles cover both anonymous information and personal data, and go further than the requirements of the UK Data Protection Act 1998 and the Privacy and Electronic Communications Regulations 2003 as defined in the European Directive 95/46/EC. The American Association of Advertising Agencies (4A's) developed similar codes. As a trade association and lobby group they are clear in their intentions to protect the advertising business from what they see as undue government intervention and to maintain an opt-out model for web-based behavioural advertising. They have been instrumental in developing a self-regulatory framework and building alliances between interested parties including the Association of National Advertisers (ANA), the Direct Marketing Association (DMA), the IAB and the Council of Better Business Bureaus (BBB) who together represent over 5000 companies. Importantly, both the 4A's and the IAB's principles are highly vague on opt-in or opt-out mechanisms. There is also little clear discussion of enforcement, sanctions or punishment for those who break the rules, although members are to be monitored for non-compliance and disclosed to the public should they breach the rules. In 2009 (before the 4A's framework was properly deployed) 10 out of 35 member companies broke the rules with the NAI's 2009 annual compliance report finding that some of its members, mostly advertising networks, were not in line with its guidelines for the collection and use of personal data for online behavioural advertising (Quenqua, 2009).

A Balancing Act

This book agrees with van Dijk's (2006) assertion that self-regulation guided by legislation is a desirable outcome and that legislation, self-regulation and technological solutions, are most effective in combination. Moreover, he makes a reasonable argument in regards to user-oriented responsibility where users 'should use their own expertise, actions and technical means such as filtering with software and using browsers to help them negotiate their personal data with online service providers' (ibid., p. 119). However, such an approach is predicated on the notion of a rational self with time, aptitude and inclination to read extended ISP agreements and/or opt-out web sites. While the premise of the self as a voluntary party is fine in principle, the complexity of the contemporary information society demands that effective legislation and self-regulation be applied and enforced on an opt-in and choice-oriented basis. Debates over opt-in/opt-out go to the core of users' implicit contracts with advertising, media companies and ISPs today. They represent a struggle over both technical and social standards that will frame the reality of advertising facilitated by behavioural profiling for the foreseeable future. Unsurprisingly businesses have pushed for an opt-out approach although a survey carried out for the IAB 2009 notes that 81 per cent of respondents were not aware that they could opt-out, stop or decline online behavioural advertising (IAB, 2009c). European legislation is clear that all identifiable data sharing must be on an opt-in basis and that users are provided with clear and comprehensive information (see Privacy and Electronic Communications Directive 2002/58/EC). The extent to which users have been consulted about 'non-identifiable' information is unclear and we are in a position where infrastructures of data collection have developed and/or been put in place without consultation. Discussing profiling in relation to democracy (and beyond the remit of critical accounts of behavioural advertising), Gutwirth and Hert (2008) state that data protection should apply to group profiling due to the accumulation of power that may occur and that these profiling processes should be made transparent. As such, if the definition of personal data has to do with an 'identified and identifiable natural person' as found in Directive 95/46/EC, this should not be a reason to discard data protection but rather that a new generation of data protection is required. Hildebrandt similarly argues that: 'Individuals need protection regarding the *knowledge* that is constructed through profiling techniques on the basis of their and other data, whether personal or not' (2008b, p. 320 [italics in original]). Moreover,

> Profiling may be perceived as a risk because it normalizes and customizes us without adequate feedback on what happens to our data and what

types of profiles may be applied to us. This feedback – or rather the lack of it – is the central problem of the Directive's limited application and its mistaken focus on data instead of knowledge. (ibid., p. 323)

Organizations such as NoDPI and the ORG are concerned that whereas identity once had to do with demography, geography and knowledge of a particular person in an area of space and time, such definitions are increasingly unstable as data mining tools grow more sophisticated in their ability to cross reference large data sets. Richard Clayton, the University of Cambridge security specialist who examined Phorm's systems, argues that data protection and privacy have been confused. Although data is protected, this does not mean Phorm are compliant with privacy ethics. To quote:

> Phorm says that of course I can opt out – and I will – but just because nothing bad happens to me doesn't mean that the deploying the system is acceptable. Phorm assumes that their system 'anonymises' and therefore cannot possibly do anyone any harm; they assume that their processing is generic and so it cannot be interception; they assume that their business processes gives them the right to imperson-ate trusted websites and add tracking cookies under an assumed name; and they assume that if only people understood all the technical details they'd be happy. (2008b)

The issue then, in part at least, becomes again one of choice and if Phorm's and other behavioural advertising systems are useful, then the consumer may choose to opt-in so as to fulfil classical conceptions of consumerism and advertising-based relationships involving mutual self-interest between voluntary parties. Of course, what behavioural advert-isers depend upon is that the majority consumers are unlikely to be aware of the immaterial labour, production and surplus value they generate.

Conclusion

In contrast to critical accounts of information societies that see techno-logical development as being solely guided by the market, the situation presented here is demonstrably more complex. In addition to the activit-ies of privacy campaigners detailed in Chapter 2, there is a wide variety of legislation that guides the practice of behavioural advertising, although the authority and application of this is also less than clear-cut. Of pivotal importance to the construction and implementation of regulation and legislation is the manner in which society conceptualizes the user, and the extent to which he or she is responsible for their web- and internet-based activities. These issues have been discussed against a backdrop of classic liberal conceptions of the self within market-oriented societies predicated on self-interest. This premise is unworkable in an informational context, perhaps most obviously because within contemporary information societies, cards are stacked against citizens and users who are unable to understand the scale of the data-mining industry and the extent to which data fuels the digital economy. In contrast to classical conceptions, contemporary web-based behavioural advertising does not represent the behaviour of two voluntary partners engaging in mutual advantage. This would instead be found in opt-in relations and arrangements. Where users' data is to be used, the onus ought to be on behavioural advertisers to pitch the value of their systems to consumers and to establish the utility of behaviourally targeted advertising, and for users to freely give specific and informed indication of their wishes. Proper consent takes on extra significance in the case of an attempt to re-introduce DPI-based advertising where examination and insertion of advertising at the centre of the network represents a tampering with communication and networks.

Chapter 4

Artificial Barriers?

Although relative speeds of technoculture may give the impression that digitally mediated societies are a customary way of life, we are in the early days of digital living with many norms, standards and boundaries remaining open to being defined. Privacy is a dynamic concept and in a culture predicated on digitally based information, it rightly maintains centre stage of the social register. Privacy issues are at the core of concerns over behavioural advertising and the aim of this chapter is thus to account for privacy in relation to behavioural advertising, and to recognize that privacy is not a static notion but rather one that is dynamic and subject to ongoing reconceptualization.

Demarcation

Privacy concerns revolve around the challenging of the distinction between public and private life. Such matters bring to light issues of maintaining public inaccessibility to parts of our lives, the right and capacity to be left alone, and the extent to which we can determine both what is held about us and the accuracy of such data (LaRose and Rifon, 2006). Such a conception of privacy derives from modernity and the post-Enlightenment premise of a sovereign individual able to participate freely in a democratic order and possessing exclusive control over her or his own body and life. Privacy is legally embedded in the idea of democracy and protects individuals from interference from both the state and private actors. Indeed, the legitimacy of democracy stems from the centrality of autonomy and utmost respect for each citizen's individual liberty (Gutwirth and Hert, 2008). The UK has a long history of interest in the legal role of privacy, harkening back to fourteenth-century England and the Justices Of The Peace Act in 1361 that provided for the arrest of peeping toms and eavesdroppers. In more recent years, as argued in

McStay and Bakir (2006), privacy is often viewed as both a consumer right (Goodwin, 1991) and a political right (Reidenberg, 2000). Westin offers what has now become a canonized definition of privacy, namely: 'Privacy is the claim of individuals, groups or institutions to determine for themselves when, how, and to what extent information about them is communicated to others' (1967, p. 7). Privacy is difficult to ensure in new media environments, although the recognition of this is not a novelty. Use of information technology storage capacities for surveillance purposes by public and private organizations were recognized at least as far back as the 1980s (cf. Lyon, 1988). In the current commercial setting, information about people is becoming increasingly relied upon as both fuel and enabler for the economy, and there is much work to be done in assessing and addressing the balance between commercial imperatives and individuals' boundary rights when digital techniques of harvesting, processing and sharing information have increased so exponentially. As noted in Chapter 2, in the case of the vision of Digital Britain, concerns over privacy may for many businesses and some policy-makers represent an 'artificial barrier' to market growth in advertising, profiling and consumer-data intensive industries. From such a standpoint, privacy issues represent: hindrances to the flow of information; higher economic costs and an impediment to the ability of the market system to deliver maximum benefits and perform optimally (Norberg et al., 2009). This line of reasoning underpins arguments made by trade groups and lobby groups such as the IAB and the 4As, where any outside regulation, particularly of the opt-in sort, to curb freedom of the movement of information corresponds to intrusion from a hampering hand.

Reconciling autonomy with commercial networks

Whereas traditional media such as press, television and other forms may be used in relative anonymity, newer media tends to be bound to networks that necessitate some form of registration or co-optation. While tactical resistances to marketers' and advertisers' data-gathering endeavours exist, one risks the life of digital hermitage in doing so. In regards to media and data-harvesting, we are also presented with an interesting contradiction: unlike television viewing which is often based on group and ritualistic viewing, use of the web is often solitary, cocooned and intra-temporal. Even the computer screen itself is a site of duplicity given that the verb – to screen – means to both show and to conceal (Taylor, 2001). The simple construction of online advertising that utilizes behavioural techniques belies a multitude of processes involving presence and absence, at least in regard to awareness of data processes and the relationships behavioural systems seek to strike with us. Likewise, the internet is an open structure and by logging-on we potentially expose ourselves and our data traces to the entire internet. Boundaries between private and public are utterly blurred and it is perhaps the inability or unwillingness to process this idea that leads to lack of proper care over personal data. Such difficulty in conceptualizing the scale of network effects sits alongside pronouncements from figures such as Facebook's Mark Zuckerberg who in 2010 publicly claimed that privacy is no longer a 'social norm', and who seeks to mine and commodify, not just interests, but human connections. Although this book maintains a different viewpoint on privacy, Zuckerberg is right in his assertion that privacy is a concept that is evolving. How we legislate and conceive of privacy must change, particularly in light of profiling machines that depend little on personally identifiable information yet may impact corporeally and increasingly determine much of daily life. Although profiling and inductive categorization is a core human trait of how we order and negotiate the world, profiling is best understood as 'a set of technologies, which share at least one common characteristic: the use of algorithms or other techniques to create, discover or construct knowledge from huge sets of data' (Hildebrandt, 2008a, p. 17). These profiles then may be used for the purposes of making decisions that may be made by machines alone or also include some sort of human intervention. For Koops and Leenes (2005) it is this automated aspect that causes the most concern as people may be treated more as an assemblage of informational fragments than individuals. Moreover, we are increasingly becoming defined by the data that is held about us and this invokes questions about informational self-determination. The concern is not so much privacy horror stories of data loss (although these occur with undesirable regularity) but rather the incremental invasion of profiling and a sense of being out of control, particularly when interaction with commercial entities is premised on a world that, in many ways, relies on consumers to manage their own privacy. Hildebrandt (2008b) somewhat scathingly and rightly draws attention to the fact that keeping track and correcting one's data trails, storage, processing and processors is nigh on impossible. Control is thus an illusion and current incarnations of consent prove a burden for both the data subject and controller alike. Apprehension may also take the form of being uncomfortable with being judged by profilers resulting in a changing of behaviour. Koops and Leenes (2005) frame this in terms of lack of scope for self-realization when there are ever fewer spheres and situations in which one can feel unobserved. Other concerns revolve around price discrimination and marketing, differing levels of service according to profiling, judgement of worth and eligibility, and pricing on ability and willingness to pay thorough the creation of categories and niches where decisions are made through automated processing (Burrows and Ellison, 2004; Beer, 2009). As discussed in more depth in Chapter 6, these categories are not neutral, self-sorting or teleonomic, but rather are inherently political, judgemental and human. Moreover, a problem for all interested parties is a lack of clear information over data-practices, thus opening the door to phantasms and less than salubrious behaviour. As privacy matters stand, we are in a situation akin to obtaining sex education in the playground with vital information not being passed on, and matters being distorted and bent out of proportion. Likewise, in specific reference to the role of behavioural advertising technologies, Kent Ertugrul, founder and CEO of Phorm, stated at a London 'TownHall' meeting at the London School of Economics (LSE) in 2009: 'Users care about privacy. There's been an attack on deep-packet inspection – but privacy is about practice and not technology' (McStay, 2009b). Privacy is somewhat paradoxically then an intensely social issue. Outside of advertising, privacy discussion is taking place in regard to a number of platforms and technologies, for example the control of profile information on social networks (particularly in regards to children) or the development of an 'internet of things' that represents a wide suite of interconnected objects ranging from books to cars, from electrical appliances to food, and communicating via Radio Frequency Identification (RFID) technology (NORDICOM, 2009). Viviane Reding, EU Commissioner for Information Society and Media, argues that such developments will only manifest at a ubiquitous level if they are accepted by the populous and privacy risks are addressed (ibid.). In September 2009 these issues were discussed at the European Dialogue on Internet Governance where one of the conclusions of the workshop was that 'Data retention must be considered a threat to privacy and to basic human rights' (EuroDIG, 2009). Participants also called for countries to 'adopt and enforce data protection laws covering all sectors, both online and offline, based on International Privacy standards that are built on the rule of law' (NORDICOM, 2009). Such actions and measures reflect Andrejevic's (2009) line of reasoning that goes as far as asserting that control over personal information is the 'database era analogue of control over labour power in the industrial revolution' (2009, p. 326), and that as businesses and the market did not eliminate child labour, limit working hours or set minimum wages, nor will it set limits to data collection and sorting practices. Others, including the UK's ICO, have called for 'privacy-enhancing technologies' (PETs) where technological safeguards are built into the design of data gathering systems that may reduce the need for law and regulation to protect privacy, although this has also come under scrutiny with urges 'to avoid assuming that a "technological fix" or "silver bullet" can be applied to what are essentially social and human rights issues' (House of Lords – Select Committee on the Constitution, 2009, p. 79). Although precise definitions may vary, democratic governments around the world have unequivocally declared that protection of citizen privacy is essential to the robust development of e-commerce (United Nations, 2001). A key concern over privacy is the right to informational self-determination (see for example Directive 95/46/EC on the protection of individuals with regard to the processing of personal data and on the free movement of such data) whereby users have rights to the image of their personalities. Putting to one side the operational difficulties of such a proposition (for example, assessment of credit risk), it does highlight the need for greater transparency over how our data selves are constructed. LaRose and Rifon (2006) highlight that privacy has been conceived of as a state of solitude or reserve (Westin, 1967), a concern (O'Neil, 2001; Phelps et al., 2000; Sheehan and Hoy, 1999), a preference (Marshall, 1974), a process of boundary maintenance (Altman et al., 1981; Petronio, 2000), and a need (Pedersen, 1997). It is worth noting that these have to do with autonomy rather than secrecy. Privacy has to do with seclusion of certain areas, starting with the body and extending into private life. Van Dijk (2006) posits three accounts of privacy. The first involves 'the right to selective intimacy' involving one's own body. Although without apparent reference to ICT, when one considers the potential of behavioural health advertising the relevance becomes even more apparent. The second has to do with 'the right to make contacts selectively'; this is a weaker form of privacy that has to do with behaviour and conducting relationships in one's private life at home, at work, while travelling and other less private spaces. According to van Dijk (2006) it is a fundamental right of freedom to determine one's own personal relationships, and conduct them without observation or interference. He argues that this may be threatened by the use of communication networks and information systems that register behaviour and relationships at a distance. This proves a hindrance for companies that wish to make revenue from sociality. For users of social networks this definition has particular resonance, given that they are predicated on traceability and transparency of data for advertisers and marketers, the weakening of distinction between private and public, and commodification of networked relations and the ever nebulous 'third party' entities. This definition also encompasses the tracking and monitoring of internet traffic, and most certainly the use of DPI. The third account involves 'the right to selective disclosure' and refers to the control that one has over personal data and how data is handled. This has to do with fear of unintended consequences and that in the digital domain, control is difficult to achieve, particularly as data may be aggregated, remodelled, passed and sold-on (Lyon, 2001). Van Dijk (2006) argues that traceability of actions across public networks concerns people most. In informational environments where companies trade in digital footmarks each zone or web space represents a commercial opportunity to better understand and profit from mobility. What is at stake with behavioural advertising and profiling is further incursion of advertising into private spheres of communication, leisure and anything else people may legally care to engage in digitally. With specific reference to data brokers, Gomez et al. find that consumers demonstrated great discomfort with the ability of data broker portals to sell data to anyone as this meant that 'in reality, no one is in control of the data' (2009, p. 30). It is then unclear to the user, and unfair to expect them to know, how broad-ranging a company's interests and subsidiaries are. Moreover, the discourse of transparency that permeates the language of organizations such as Facebook is one-way. Whereas such organizations would like us to spill interiority for the purposes of targeting and revenue generation, albeit ensconced in the language of community and sharing, where is the transparency of Google, Facebook and similar organizations? As boyd (2010) highlights, people's conception of who can see what do not match with reality and the notion of informed consent is problematic at best, particularly in regards to the level and type of data sharing. Despite the rhetoric of transparency, companies such as Facebook are not transparent about what the data gathered is used for, and instead a vague void of discomfort exists. Google, eBay and Amazon maintain a similar silence over their data-mining activities and although this is due in part to a perceived need to protect trade secrets, processes and competitive advantage, it still means that transparency by default is fine for one but not the other. This has the concurrent effect of potentially making consumers more nervous than they need to be. Often, however, the case of privacy disclosure is unworkable and it is a mistake to see data mining as inherently malign. Modernity itself has in part to do with abstraction as business is carried out at a distance (as opposed to face-to-face) where tokens and identification numbers operate as signifiers of trust (Lyon, 2001). More specifically, as Cate (2007) highlights, credit ratings are predicated on banks being able to collect information that is hidden from the consumer. If consumers were able to block unfavourable reports, this would make credit ratings systems unworkable. As such, full disclosure of information flows may not be a desirable outcome when all is considered. What then is required is trust and the confidence of the public that their data is being used for worthwhile ends that benefit them in some way, and is subject to meaningful protection.

Privacy issues do not exist in isolation but rather overlap, intermingle or are entangled both synchronically and diachronically. Unease over organizations such as Phorm involves not only the behavioural advertising model that tracks information over a period of time, or the technology of DPI itself and its use within communicative gateways, but also their discursive construction and the manner in which such practices are mediated. It is difficult to discuss such matters without recourse to the examination of the assemblage that inform citizens' thoughts on privacy matters, particularly as a large portion of people do not know what online behavioural advertising is (IAB, 2009c). If privacy and processes such as DPI are not technological then they have to do with the social construction of privacy and the battleground for trust, in addition to how we imagine technology. As Bogard highlights, surveillance possesses qualities of fantasy and simulation 'where the imaginary and the real coincide' (1996, p. 9). To comprehend perceptions of surveillance, one has to engage and understand the discourses that feed into constructions and simulations of surveillance. This involves the leveraging of imagination, readily stoked by a zealous entertainment industry that capitalizes on postmodern pessimism, anxiety, menace and broken promises that high technology arouses. Such wide-ranging sources of dystopia indicate a less than coherent view of paranoia, although they do tend to group around conspiratorial discourses (Holm, 2009). As well as being a democratic right, privacy is also an assemblage comprised of threads, traces, histories and experiences all suffused with an unhealthy dose of generalized anxiety. In addition to unease over corporate data mining, governmentality also has a role to play and Phorm's agenda was arguably marred by controversy over the proposed and subsequently shelved UK Communications Data Bill that involved the collection and retention of internet data, and contacts between people as part of a modernization of UK police surveillance tactics (House of Commons, 2009). Widely reported in the UK national media in 2008, it would have allowed authorities to gather and hold on to details of internet sites people have visited, every phone number called or texted, as well as addresses to where emails have been sent. It intended to transpose EU Directive 2006/24/EC[1] that addresses the retention of data generated in connection with the provision of publicly available electronic communications services or of public communications networks into UK law. This proposed Bill would have extended powers of interception granted by the RIPA which can be invoked by government officials on the grounds of national security, and for the purposes of preventing or detecting crime, preventing disorder, ensuring public safety, protecting public health, or in the interests of the economic well-being of the UK. The government however back-peddled on this in April 2009, stating that it 'recognises the privacy implications of a single store of communications data and does not, therefore, intend to pursue this approach' (Home Office, 2009, p. 4).

Privacy and Decision-making

Our privacy-oriented behaviour is riddled with contradiction. Schwiderski-Grosche (2006) highlights that users themselves are the weakest link in the security chain and the ideal user who uses up-to-date antivirus software, personal firewalls and patches their operating systems regularly does not exist. Such an exemplar would also use different passwords/PINs for different authentication scenarios and would take advantage of secure software and hardware wherever possible. This paragon would also not open email attachments or download software or applications from dubious sources. However, this user rarely exists, and in addition to the lack of user protection employed, end users according to Schwiderski-Grosche (2006) are not willing to pay any extra for security. Security is taken for granted – at least until individuals experience major drawbacks from the lack of security in their personal life. The number of security-related activities users are asked to carry out compounds this in that they are required to update virus protection, attend to security settings, download patches, install firewalls, screen email, shut down spyware, control cookies, deploy encryption, fend off browser hijackers and block pop-ups (LaRose and Rifon, 2007). Both in regards to legal and illegal intrusion, users are required to be responsible for their internet and web usage. If internet-based platforms and protocols are media channels, then they come with vastly different user expectations to television, radio, cinema, press and outdoor media. One method of assessing to what extent users care about privacy is through the degree of resistance displayed. As Marx (2003) explores, users employ 11 forms of privacy self-protection. These include: discovery of surveillance; avoidance; surreptitiously piggybacking on identifiable users; switching identities; distortion; blocking information; masking information; breaking (sabotaging) the system; refusal; cooperation with other surveillants and counter-surveillance. However, users may not be aware of when their data has been breached as much legal and illegal collection of data is a behind-the-scenes activity. Furthermore, even if a breach is noted, tracing it is highly problematic in many cases. We are open to attack both from within and externally and as data accidents both in the public and private sector reveal, open to human error as well as technological failings. Data as commodity may be sold and passed on and then aggregated; this means it is difficult to trace back to the original leak or hack (Nehf, 2007). Norris and Armstrong (1999) have coined the term 'expandable mutability' that refers to the capacity of surveillance cameras, installed for one purpose, ending up carrying out other tasks also. Ball et al. (2006) similarly describe this as 'function creep'. The concern for many users and privacy activists is that data gathered from the mining of consumer data will end up utilized for another purpose, merged or data-matched with other data-sets to create a wider picture of consumer activities. Although legislated for in Article 6 of the EU Directive 95/46/EC that states that data may only be collected for the original purposes intended, ubiquitous and networked computing environments offer the potential for increased function creep (van der Hof and Prins, 2008). Although there are tools, software and behaviour that users employ to guard against external threats, more difficult to guard against are internal ones. In the United Kingdom the House of Lords Select Committee on the Constitution (2009) cite what they consider to be one of the most detailed survey (Flash Eurobarometer, 2008) carried out highlighting that 76 per cent of UK respondents were very or fairly concerned about how public and private organizations protect the privacy of their personal data (a figure that has remained fairly constant since 1991). Only 35 per cent thought that their personal data is properly protected; 79 per cent worried about leaving personal information on the internet and 69 per cent did not think that our legislation could cope with the growing number of people leaving personal information on the internet. Moreover after Greece, UK citizens were also the most likely to disagree that their personal data was properly protected in their country. Similarly, Meglena Kuneva, the European Commissioner for

Consumer Affairs ordered research into internet use. She found that around 80 per cent of young internet users believed their personal data was being shared with third parties and used without their knowledge. These under-25s were suspicious of the internet, comparing their internet use to the drinking of water they knew to be toxic. Meglena Kuneva added: 'We would not allow such a situation to exist in the market for water, or cosmetics, or toys' (Traynor, 2009). Research conducted in the United States by Gomez et al. (2009) illustrates that users desire control over who can collect or see data about them and for what purposes information is being harvested. They cite a range of studies both academic and those carried out by organizations such as the Harris Poll, TRUSTe, Consumer Reports, Annenberg Public Policy Center, and the Pew Internet and American Life Project all of which state that the majority of users sampled are concerned about what happens to their personal data. While aware that information about their surfing habits is being collected online, many are not aware of what companies are able to do with their information and how commonly it is sold by companies without their knowledge. For example, the Consumer's Report Poll observes that 61 per cent of US citizens sampled trust that what they do online is private and not shared without their permission, and that 57 per cent incorrectly believe that companies must identify themselves and indicate why they are collecting data and whether they intend to share it with other organizations (ConsumersUnion.org, 2008, cited by Gomez et al., 2009). In addition to confusion over practices, there is also anxiety: the poll also states that 72 per cent are concerned that their online behaviours are tracked and profiled by companies; 53 per cent are uncomfortable with internet companies using their email content or browsing history to send relevant advertisements; 54 per cent are uncomfortable with third parties collecting information about their online behaviour; 93 per cent think internet companies should always ask for permission before using personal information and 72 per cent want the right to opt-out when companies track their online behaviour.

Research from New Media Age describes that the number of consumers interested in relevant advertising increased in 2009 to 69 per cent, from 58 per cent a year earlier, but 66 per cent of people still object to advertisement targeting on privacy grounds and a further 7 per cent are opposed for other reasons (Bearne, 2009). However, an analyst for Forrester/Jupiter Research, Rebecca Jennings, observes that: 'Generally we find consumers are far less concerned about this than people think they should be. Often they want to see well targeted rather than random adverts' (BBC, 2009a). Google offer a similar account describing that relatively few users visit their advertising preferences page, and among those who do, only a small fraction opt out. Nicole Wong, Google's deputy general counsel, states that tens of thousands of individuals navigate to the page and that of those who visit, four times as many people revise their targeting profile as opt out of targeting entirely (Rodgers, 2009a). It is not the remit of this book to discuss the robustness of respective results, but rather to raise questions over the findings as to: How do we account for what users do; what happens when their stated preference for privacy conflicts with their online behaviour that does not reflect their privacy ideals; and what is the nature of users' relationships with behavioural advertising systems? Nehf, for example, highlights that most consumer behaviour involves low-effort decisions and that 'in making decisions about interactions with Web sites, consumers pursue other goals that render privacy less salient than other attributes' (2007, p. 356). Furthermore, when trying to achieve a given goal most people will choose the apparently easiest option and expend as much energy as necessary to reach a satisfactory, rather than best possible, outcome (Garbarino and Edell, 1997). Time is also a key factor, particularly in an environment when people expect instantaneous action and feedback. In this environment then, behaviour is more likely to be of the sort that facilitates immediate informational, consumeristic and entertainment-based gratification.

Privacy for Prizes

Privacy exists on a continuum and we regularly offer up insight into ourselves for all sorts of gains. LaRose and Rifon see privacy as behaviour, and that 'information disclosures are said to be weighed in relation to monetary benefits and to expected negative consequences' (2006, p. 102). Ang (2001) describes this as the market mechanism and technology view (as favoured by industry and those who would opt for higher levels of self-regulation) where privacy is a negotiable item, like property, instead of an inalienable right. This property-based view (also see Lessig, 2006) where privacy is dynamic and negotiable may also be seen as a form of boundary control taking place between oneself and one's environment (Hildebrandt, 2008b). Hirshleifer (1979) also argues for the privacy-as-property-argument highlighting that privacy has not to do with solitude but rather the rights of the individual in reference to others, and that this may be conceived of in terms of private property. This perspective on privacy is also a useful reminder of how entities such as internet search engines, credit reporting forms, direct mailing lists suppliers and of course advertising networks conceive of personal information: once it is in their hands, it is their property and not ours to own or control (Norberg et al, 2009). Such a perspective requires that consumers be responsible for their online behaviour so to protect their privacy (Milne et al., 2009), although most of us also readily offer up privacy in exchange for enticements, convenience and cookies so as to enter details for us and remember our profiles. Indeed, Miyazaki (2008) found that cookie use, when disclosed, greatly reduces negative reactions to their use, although this should be tempered with research finding that many consumers are unable to identify what cookies are (Ha et al., 2006). Like other pleasures, once sampled, the gratification offered by modern technology form habits that are difficult to break (Munro, 2001) and, as Acquisti and Grossklags (2007) find, such user behaviour is also reflected in hyperbolic discounting theory that in behavioural economics means that people prefer smaller, more immediate payoffs, to larger payoffs that come later. As willing participants in our own surveillance we regularly offer up personal details for services and rewards, although as Lanier and Saini (2008) highlight, such incentives can only be truly ethical and voluntary when consumers fully understand the nature of the bargain they are subscribing to, and when this involves full disclosure and transparency. With imperfect information the user is unable to calculate possible outcomes, their likelihood of occurrence, and may not be able to assess the significance of these probabilities. Such a proposition is an unfair exchange. Koops and Leenes (2005) also draw attention to problems regarding the mechanics of data and information management involving questions regarding how someone controls personal data when it has entered the opaque profiling market. While many myopic and cavalier users are unconcerned and take little notice of privacy notices, this is perhaps a question of value, and lack of recognition and estimation of their commodity value as profiled audience members. As short-term decision-making plays a role, so does the appearance of apathy, where despite their privacy concerns internet users seldom engage in self-protection, with privacy concerns apparently having little impact on users' online habits or e-commerce (Miyazaki and Krishnamurthy, 2002; LaRose and Rifon, 2006). Although it can be posited that this means consumers do not care about privacy, a rival hypothesis for the majority of privacy notifications is instead advanced: the situation is too complex for users to understand. LaRose and Rifon (2006) cite Turow (2003) who gives credence to this proposition. For example, Turow found that 64 per cent of his sample never sought instructions on how to protect personal information and 40 per cent knew almost nothing about how to prevent websites from collecting it. Likewise, in contrast to alienation, 'over-confidence is also a problem as 66% of those who are confident of their understanding of privacy policies [57% of the total sample] also believe[d] (incorrectly) that sites with a privacy policy won't share data' (Turow, 2003, p. 4). While many industry representatives note low level of complaints about data gathering, Gomez et al. (2009) argue that the number of complaints simply conforms to the hypothesis that users file complaints only when two conditions are met: (1) they perceive an invasion of their privacy and (2) they know where to file a complaint.

Privacy and Trust

Where we disclose and expose, there are forms of trust in operation. The online behavioural advertising industry sees consumer trust and confidence as necessary and something to be won so as to create a fertile environment for their practices. They argue that this is achieved through educating audiences about their activities and by making privacy 'business as usual' (IAB, 2009c, p. 35). Trust is one of the defining social features of late modernity and, as Luhmann in the 1970s argued, we should expect trust to be increasingly in demand as a means of 'enduring the complexity of the future which technology will generate' (1979, p. 16). This premise is all the more relevant today: trust is something that may be addressed from a rational instrumental point of view having to do with calculated self-interest, active consent and as a means of achieving something more quickly, cheaply or efficiently. It may also be conceived of as a moral issue having to do with duty and obligation (Lauer and Deng, 2007), although as Lauer and Deng later describe, there is little in the way of certitude that respect for consumer privacy yields business benefit. For example, it is clear that there are at least short-term financial benefits to less than ethical approaches to privacy as demonstrated by the multitude of adware companies once in operation. Although most have rebranded (as in the case of 121Media into Phorm) or have simply been edged out of the market by browser and software developments, they are a testament to the fact that there is little hard evidence that ethical behaviour equates to trust and higher revenue. However, in the longer term, relationships between businesses and consumers characterized by trust and sincerity would presumably involve more disclosure and therefore more valuable data. Bakir and Barlow (2007) summarize that explanations of trust favouring rationality argue that we are trustworthy because we individually and collectively benefit from it, often invoking assessment of probabilities based on past performance, and shared commitment to consensual norms of moral behaviour (Durkheim, 1964; Gambetta, 1988; Mistzal, 1996). This for behavioural advertising would involve a business commitment to transparency and opt-in approaches. Such trust-based benefits include the generation of social capital that lubricates economic and political cooperation (Putnam, 1993; Fukuyama, 1995; Sztompka, 1999); and the management of social complexity, uncertainty, and risk characterizing contemporary modern society (Luhmann, 1979, 1988; Shapiro, 1987; Giddens, 1990; Beck et al., 1994). Explanations that favour the 'irrational' variously argue that trust involves an 'element of socio-psychological quasi-religious faith' (Simmel (1990 [1900], p. 179) or 'suspension', the mechanism that brackets out uncertainty and ignorance (Möllering (2001, p. 414). Mayer et al. (1995) delineate a number of trust-oriented characteristics including: integrity, which involves a perception that the trustee is dependable; benevolence, the belief that the trustee cares at an interpersonal level; and ability, the belief that a trustee is competent. Robertshaw and Marr (2006) similarly demonstrate that people tend to exclude information they consider sensitive if they do not trust that a company will take what they perceive as adequate measures to protection their data on salary, health and life insurance information. Relationships of trust are feedback-oriented affiliations whereby the trustor's risk-taking behaviour, or leap of faith, will influence the trustee in a mutually advantageous cycle. As has been demonstrated time and again, trust is central to advertising and wider e-commerce transactions, particularly where contact between buyer and vendor is at a minimum and where a merchant's word is relied upon to not take advantage of the consumer's vulnerability (Geyskens et al., 1996; McStay, 2007b). Lauer and Deng (2007) similarly find that consumers' trust in a company is intimately tied to the company's respect for privacy and this is made manifest through increased sales and purchases, willingness to try new products, and moreover the willingness to offer up more personal information. Joinson et al. (2008) similarly argue that there is a symbiotic relationship between privacy and trust and this helps explain why people may forgo privacy concerns when faced with a trusted requestor, and why privacy is important when faced with a request from an organization or individual one does not trust. In addition, large numbers of businesses have failed in the online environment because they have been unable or have not attempted to win consumer trust (Urban et al, 2000). The corollary of trust is risk and many sociologists have reflected upon the necessary yet fragile nature of the risk-trust relationship in late modernity (Luhmann, 1979, 1988; Giddens, 1990; 1991; Beck et al., 1994; Urry, 2007). Beck famously sees risk society as a confrontation with industrial society and reflexive modernization as a 'self-confrontation with the consequences of risk society which cannot (adequately) be addressed in the system of industrial society' (1996a, p. 28). It involves tensions and contradictions (or 'externalities') that arise out of the pursuit of industrial life that come back to haunt the system (Adam, 2003). Latour maintains that reflexive does not mean that people know more or have mastered awareness of risk as the adjective 'reflexive' implies, but rather an awareness that mastery over events and actions is a fiction from the first modernity which as Latour cautions, is itself full of contradictory definitions. In what Latour loosely calls the second modernity, 'we become conscious that consciousness does not mean full control' (2003, p. 36). Stiegler argues that it is easier to innovate than it is to manage and understand the outcomes of any given technology, observing that industrial society and a sense of urgency go together. This involves a state of being where urgency exists because the 'immediate future is violently introduced to the present as the undetermined but immanent possibility of an accidental, unforeseen event' (2009 p. 138). Perception of the degree of risk and danger involved is influenced by how risks are defined in society's recognized and unrecognized arenas of public discussion. For example, Phorm's Privacy Impact Assessment report frames risk as being a matter of perception, despite arguing that its systems provide high-levels of data protection. It states that

> risk arises from three key phenomena: the plethora of invasive products and programmes currently being deployed across the Internet, the belief that the 'fact' of online tracking is inherently invasive, and the lack of knowledge the majority of people have about online tracking. The fact of having one's Web activity analysed will, in the minds of some, be an intrusive act, regardless of legal analysis. This is a perception Phorm should take seriously. (80/20, 2009, p. 8)

Risk issues are particularly susceptible to social definition because, by their nature, they generally remain invisible, may be changed, magnified, dramatized or minimized and are open to social designation and construction. In the most intense period of the media-storm and privacy campaign waged against Phorm, it experienced difficulty, having to combat a number of trust-oriented threats to its reputation and business. Ironically, Phorm engaged in many of the correct activities (as perceived by risk communication specialists), particularly in regards to public consultation. As Benediktus and Andrews (2006) discuss in relation to winning trust, businesses should present a larger amount of up-front information and give consumers a more accurate representation of the product and the firm's policies. They should also: clarify their product description and make it as simple as possible for the layperson to understand; establish accurate service expectations (in Phorm's case this revolved around clear opt-out options) and create opportunities for customer-employee interaction (which Phorm did to some extent through their blog, although there was little in the way of two-way communication). They also addressed customer concerns promptly in an unambiguous manner through their video representations of the OIX 'Webwise' system[2], although their 'stophoulplay' endeavour gave an appearance of desperation. However, despite its Webwise pages being clear and well laid out, Phorm was somewhat insincere in its presentation by playing down its advertising system and sugar-coating it through the prioritizing of anti-phishing features (this has since been reversed). While lay consumers' concerns may have been allayed, in an online environment where Phorm was being monitored by both mainstream media and privacy campaigners, there was no space for ambiguity or disingenuousness. Ideally Phorm would also have generated the word-of-mouth peer reassurance necessary to maintain or improve its reputation, although this proved more difficult due to activities of privacy campaigners who mostly managed to set the media agenda. Activists were also quick to capitalize on intertextual concern over data mining, governmentality, consumer profiling and privacy concerns over both private and public organizations.

The Role of Privacy Policies

Privacy then has to do with consumer behaviour and privacy policy statements are part of the arsenal at marketers' disposal in attempting to foster confidence in online industry practices. From a laissez-faire point of view they are a vestige of light-touch regulation from the 1990s intended to help nurture an emerging industry. As Turow et al. (2008) establish, studies consistently show that users are concerned about data and companies extracting value, and learning information about them, but rarely, if ever read privacy policies or utilize measures to guard their personal information while online (also see Nehf, 2007). As highlighted, empirical studies also indicate that user actions are governed more by situational than dispositional factors (pre-existing attitudes), and that although users may demonstrate greater concern about privacy, this rarely translates to privacy-enhancing behaviour online (Joinson et al., 2008). Although many companies claim they offer users choice in their privacy policies and opt-out arrangements, this is often an unreasonable choice given the lexicon and complexity of the data gathering practices. As Thomas and Walport argue in recommendations on data sharing to the UK prime minster: 'Much could be done to distinguish more clearly between genuine consent and consent that is simply enforced agreement' (2008, p. 1). In the United States, Fernback and Papacharissi also describe that privacy statements they analyzed offered little protection to the consumer, instead serving to authorize business practices that allow companies to profit from consumer data. Instead these serve as a marketing tool utilizing the rhetoric of protection and safety. They observe:

> Privacy statements generally serve two major purposes: to mollify consumers wary of conducting transactions online for fear of privacy violations; and to convince regulators that further legislative initiatives to guarantee consumer privacy are unnecessary, since the industry self-policing efforts sufficiently protect citizen rights. (2007, p. 719)

They further argue that when the burden of securing privacy falls to the individual or the public, this is a misleading right to privacy and that '[a] right without a legal remedy is an illusory right' (ibid., p. 718). Other systems have also been found wanting, particularly with seal-based self-regulatory programs in the United States. These are marks or badges awarded by third parties placed on a website intended to assure users of an organization's compliance with the law and industry agreed standards on privacy. Somewhat worryingly, LaRose and Rifon (2006) find that websites that use privacy seals are actually more likely to infringe upon their visitors' privacy in regards to the amount of personal information that they request from consumers. In examination of websites that were both supported and not supported by privacy seals, they found that there were few differences in the privacy practices between seal authorities. For example, TRUSTe and BBBOnLine, two of the largest organizations offering web seals, offered users about the same degree of privacy protection assurances, and they were equal with regard to the amount or depth of personal information they requested. Interestingly, unsealed sites offered 'nearly equal privacy assurances and made fewer personal information requests than the sealed sites' (2006, p. 1009). However, when compared to European standards, neither seal program partici- pants nor non-participants offer adequate protections. Gomez el al. (2009), for example, studied the policies of the top 50 US most visited websites to better understand disclosures about the types of data col- lected about users, how that information is used and with whom it is shared. They found that the majority of these had unclear privacy poli- cies regarding 'data retention, purchase of data about users from other sources, or the fate of user data in the event of a company merger or bankruptcy' (2009, p. 4). Such behaviour leads to what Vila et al. (2003) describe as a 'lemons market' for privacy. As Akerlof (1970) explains a lemon market[3] is one where a buyer or user is in an asymmetric informa- tion relationship with a vendor. Because the buyer does not know whether goods are of good or poor quality, he or she will only be willing to pay an average amount. In terms of privacy and potentially risky relationships, users will only offer the minimum information resulting in good vendors being forced out of the market and the bad driving out the good. Many of the sites examined by Gomez et al. (2009) contained 'web bugs'. These are third-party tracking tools employed by companies such as Google, Omniture, Doubleclick, Statcounter, AddThis, Quantcast, OpenAds, Wordpress Stats, among others. Gomez et al. (2009) argue that this appears to be a significant loophole in privacy protection and that language used to describe how information is processed and shared is unclear, for example the distinction between marketing partners, corpo- rate affiliates and subsidiaries. Their analysis of privacy policies found that many stated that they do not share data with third parties, but do share data with affiliates. This suggests they only share data with compa- nies under the same corporate ownership. However, many of these websites also allow third parties to track user behaviour directly through the use of web bugs. The authors cite a conversation with a website's Chief Privacy Officers who claimed they consider the advertising server Doubleclick a marketing partner and not a third party (ibid.). Web bugs have the effect of circumventing policies that state websites will not share information with third parties. They are embedded in a webpage's HTML code, often in the form of tiny graphics that are usually invisible to the user and assess: the IP address of the computer that fetched the web bug; the URL of the page where the web bug is located (which essentially reveals content); the time the web bug was viewed; the type of browser that fetched the web bug image and a previously set cookie value. They are difficult to block and not all web browsers allow the blocking of third-party cookies. Google had a web bug on 92 of the top 100 sites, and on 88 per cent of the total domains reported in the data set of almost 400,000 unique domains. Evidence of web bugs may be seen by employing Firefox as browser of choice along with Ghostery, an add-on. For example, the UK's *The Guardian* newspaper website reveals five trackers in operation including AudienceScience, Doubleclick, Google AdSense, Technorati Widget and Omniture. A visit to *The New York Times* website reveals that comScore Beacon, Doubleclick, NetRatings Sitecensus and WebTrends are all collecting information about user behaviour. While some of these analytics companies are employed so as to measure usability and performance of respective websites, it is highly unclear which are sharing data and which are not.

Conclusion

All interested actors will agree that clarity over the practice of behavioural advertising is required, even if they will not agree over definitions and implications, or how internet users should be educated. Whether the answer is regulatory, technological or a combination of both, accounts of behavioural advertising that confuse actual practices with those of a dystopian nature serves only to foster Big Brother-type phantoms. These help neither critic nor promoter when, as Kent Ertugrul highlights, conceptualizations of behavioural advertising have more to do with sociology than technology itself. To this end, the following chapters offer a wider-ranging cultural critique of behavioural advertising so as to better explicate the novel way in which audiences and online behavioural advertising systems relate and interact with each other.

Chapter 5

Controlling the Mood of Information

Having offered a detailed analysis of the Phorm case study and online behavioural advertising in terms of political economy and privacy, this chapter moves towards a more novel understanding of advertising systems based on networks and feedback. It initially delineates a technocultural account of control systems understood through goal orientation and then proceeds to elucidate the nature of behavioural advertising utilizing biological metaphors of autopoiesis and self-replicating systems, moving on to inquire into the relationship between behavioural systems and experience understood phenomenologically.

As discussed in Chapters 3 and 4, digital communication streams offer a multitude of opportunities for businesses and governments through the monitoring and profiling of consumer and citizen data for purposes of tailoring content, marketing, promotions, goods and advertising. Adopting a broad view of media and technological history, of one thing we can be sure: we are in transition to a society underpinned by networks, ubiquitous computing and significant capital generation expressed as the outcome of relationships between users as configured within advertising systems that to some extent are self-organizing. To understand the centrality of digital culture to the economy we only have to look to the United Kingdom and the vision of Digital Britain that sees the internet as vital as water and gas. Gordon Brown, UK prime minister (2007–2010), writing for *The Times* (UK) states:

> Just as the bridges, roads and railways built in the 19th century were the foundations of the Industrial Revolution that helped Britain to become the workshop of the world, so investment now in the information and communications industries can underpin our emergence from recession to recovery and cement the UK's position as a global economic powerhouse. (Brown, 2009)

Similar sentiments have been recognized by political and business leaders the world over. As alluded to in Chapter 3, in reference to information societies, such characteristics draw impetus from modernity itself that has to do with speed, movement, communication, precision, the refinement of bureaucracy and a more technical way of being than prior civilizations. The identification and reliance on such technologies are key signifiers of modernity, potentially best defined as 'that moment when enormously powerful machines are imbricated within human experience' (Urry, 2007, p. 93). Like other modern technologies, digital is no different as we reach a point where modern humans would struggle significantly without such machines and they, both increasingly occupy the foreground of many people's lives, and also facilitate background processes. Bureaucracy finds contemporary expression in having influence over the networks and the extraction of revenue to reward investment in hardware, software and applications that organize, carry and route information, and monitor and reallocate information flow. To this end, networks have to do with processes of control, although not necessarily of the dystopian type often described in relation to digital media. When notions of 'control' are raised, most common are repressive parallels with Orwellian (2004 [1949]) depictions of surveillance societies. Given their political orientation involving Stalinism, centralization and propaganda, these prophecies do not graft well onto contemporary concerns of commercial data mining. Moreover, dystopia itself is a political vision referring to John Stuart Mill's (2008 [1868]) critique of conservative observations that a perfect society may be reached through intensification of rules for citizens and their social, political and economic interactions. Rather than this being some form of utopia, Mill created the term 'dys-topians, or caco-topians' to refer to social tyranny (also see Trahair, 1999). Less discussed in relation to control is Huxley's (1994 [1932]) vision of a *Brave New World* where control is based on pleasure. There is more merit in this, although there remains an element of forcing reality to fit the metaphor. Instead of control being an oppressive force, it must offer something we covet, desire or wish for. Huxley's parody of utopia was born out of a re-formation of the world, at least in the technologically advanced West, predicated on a growing popular culture and all that it entails. Consumption, advertising, prescribed lifestyles and massification all had their role to play in this vision. Huxley may also have had much to say about the changing modalities of advertising and the growth of digital marketing and advertising predicated on behaviour. Fascinated with Pavlovian notions of conditioned reflexes, behaviourally targeted advertising would surely have made an appearance had the internet been a feature of his brave new world. Orwell and Huxley were not the only people to concern themselves with what modernity and the bureaucracy of everyday life wrought. As Jameson (1996) highlights, conceptions of dystopia have been shaped by literature since the nineteenth century and have evolved into a critique of high modernism itself, thereby extending the remit of the expression beyond political matters. As such, post or late-modern narratives involving privacy concerns, depictions of dystopia and visions of a 'control or surveillance society' derive impetus from fictional writings from the later 1800s and early 1900s from authors including Dodd (1887), Forster (1909) and perhaps, most influentially Kafka (1994 [1925]) and *The Trial*. In contrast to definitions of control that revolve around the idea and practice of domination, Beniger, inspired by cybernetics, understands control as representing 'purposive influence toward a predetermined goal' (1986, p. 8). Although citing older cases of technology and control, his notion of a control society derives from industrial transformations and the industrial revolution, as popularized by Toynbee's (1884 [1920]) lectures on industrial England. In addition to muscle forged through advances in engineering, control is also organizational. For example, Tilly (2007) in regards to nineteenth-century political structures and communication describes US governmental communication and control systems stretching from central institutions to localized ones and back again. Feedback here took the form of tax codes, large-scale postal services, professional civil services and national military conscription. Urry (2007) also highlights time as a characteristic of control, particularly in relation to the abolishment of time variances in the United Kingdom. Such transformation intensified the time disciplining of travellers, school children, prison inmates, holidaymakers and the general infiltration of a discourse around the need for time to be timetabled, banked, organized, monitored and regulated. Although previous societies maintained characteristics of modernity, the pace of change experienced from the seventeenth century onwards across political, social, economic and technological fields is unparalleled (Giddens, 1990). The ramifications of modernity and societies of control are also well accounted for by the sociologist Max Weber who was interested in the growing rationalization and bureaucratization of everyday and working life in the late nineteenth and early twentieth centuries. He observes that as a control system bureaucracy has five features: hierarchy of authority; centralization of decision-making; formalization of rules; specialization of tasks and standardization of actions (Weber, 1922). Although central-ized administrations have occurred in other societies and historical epochs, these saw intensification by the late modern industrial period (around the mid-1800s onwards) that resembles our own administrative systems. Both governmentally and in the workplace, such processes had significant effects resulting in increasing surveillance and monitoring of workers' habits and Taylorist routinization, as well as more efficient monitoring of citizens, consumer habits and later the formation of market research firms.

Discursive Constructions of Bureaucracy

De Landa (1997) comments that bureaucracies arise to effect a planned extraction of surpluses of energy whether these be in the form of taxes, tribute, rents, forced labour or, in our case, some sort of data mining. The will today then to quantify, rationalize, predict, pre-empt and create found its initial expression some years ago. Ellul (1964) phrases this impetus slightly differently referring to a technique, or technical imper-ative, that encompasses bureaucracy and is independent, autonomous, self-determining and integrates machines into society. For Postman (1993), bureaucracy has long ceased to be a servant of modern institu-tions and has instead become their master. As well as solving informa-tional problems, it also creates them. According to Postman, bureaucrats take no responsibility for the human consequences of their decisions, but only for the efficiency of their part of a bureaucracy, which must be maintained at all costs. This leads to a scenario where no one takes responsibility for the meta-system. In addition, the fact that bureaucracy involves workers operating as cogs (or nodes to use a more contemporary metaphor) of a larger machine whose entirety they will never under-stand, means that bureaucrats may issue orders without understanding the nature or implications of their effects. This, in turn, implies an abdica-tion of responsibility. However, are these metaphors and visions apt? As Beniger (1986) notes, it is in the informational nature of life itself where the paradox of information societies lies: the bureaucratization of social life is resented as being dehumanizing, while work in DNA and informa-tion processing address the core fundamentals of what it is to be human. Du Gay (2000) provides a refreshing defence of bureaucracy that is per-haps too readily or easily attacked and, although not discussing control societies per se, makes an important point in relation to ethics, and the social imagining of organizations. Detailing arguments against bureaucratic structures Du Gay describes the schism that bureaucracy is forced into. For example, bureaucracy is, both academically and in the popular imagination, cast in opposition to the emotional, the sexual and so forth. Instead we have the 'typical bureaucrat' more concerned with regulation and innovating new forms of systematic control. Du Gay further queries the romantic belief that the 'full and free exercise of personal capacities is akin to a moral absolute for human conduct' (2000, p. 3). This represents the benchmark that organization, specialization and regulation are required to define themselves against. Another way this can be framed is through oppositions of ethical versus the technical, the spiritual versus the soulless, the sexual versus the lifeless and so on. This is perhaps unfair when a rear-view mirror check of organizational history offers the notion of harmony, as well as the notion of a dead and passive universe characterized by automation (Prigogine and Stengers, 1984) and Hegalian (1969 [1812]) criticisms of reductionist world views. In the mid-eighteenth century for example, Diderot in a discussion of rationality, the art of governing and the ordering of parts observes that harmony is 'the general order that prevails between the various parts of a whole' due to which components 'work together as perfectly as possible' (Mayr, 1986, p. 79). Further, from the fourteenth to the eighteenth century the regularity and ordering of the clock (emblematic of such ordering) gave rise to Paley (1986 [1802]) and the argument by design for God as a divine watchmaker, particularly in mainland Europe. Thompson describes that in Elizabethan times (mid-1550s) images of time as 'a devourer, a defacer, a bloody tyrant, a scytheman', had been prevalent for some time, although there was a new immediacy and insistence generated by the clock (1967, p. 57). By the seventeenth century it had become woven into conceptions of the universe itself, as well as in the homes of the well-to-do in the 1650s, where pendulums began to swing. Thompson (1967) also details that although watches were available before 1674, they were of dubious accuracy until improvements in the escapement and spiral-balance spring. Such technology bridged the realm of magic and rationality, ushering in thinking predicated on cause and effect that ultimately led Europeans to think mechanically and conceive of the world or universe as a machine (Mayr, 1986). Such manufacturing of time and a common temporality gives rise to bureaucracy and the establishment of order as a replication of processes found to exist in the cosmos. Similarly, Du Gay calls for interrogation of the polar ideological views of humanism versus bureaucracy arguing that there is nothing inherently morally bankrupt about the bureaucratic process. In discussion of extreme and postmodern views of bureaucracy, Du Gay (2000) cites Bauman who maintains:

> [. . .] the bureaucratic culture which prompts us to view society as an object of administration, as a collection of so many 'problems' to be solved, as 'nature' to be 'controlled', 'mastered' and 'improved' or 'remade', as a legitimate target for 'social engineering', and in general a garden to be designed and kept in the planned shape by force (the gardening posture divides vegetation into 'cultured plants' to be taken care of, and weeds to be exterminated) was the very atmosphere in which the idea of the Holocaust could be conceived, slowly, yet consistently developed, and brought to its conclusion. (Bauman, 1989, p. 18)

Bauman's reading of Weber thus revolves around an understanding of bureaucracy as something that demoralizes and is characterized by a loss of moral evaluation caused by instrumental rational criteria. It is one that ends in a schism of passion, spontaneity and actions without purpose on the side of morality; and reasons, calculation of interest and utility with immorality on the other (Du Gay, 2000, p. 59). As will be developed in this chapter, networked technologies bring about a different conception of mastery of people, space, time, temporality and information. As opposed to centralized and unified experience, control is now more often dispersed. Contemporary control and bureaucratic power is predicated on de-centralization and disrupted illusions of shared space instead invoking heterogeneous temporality and unique mediatised experiences. Whether we consider traditional or more recent incarnations of bureaucracy as positive, negative or even if we are indifferent, it is worth bearing in mind the discursive construction of bureaucratic systems and the cultural and historical traces that feed this critical point with which contemporary informational arrangements may be explained.

Technology and Innovation

The essence of technology has to do with the capturing of phenomena and putting them to work (Arthur, 2009). It also involves the programming (or organization) of phenomena for some specified purpose. As we can see with technologies of bureaucracy, technology need not be a physical process but instead may also be a technique. Indeed, it is in organization and the structuring of relations that we find the impulse of technology. Related techniques and technologies include the monetary and legal system, education and quite arguably advertising itself, with all being systems with purposes. Technology has to do with innovation that has to do with the trying out of new ideas and by extension, co-opting inventions into commercial use (Arthur, 2009). This may involve new solutions to problems, new technological categories or new elements within existing technologies. The contemporary milieu of innovation and progress versus caution and suspicion is not a new one, nor is concern about the political and cultural investment in machines. Nevertheless, despite political interest in new technologies, the distance between technical systems and social organizations, and the extent to which we are able to tame them, continues to widen. Sismondo (2004) describes technological determinism as a position that privileges material forces, their properties and the capacity for technologies to determine social events. Through this history is constrained, as are the limits of human endeavour. Postman (1993) takes this view of tools and technology one step further by arguing that mechanization invoked a technocracy, a situation where technology steps to the forefront in determining cultural life. In a technocracy, or a period of invention and innovation, tools are not incorporated into the culture; they assail the culture. Postman argues that they bid to become the culture attacking tradition, social mores, myth, politics, ritual and religion. In some contrast, this book argues for a softer determinism in that fully-fledged hard technological determinism makes little plausible sense due to agency being wrongly ascribed to hardware and software. Smith and Marx highlight this well commenting that sentences in which 'technology' or some surrogate is made the subject of an active predicate are illogical. Examples include: 'the automobile created suburbia', 'the pill produced the sexual revolution' or 'the internet caused students to stop reading books' (1994, p. xi). In all cases, complex phenomena are deemed as having followed from the technology itself, or that the technology is credited with undue agency. Smith simplifies this further observing that technological determinism is 'the belief that social progress is driven by technological innovation, which in turn follows as an "inevitable" course' (1994, p. 38). Another way of looking at this is to ask: Has a technology ever initiated an action not pre-programmed by humans? The answer is no, but the answer is complicated by recognition of the feedback loop or reciprocal stimulation that occurs between institutions and technologies they produce

(De Landa, 1997). It is also worth quickly interrogating the word 'technology' itself. As Marx (1994) describes, the signifier 'technology' as we understand is a relatively recent one. It is a word devoid of a referent or specific adjective: it does not refer to an institution, place, persons, group of people, class or gender. Instead it is a vessel into which a variety of discourses are injected. When intellectual, social and scientific developments converged in the Enlightenment, for the upper classes, mechanics was a low art deemed as useful, practical, industrial, having to do with crafts and the skills, getting hands dirty, the physical, tools and ultimately was a derogatory expression, particularly in England. It was distinct from the creative, high or fine arts. The distinction also served to keep apart things and ideas, the physical and the mental, or making and thinking. The word technology was thus implemented to mask mechanical technique with a sign imbued with refinement and neutrality. Similarly, science and technology are also relatively recent bedfellows and it is only since the mid-1800s that technology has utilized and borrowed from science, particularly in regards to phenomena inaccessible to the human eye, for example, those of a chemical and electrical form (Arthur, 2009). In the nineteenth century there developed a profound belief in the rallying cries of innovation, invention, objectivity, efficiency, expertise, standardization, measurement and progress, arguably at the expense of tradition (Postman, 1993). In this view of the relationship between technology and society the main goal of human work is efficiency, calculations are superior to human judgment and phenomena that cannot be measured do not exist or are considered unimportant.

Feedback Machines

Castells (2001) similarly describes two industrial revolutions, that of steam and the second of electricity, both guided by the application of scientific knowledge. The first started in the latter half of the eighteenth century and involved James Watt's improvements on Thomas Newcomen's steam engine, James Hargreave's spinning jenny that augmented cotton production, Henry Cort's process of metallurgy and the refining of iron ore, and, more broadly, the replacement of handheld tools with machines. The second, around one hundred years later, revolved around the development of electricity, the internal combustion engine, refined science-based chemical and pharmaceuticals, efficient steel casting, telegraphy and the laying of telegraphy cables across ocean floors, the telephone and wireless telegraphy or radio. In these Years of Progress stereotyped as a society in rapture over reason and invention, feedback-based technological developments that aided in the organization of production, distribution and consumption of goods and services include closed-loop feedback devices like James Watt's steam governor (1788) that regulated the amount of fuel (or other necessary liquids or gasses) admitted. These were preceded by a range of other modern self-regulating systems including Cornelis Drebbel's thermostat (1620s), Denis Papin's steam pump and safety valve (1688) and a range of windmill designs awarded UK patents that used self-regulatory techniques to take full advantage of wind; for example, Thomas Mead patented the centrifugal pendulum (1787) to control the speed of grindstones in a mill driven by wind. Other technologies that involve production and codification include pre-programmed open-loop controllers like those of Joseph Jacquard's loom (1801/patented 1804) that was to spark the 'information age'. This was a mechanical loom used for textiles production that involved use of large punched cards that correspond to a hook in the loom that guided, raised and lowered threads to allow for different patterns of textiles. As Essinger (2004) describes, the central innovation here was that the loom was programmable through punched cards so that the loom continually fed itself with the information it needed to carry out the next row of weaving or set of operations. Weaving webs of information, Jacquard's loom provided a key technological platform for others including Charles Babbage and his endeavours to create the Difference Engine (proposed in 1822) and the Analytical Engine (first described in 1837). The former had the purpose of being a *reliable* and rapid mathematical calculator and the latter a more general 'computer'. Famously, the Analytical Engine was never built due in part to lack of funding. The importance of the Analytical Engine is summed up by Ada Lovelace who wrote: 'We may say most aptly that the Analytical Engine *weaves algebraical patterns* as the Jacquard loom weaves flowers and leaves' [Lovelace's italics] (Essinger, 2004, p. 141). However, as Mayr (1986) reminds us, the history of feedback technologies does not begin with the West but can be sourced in the history of Islam as far back as the thirteenth century, and arguably back to Hero of Alexandria (circa 10–70 AD) who created a rocket-type steam engine called the aeolipile, as well as the float-level regulator that forms a well-known practical example of feedback systems. In their history of automatic control, Dorf and Bishop (2008) look back even further to Greece and the water clock of Ktesibios

(300 to 1 BC) and an oil lamp devised by Philon around 550 BC that used a float regulator to maintain a constant level of fuel. Although these technologies represent important developments in the history of feedback technologies, they are still identifiable as representing natural laws rather than having feedback loops of information as their driving force. Facilitating the growth and cultural logic of network society, communication and feedback, there are a number of key innovations that have directly contributed to contemporary technoculture and information management systems. In addition to punch-cards, relevant media and communication technologies include innovation of photography and telegraphy (1830s), rotary power printing that uses impressions curved around a cylinder to print on long continuous rolls of paper or other substrates (1840s), the typewriter (1860s), transatlantic cable, first laid between Ireland and the US used for telegraph communications (1866), the telephone (1876), Kelvin's tide-predictor that proved the feasibility of replacing calculations performed by people with computations by a machine (1876), motion pictures (1894), wireless telegraphy (1895), magnetic tape recording (1899), radio (1906) and television (1923). As Virilio (1994) describes, such technologies either played a part in facilitating or directly enabling people to 'write at a distance' and with the arrival of television we saw the coming together of the transtextual and the transvisual. In regards to storing, ordering and accounting for data, the Hollerith machine, designed in 1890 by Hermann Hollerith, was used to tabulate the 1891 US Census, although this was in many ways based upon Charles Babbage's unbuilt Analytical Engine as well as the Jacquard Loom. Essinger (2004) observes that whereas Babbage laid the conceptual ground between the Jacquard Loom and the computer, Hollerith made it a practical reality. Hollerith also used punched cards to record information and designed a tabulator and sorter to mark the results. For census purposes, Hollerith machines not only saved the taxpayer time and money, but they also allowed early data miners to establish interrelationships between data sets. Private and public bureaucracies and organizations alike adopted these machines globally. In World War I they were used far beyond their original vision to control and manage activities such as food supplies, but also to chart the activities of German U-Boats. The success of Hollerith's electro-mechanical machines led to the formation of International Business Machines (IBM) in 1924[1] and the growth of information technology as an industry. In addition, Hollerith systems were used by Nazi Germany in the registering and surveillance of Jewish people throughout the holocaust

(Black, 2002, p. 131–32). Gere similarly observes, 'Hollerith's invention also helped found a connection that continues unabated to this day, between digital technology and methods of surveillance, control and discipline' (2002, p. 38). As Elmer (2004) highlights, such innovation in inventory systems also found expression in the 1970s through the Universal Product Code (UPC), or bar codes, and more recently the widespread use of RFID. The bar code and associated scanning technology greatly facilitated computerized feedback loops through understanding of shopping preferences thus shortening feedback times immensely when compared to paper or observational feedback to store owners or data managers. Along with the intensification of feedback as a social modus operandi, these early (along with more recent) developments in data processing and sorting represent an order of control that contributes to technical mastery over time and space conceived of both in terms of homogeneity and heterogeneity. However, while many of these creations contributed to new methods of bureaucracy, organization and data management, the intensification of computer network development encompassed all of these and almost literally created the backbone for online behavioural advertising.

By World War II there were a range of modern computers in operation (Wurster, 2002). Although far from resembling the machines we are used to today, these developments in the 1930s centred in Europe and the United States laid the basis of the intellectual environment of which contemporary computing is still a part. Developments are too vast and wide to account for in detail here (see Rojas, 2002), but key innovations and developments include: the differential analyzer of Massachusetts Institute of Technology (MIT) engineering professor Vannevar Bush (1930); the 'mechanical programmer' from Wallace Eckert (1933) that linked various IBM punch-card accounting machines; Bush's electrical analog computer (1935) with punched-tape programming; an electronic analog computer (1938) devised at the Foxboro Company; a working prototype of an electronic calculator that used Boolean logic (1939) developed by John Atanasoff at Iowa State University; Konrad Zuse and his Z1 that was a binary rather than decimal mechanical computer that importantly used Boolean logic programming rules (1935–1938); the Bell Laboratories Model I or the Complex Number Calculator (1940), built by George Stibitz and able to send commands via telephone lines (AT&T claimed this to be the first digital computer); and the Electronic Numerical Integrator And Computer (ENIAC) announced in 1946 employed for military and ballistic purposes (Winston, 1998). Although the ENIAC lacked a central processing unit (CPU), it is nonetheless more commonly recognized as the world's first all electric digital computer (Essinger, 2004). Von Neumann would later contribute the ideas that led to the development of the CPU, internal memory and binary mathematics (Barney, 2000). Howard Aiken's design and IBM's engineering led to the Harvard Mark I (otherwise known as IBM's Automatic Sequence Controlled Calculator) in 1944 that was the first operating machine that could execute long computations automatically and was America's first program-controlled, general-purpose digital calculator. Such developments laid the foundations for a network society and invoked the understanding that contemporary computers are crippled if they cannot communicate with one another and that the future lay in connectivity.

Ubiquity of networks

Highly dystopian, Virilio (1997) paints a scenario of citizen-terminals characterized by inertia, where interactivity has shrunk the planet so nothing is left but the teletechnologies of generalized interactivity. For Virilio, travelling without moving stands in contrast to the transportation revolutions of prior centuries that were characterized by the mobilization of people. This dichotomy is a false one, particularly given recent innovation and popular adoption of locative computing, smartphones and the colliding of virtual and real experiences as found with augmented reality applications. There are however general lessons to be taken from Virilio's insistence on interactivity, telepresence and the opening up of relativistic space as defining features of the contemporary media environment. From the vantage point of 2011, it certainly seems van Dijk (2006) is right in asserting that the twenty-first century is nothing less than the age of networks. They have become the nervous system of our society supporting not only advertising and media, but core societal infrastructures translated into bits and packets. Although the history of the internet has been told many times over (see the Internet Society (2010) for an authoritative and extended description), it is worth a quick recount of core principles given the centrality of DPI to this book. In the early 1960s packet switching was conceived as a means of communicating across networks. Instrumental was Leonard Kleinrock (1961) and his PhD work that addressed problems associated with information flow across networks consisting of nodes that receive, sort, store and transmit messages. Another significant leap came from RAND Corporation's researcher

Paul Baran, supported by earlier work in Information Theory. As discussed in relation to packet switching, Phorm and DPI in Chapter 2, in the 1960s Baran (1964) wrote a paper detailing the process of breaking up information into 'message blocks' able to be sent in packages throughout a network. These developments were set against concern over destruction of centralized (or star type) networks and the potential of thermonuclear war. Showing that networks fall into one of two categories, centralized and distributed (grid or mesh types), he points out the capacity and flexibility inherent in decentralized networks, as they facilitate transmission between any station within the network, provided a path can be drawn for data to travel along. This was described as a self-learning network of unmanned digital switches without a vulnerable central control point where, should a network suffer damage, the routing doctrine would find the shortest possible path available to a destination for information to be reassembled. Although primarily conceptualized in defensive terms, Baran's paper also posits the potential for civilian uses. Donald Watt Davies had a similar innovation while working at the National Physical Laboratory (NPL) in London, but instead of calling his messages 'blocks' he used the now standard expression 'packets', and the process of breaking up and recompiling messages and/or information, 'packet switching'. There remained however the issue of how networks should talk to other networks. In 1962 Joseph Licklider introduced his 'Galactic Network' concept framing a globally interconnected set of computers through which all may quickly access data and programs from any site (Leiner, et al., 2003). In the early 1970s there were a handful of networks (for example, ARPANET; the Watt Davies network at NPL; ALOHANET; the emergent French network, Cyclades; and the satellite network, SATNET) but with no common protocol to build a 'network of networks'. In 1973 Vint Cerf and Bob Khan presented draft protocols and a year later these became Transmission Control Protocol (TCP), the fundamental programme at the heart of what became the internet (Leiner et al., 2003). Key access points were limited to university computer science departments, although 46 of 62 ARPANET sites themselves were located within the military-industrial complex. Winston (1998) describes that in the mid-to-late 1970s there was a sense within the ARPANET realm of a failure of its authorities to impose their will on emerging structures and address the increasing need for coordination mechanisms. It was not until 5 years after the TCP protocol was agreed in 1974 that ARPA (who were redesigned as the Defense Advanced Research Projects Agency (DARPA) in 1972) created an Internet Configuration Control Board

(ICCB) in 1979, although that only had a limited effect as a control measure. In 1983 DARPA introduce the domain name system, or the 'phone book of the internet', with 'edu' for universities, 'com' for commerce and 'mil' for military and in the same year the military sites of ARPANET became MILNET (and integrated into the Defense Data Network). By 1988, the internet (the network of networks) was an essential tool for communications, and in 1989, ARPANET was closed down. The internet has then undergone three significant developments: the ARPA phase between 1969–1990; National Science Foundation (NSF) phase between 1990–1995 and the commercial phase from 1995 to the present day. In the first stage ARPANET traffic was of a military nature, yet by the middle of the 1980s, other players started to build around the ARPANET and by 1984 the NSF started contracting for the building of a national backbone to connect research universities, the NSFNET. Concurrently other government agencies, and some commercial agencies and academic institutions began building regional networks. However, the NSF's 'Acceptable Use Policy by the end of the 1980s limited some uses of the Internet by commercial interests. By 1995, with the private, commercial market thriving, NSF decommissioned the NSFNET, allowing for public use of the internet.

Innovation in transporting information, communication and routing has resulted in an implosion. As Baudrillard writing in the 1980s put it, we have collapsed 'into a space which is reduced daily as a result of increasing mobility made possible by airplanes and the media' (1987, p. 39). The expansion of communication networks contributed to the voiding of the space information travelled along by dint of near effortless movement. First with telegraphy, radio, the telephone and then television, reliable instantaneous communication became the norm. Networks, internet protocol, the web, and go-anywhere locative online media, subsequently facilitated higher degrees of network-based interaction and participation. Such communicative innovation engendered the displacement of body and the abolition of space that Virilio describes as having been obliterated, and as now characterized by relativity as a mode of understanding space-time. Contrast this for example with the observation that news of the fall of the Bastille in 1789 took a fortnight to cross 83 miles and reach the citizens of Peronne (Roberts, 1972). Virilio's ideas sit within a wider late modern/postmodern interest in time-space compression and the primacy of information flows as a means of shrinking real space (also see Harvey, 1990; Giddens, 1990). Modernity is predicated on speed when, for example, people can outrun animals by dint of machines. Network society theoretically operates at the speed of light, although daily experience tells us there are numerous bottlenecks, barriers, periods of lag and differentials of connection speed that affect this unrealizable claim. Virilio (1997) discusses speed in terms of *dromology*, meaning the science or logic of speed. When we think about the world we often conceive of it in terms of distribution of wealth, finance and military might. Virilio (1986) instead examines speed as it relates to power, for example, in the velocity of dispatching information. Whereas forces such as the military sought to speed up the movement of troops (as well as communication to and from these), acceleration has now more to do with information and the attainment of real-time understanding and transmission. This real-time understanding manifests in the replacement of the physical journey to one of constant arrival. By this Virilio (1997) argues that as the last transport revolution began to eliminate delay and change, it still took a long time to arrive somewhere. What he proposes in an era of information travelling at the speed of light is that we see the beginning of a scenario of 'generalised arrival' (1997, p. 16), and that the journey loses its components in favour of arrival alone. Both Marx, and later Lefebvre, discussed the relationship between time and space extensively. In *The Grundrisse* (1973 [1939]) Marx articulates the propensity of capital to annihilate physical space with time, and the propensity of transport and communications to effectively diminish the significance of physical spatial distance, particularly as an obstacle to the expansion of capital flows. That is to say, the role of physical place becomes much less important due to new communicative faculties, and that notions of space and division have imploded, folded in on themselves and taken on void-like qualities. Such compression also highlights the malleability of space in human hands and the problems with naturalized theorization of space. Accounts of communicative implosion are thus founded on the belief that space/time has for all intents and purposes been abolished and what is left is the perception of real-time interactivity. Lefebvre (1971; 1991 [1974]; 2003) describes spatialization as the process of overcoming the constraints of space and time in social life, and that space itself is a social (and economic) construction. In discussion of socio-spatial dialectics Soja (1989) similarly argues that space is a social construction and is not fixed; much in the way that time is articulated through social transformations. He argues that:

The geography and history of capitalism intersect in a complex social process which creates a constantly evolving historical sequence of spatialities, a spatio-temporal structuration of social life which gives form to and situates not only the grand movements of societal development but also the recursive practices of day-to-day activity. (1989, p. 127)

Space then is a material product and not a chance happening or fixed phenomenon (Castells, 1977). It is a manifestation of a particular societal arrangement whose principles we should better understand. Citing debates in science about relative versus absolute space, Soja argues that between space as established in nature and space as understood through one's own mental cognition is socially produced space. The three – physical, mental and social spaces – overlap both in Soja's accounts of urban space and here in regards to digital space and the structures that underpin it. If digital (and analogue) communications operate in what people perceive to be of the moment than we have created what is effectively relative space. It is in this space of interactivity and telepresence that Virilio (1994; 1997) targets his critique of a communications and transportational culture predicated on the abolition of traditional conceptions of space-time, and where we find the technocultural basis for advertising based on exponentially higher levels of control, feedback and information management. Like space, time is rendered relative where networks engender a multiplicity of time-based experiences that have little to do with clock-based regimentation. Time here is understood in relation to difference between elements (Latour, 1997b), and although it may be tempting to see behavioural advertising systems as being the meter, clock or measure of 'time', what they instead represent is what Leong et al. in reference to wider online systems describe as 'not one isochrony but a multitude of timings' through which localization and heterogeneity is maintained (2009, p. 1280).

Beyond Philosophy and Stimulus-response: Cybernetics

Heidegger, in an interview with *Der Spiegel* magazine in 1966, when asked what had taken the place of philosophy, responded, 'cybernetics' (Zimmerman, 1990). Having a dystopian view of modern technology and the imperatives that drove it, he argued that the cybernetic-computer revolution was indicative of the submission of the primordial *logos* to logistics, and that the role philosophy had traditionally played in guiding and revealing the world had been taken over by the sciences.

Franchi and Güzeldere (2005) discuss Heidegger's forecasts in terms of a concession of dominance where cybernetics represents the liquidation of the humanities in general. For Heidegger, it is in the equivalence of spheres where cybernetics derives its power and effectiveness. That is to say, whereas traditionally Western philosophy had divided reality up into the physical, the psychical and the biological, cybernetics sought a control-oriented system that would unite these categories conceived in technical terms in which there is little need for the concerns of humanities, philosophy or 'thought' in general. Lyotard (1979) makes a similar point in *The Postmodern Condition* involving the operationalization and instrumentalization of knowledge and the translating of 'abstract' understanding into informational form subject to ease of goal-oriented manipulation. In the construction of a technological universe Heidegger saw a waning of spirit. His concern was not so much with science, but rather the scientific method. For Heidegger this found its most profound expression in cybernetics[2]. Such fears over pragmatism and technological operation and manipulation were at least in part based on the conclusions of Claude Shannon (1976 [1938]) and others who demonstrated that information can be treated like any other quantity and may be subjected to the manipulation of a machine. Information for Shannon meant that it had no materiality, no dimension of its own and no innate connection with meaning. Shannon's close colleague, Warren Weaver also later observed that 'two messages, one of which is heavily loaded with meaning and the other of which is pure nonsense, can be exactly equivalent' and information should not be confused with meaning (1949, p. 5). This led Shannon to be dubbed, the 'father of information theory'. It is this link that is vital to the notion of bureaucratic control as not only could machines compile statistics, but they also offered more profound capabilities for processing data relating to people. Information theory thus stripped away semantic meaning from information. Post-World War II, Norbert Wiener (1948) was working on cybernetics popularizing terms such as 'feedback', 'input' and 'output' in describing the actions of machine, man and animal, and the enterprise of communications engineering. He sought to understand objects in terms of communication, statistics and control, choosing to reject humanist ideas of subjectivity, instead focusing on humans as parts of systems with actions measured through behaviour rather than introspection. This is not to suggest that Wiener looked to understand people in terms of machines, his interest rather was in the potential for machines to function like people. The intellectual eruption of cybernetics was a major paradigm shift, although one that Wiener himself recognizes as stemming back to Leibniz (2005 [1686]) who in the late 1600s, among other innovations and theorization, documented the binary number system and discussed the notion of feedback. Franchi and Güzeldere (2005) describe that the term 'cybernetics' originates in the writings of André Ampere (in *Essai sur la philosophie des sciences*) in the form *cybernétique*, meaning the 'science of government or control'. For Wiener, Leibniz envisioned for the future the possibility of a symbolic logic (the calculus ratiocinator) operable by machine (the machina ratiocinatrix), which would handle mankind's logical problems (Masani, 2000). Leibniz, a true polymath, was not alone in conceiving of feedback systems. For example, Thomas Willis (a medical doctor) was also interested in man-machines, transmission, reception and communication within feedback systems also coining the term neurology and providing the germs of cybernetic understanding (Muri, 2007; also see Booth, 2005).

As Beniger (1986) describes, twentieth-century cybernetics was largely anticipated in a paper published in 1940 by a British scientist, W. Ross Ashby. Ashby's paper 'stated the fundamental ideas of cybernetics' introducing the term 'functional circuit' for negative feedback, and parts of a system that maintain the norm (Ashby, 1940, cited in Miller, 1978). Such a dynamic proposition has far-reaching consequences ranging from physical ecosystems to supply/demand-based economics. Positive feedback, by contrast, involves deviation from homeostasis, where a phenomenon increases exponentially until a resource is drained, as with the spread of a virus for example (conversely the object in question may transform, emerge, or change states). As Ashby argues, information theory and cybernetics are predicated on the notion of understanding all the possible behaviours that a situation can produce and how likely or probable one behaviour is compared to another. Specifically, Ashby states that 'cybernetics typically treats any given, particular, machine by asking not "what individual act will it produce here and now?" but "what are *all* the possible behaviours that it can produce?"' (1956, p. 3 [emphasis in original]). Cybernetics focuses on how systems use information, models and control actions to steer towards and maintain their goals, while counteracting various disturbances (Heylighen and Joslyn, 2001). This means that systems resist hindrances from outside themselves that would make them deviate from their goal or ideal condition. Whereas in Newtonian conceptions effects follow causes, cybernetics is more interested in circularity, feedback and how an effect feeds back into its cause, thus potentially making causes and effects indistinguishable. We may say the same of advertising. Whereas the majority of discussion and critique of advertising is aimed at understanding effectiveness, or the short and long term semiotics effects of advertising (Williamson, 1978; Messaris, 1997; MacRury, 2009), what is highlighted in this book is circularity and how effects feedback into causes. Rather than thinking of advertising in terms of stimuli and response it is more prudent to examine behavioural forms of advertising (and potentially other more traditional types) in terms of feedback loops and circular systems. Advertising is then best understood in terms of ecology rather than through behaviourism and its fixation on stimulus-response, and as Lash similarly remarks: 'The feedback loop is the locus of the critique of information' (2002, p. 112). Feedback must come in the form of two-way data between the controlled and the controller, and is a means of regulating for error and deviation from a particular goal that in our case involves the delivery of the most relevant advertising understood through being appropriate, meaningful or valuable to the user. Inherently it is then an imperfect system as it is predicated on correcting wrongs and it is in this will-to-learn that we find a key driver behind the teleonomic-type impulses of information that form the key social and technical drivers behind behavioural advertising. Despite the on-going novelty with which 'new media' continues to be held, many of the technological, conceptual and sociological frameworks had been laid before or around World War II, far preceding later conceptions of an information age or post-industrial era (Bell, 1973) with early cybernetic thinking having a distinct resonance with the condition of cyberspace today and its architectures of control. Management of feedback relationships through control architectures of cyberspace are vital to advertisers and marketers (Miles, 2007) and it is in this manner, as Harvey (1985) discusses in relation to social and physical landscapes, that agents of capital have remade and continue to model or influence networks so as to facilitate information flow that with artificial barriers removed readily translates to capital. Indeed, the Organisation for Economic Co-operation and Development (OECD) guidelines on the Protection of Privacy and Transborder Flows of Personal Data 1980 exist to advance the free flow of information between member countries and to avoid the creation of unjustified obstacles to the development of economic and social relations among member countries. For Davies (1998) unfettered circulation has to do with efficiency of identification, although as established in Chapter 4, this is to miss the point slightly. Marketers and advertisers care little about identity and individuals, although they crave optimization and efficiency. What is then presented is Heidegger's (1993 [1954]) 'standing reserve' that overcomes subject-object distinctions, makes no ontological distinction between entities, and in our case involves autopoietically generated information and resources available for the purposes of the generation of more advertising and further data. As with traditional conceptions of bureaucracy, signifiers that identify individuals are readily sacrificed for an efficient system. Following Harvey (1990), Elmer (2004) similarly accounts for the transition from a Fordist economy to one based on networked production, distribution and sales loops. Such flexible modes of production and 'just-in-time' inventory is reflected in identification systems that have been brought into play to allow internet servers to identify targets for online behavioural advertising. Moreover, such methods of managing advertising production reflect a scenario of immanence, deterritorialization, instantaneity and constant arrival. Such processes are not of a malevolent character but are administrative and guided by cybernetic corrective logic.

Pulse Value and Phenomenal Fields

Behavioural advertising opens up the possibility of a blurring between transmission and reception, to the extent they may become indistinct. This can be contrasted with traditional advertising forms whose cycles take much longer. What is thus valued by behavioural advertisers is instantaneity, delivery, refinement, flow and feedback, over more playful creativity as found in traditional brand advertising and more recent forays into newer media. Whereas traditional advertising has more to do with a visually-oriented semiotic logic (Williamson, 1978; Jhally, 1990; Wernick, 1991; Forceville, 1996; Odih, 2007) whose mode of address forcibly attempts to fuse often hitherto non-established links between disparate signifiers and signifieds (i.e. the creation and maintenance of brand identities for products), in relevance-based advertising, this fusion is absent or much less pronounced. As Odih (2007) describes, semiotic accounts of advertising have more to do with texts that are closed and frame an event already passed as determined by an idealized nature of the commodity-form, although these of course may be re-appropriated and/or infused with local meaning. Branded advertising, as opposed to direct mail or classified advertising for example, involves the construction of unified spaces via the language of social worlds drawing upon cultural codes to frame a particular message. They act as mini-lessons in consumption that invite their audiences into the frame so as to adopt a particular subject position. Like zip files once engaged with, they open up an array of referents and a multi-layered information structure. This is not an abstract informational structure but rather one constructed in reference to systems of signification. They occupy a position within a matrix of meaning and are understood through relationships with other signs. Further, the role of the viewer or listener is also constructed in reference to this symbolic world that is to some extent a construct of this cultural world and acts as both receiver and producer of culture. As Williamson (1978) argues, the transactional space does not exist outside but rather we constitute the terrain through participation. As such feedback relationships are not unique to behavioural advertising, although the speed with which such information is processed and circulated is. Whereas traditional creative advertising is in many ways predicated on seduction and simulacra, relevance-based online (and wider digital) advertising is more akin to an infant who knows little of the arts of misdirection, secrecy, intertextuality, semiotic trickery and holding one's cards close for the purposes of mystique. In some contrast, what is presented here involves less overt emotional or ideological investment, or visual and aural stimulation on the part of the user. Rather than advertising disengaging audiences and receivers from a given flow of time and being into one where life is narrated and ordered to the ideological wishes of advertisers and their agencies (Williamson, 1978), behavioural advertising seeks to engage with the lived experience of its recipients, or their *durée*; it does not seek to disrupt or distract, it seeks to inter-act. Its effectiveness currently derives from timing, situation-orientedness, feedback and kairos that have to do with understanding the moment and changing circumstances (Sipiora, 2002). Such approaches are of a different order to Debord's (1992 [1967]) depiction of society that places the spectacle (involving advertising, news, entertainment and other elements of the communications industry) as the dominant model of approaching media, consumption and the pre-eminence of representation. Whereas Debord places the spectacle as the leading production of present day society, in the twenty-first-century information and feedback systems are making themselves more pronounced. What is presented is not a suggestion of succession, but rather deepening and extension caused by semiotic overproduction and an advertising industry that for decades has been caught in a positive feedback loop. As the din of representational advertising reaches inertia, new dimensions are required. Increasingly we see the fields of televisual and print-based attention emptied of potency, along with advertisers' expenditure in the case of newspapers. What is required is the subtle channelling of consumer desire that users carry out on behalf of advertisers through self-regulating feedback relationships with networked and online media. As Baudrillard (1987) argues, ironically in discussion of television (the subject of much semiotic critique), there is no longer transcendence or depth but instead the unfolding of operations and the functional veneer of communications. Behavioural advertising draws less on users' reservoirs of social and cultural references, and more on the aggregated wanderings of their data-doubles. The emphasis then moves from behavioural advertising as being part of a symbolic industry (traditionally having to do with constituted units both intense and discrete) to one based on understanding of flow (and continuous monitoring) of data that make up humanly readable symbols. This indicates a shift in prominence from a language-based conception of advertising to one more predicated on technology. Whereas the former is incorporeal, the latter is more physical. In the language of Deleuze and Guattari (2003 [1987]), this technological perspective is better understood in terms of a machinic assemblage comprised of networked technologies, deep-packet inspection and/or web-based profiling, cookie droppings, dispersed bodies, acts of searching, pointing, typing, clicking, aggregation and disaggregation, and the dynamic interaction between hardware, applications and people that meld together to form behavioural advertising systems. This can be contrasted to conceptions of advertising predicated solely on assemblages of enunciation having to do with regimes of signs and language elements. While the distinction between spectacular and behavioural approaches is not entirely clear, particularly as all advertising relies on media technology to be delivered, there is a substantive difference between traditional ritualistic advertising and autopoietic behaviourally based digital advertising. Like first-wave cybernetics, concern revolves much less around what the messages mean but rather how information is most efficiently delivered and integrates with the behaviour and actuality of any given profiled user. What is more important is the competence and circulation of informational pulses, and advertising that has less to do with latent ideological structures and transcendental coding, and more to do with what preferences, interests and ways of being with which an observer engages the system. Elmer (2004) makes a similar point in his account of profiling machines choosing to focus on techniques of targeting, rationalization and customization over textual representation. Although processes of (re)production are very much alive (Arvidsson, 2006; Schroeder and Salzer-Mörling, 2006), in behavioural advertising we witness a different mode of presentation compared to semiotic/representational advertising that seeks to relay a story, event or vignette. Although display-oriented behavioural advertising is 'designed' and harnesses behaviourally targeted video-based media, rich media, as well as more traditional online display formats, what is more important is understanding the channelling of flows of desire through capillary-like networks, not the relearning of the schizoid lessons of consumer society that seek to confuse metaphor with literal expression. To focus on behavioural advertising texts would be to miss a much larger picture of processes of subjectification and how frontiers of mediation for the purposes of commercial solicitation are being augmented.

Co-production and constructivism

What is instead proposed here is a stronger account of constructivism that reflects a different ontology of brand 'communications'. Whereas mass and niche advertising sought to create or represent an external reality of transcendental brand ideals, behavioural advertising introduces a more immanent practice of co-production than found in spectacular advertising and its feedback relations. Instead of attempting to transmit meta-value, the consumer may be involved at a deeper level, where we clearly inscribe ourselves within the system. As Mary Catherine Bateson[3] (1972) remarks in the title of her book, following such a view of cybernetics, we may act as 'our own metaphor' where our interior becomes externalized, or our inner world becomes a metaphor for an outer world. Reflexively conceived advertising offers a similar result; it involves a dynamic view of consumer/advertiser relations where commercial experience is created through correspondence rather than meaning being something 'out there'. Instead, through collaboration and immanence that involves us being fully present, we are active in its construction as we negotiate, create, search and deal with information and progressively couple with behavioural advertising systems. Commercial pulses stand in contrast to other forms of advertising that involve representation and vignettes relayed through photography, radio, cinema and television. What differentiates 'classical' advertising and relevance-based advertising is that in online behavioural advertising no vista, narrative or depiction opens before us. What is instead presented is a self-referential mode of representation. That is to say, unlike advertising that borrows from other social situations, visual modes of representations, or semiotic substitution, behavioural advertising marks an end to public representation, or to spectacle. Whereas advertising from the modern era has to do with shared events and unfolding in a common temporality, we see here the realization of postmodern conceptions of polytemporality due to the unique relationship generated within advertising systems comprising users, their activities, relevant hardware and software and informational exchange. Digital relevance-based advertising is experienced as node or gateway, or to continue the informational analogies, a relay. It is hard to even call them empty signifiers as there is often little in the way of a vessel to imbue with meaning or signifieds (as is the case with link-based advertising). Although one could argue that behavioural advertising provides 'bits' of content, its nature ensures that it falls short of being part of a culture-machine with depth, richness, humour, unusual perspective, intertextuality, juxtaposition, optical illusions, provocation and other elements and means of seduction that advertising creatives concern themselves with. Purposive use of the web generates a different, more active, order of information consumption where only advertising of relevance to the user, at a contemporary moment, is likely to receive attention. Lash describes, that the 'content of the media machines is neither artifact, nor art, nor singularity, not commodity, not narrative, nor discourse, but *information* itself' (2002, p. 72 [emphasis in original]). The pulse of the signal is in real-time, at least in regards to human perception with little or no reference to a past, imagined or otherwise as is often the case with television commercials, for example. Behavioural advertising exists at present as a utilitarian form of advertising having less to do with contemplative forms of creativity or advertising agencies' conceptions of creativity. They are a stimulant, though not of a narcotic nature as so often ascribed to the semiotic version of consumer society. They are sub-rational and should not disturb but rather gently redirect flows of information and *durée*. Contemporary and nascent behavioural advertising then has to do with gateways, channels, signposting, direction or routing that guide advertising signals within a shared and coupled system. If digital advertising has little in the way of sign value, then it must have signal value. This takes us back to the origins of information theory and feedback machines which, according to Latour (1993), the user is indistinguishable from. Indeed, truly we become quasi-objects and subjects. Whereas traditional conceptions of advertising have to do with stages, step-by-step approaches, and periodic inputs and outputs (advertising-in/consumer response-out[4]), what is instead posited is a continual interaction that through the exchange of information sustains the system and ensures its continuation.

Towards an Autopoietic Understanding of Behavioural Advertising

On reflecting on behavioural advertising and the nature of the control system therein we understand that it is predicated on feedback, circularity, movement and self-sustainability. In this sense it differs from first-order cybernetic systems in that traditionally a cybernetic system will proceed in reference to its environment as it advances towards a goal (in the way, for example, that a mountain biker will proceed down a hill responding to terrain through checks and balances). However, although cybernetic systems are self-regulating, they are not self-organizing or self-reproducing. An autopoietic system is different in that it is its internal structure that determines change in a way that concurrently maintains its identity. Autopoietic thinkers do not lay claim to having discovered self-organization, but instead recognize autopoiesis as flowing from Kant's (2008 [1790]) *Critique of Judgement* and the notion of 'natural purpose' (Thompson, 2004). Specifically, autopoietic systems are 'self-producing systems – their components participate in processes of production the result of which is the very same components' (Mingers, 1995, p. 206). While a true autopoietic theorist may quarrel that it is incorrect to argue that behavioural advertising is self-propagating, we may at least use the notion metaphorically in establishing how interactions between components of a behavioural advertising system are mutually constitutive. Like cellular entities, parts of behavioural advertising are renewed over a period of time and the laws and structures that inform it remain the same unless modified from outside in some way. Behavioural advertising reproduces itself in that users and observers of advertising browse, data is harvested, relevant advertising is served, users browse further, more data is harvested, more relevant advertising is served and so on. After a time it matters little when and where the starting point began; the point is, the system is stable and continues as sustenance is derived from its environment. Advertising agencies, behavioural advertising networks, users, publishers reliant on advertising and advertisers themselves are not monolithic entities. If the system of which we as users are also exchangeable parts did not exist then these companies would not exist. The components of behavioural advertising conceived of as an autopoietic system are changing constituents and like living matter, they tend to develop, change and be replaced over a period of time until all its initial matter has disappeared although the nature, structure and organization of the components remains the system.

To pick on one component: an advertising agency, for example, is not unchanging, but rather its employees gradually come and go, office furniture changes, office buildings change and everything that it is made up of transforms over a period of time. In terms of behavioural advertising itself, its parts will be changed and replaced over a period of time and this is sustained by returns from the system itself. The system ensures the replacement of its parts and the parts of course constitute the system. The advertising text is then a manifestation or instantiation of all actors in the system, and is defined through its constituents and the relationships between these. Fitting in with discourses of complexity (Capra, 2005; Urry, 2005b), such a view of behavioural advertising highlights the shift from reductionist analyses to one more chaotic, albeit structurally stable, involving self-assembly and self-reproduction.

Autopoiesis is a key pillar of second wave cybernetics in that it is much more reflexive than the first. As von Foerster (1981) and Maturana and Varela (1980) posit, it requires that greater consideration be paid to the observer, who not only observes, but is also observed and who actively contributes to the shape and nature of the system. As Urry (2005a) highlights, such complex interactions have been likened to walking through a maze whose walls rearrange themselves as one walks past. For us interested in digitized information and advertising, this can be presented more literally in that the web changes before us as we move between pages and sites that are informed by behavioural advertising systems. These involve ourselves, other users and their own traces, mediating properties of web browsers and IP addresses, publishers' web page content, advertisements themselves, advertisers and advertising networks' aggregating processes. Importantly, it is our very presence that affects the way the web looks to us and it is our informational being that affects the nature of 'there'. Systems understood through complexity do not involve a central organizing, planning or controlling authority, but rather are defined in terms of themselves and their constituent elements. What counts more is the constancy of the relationships maintained between the parts of a system. In autopoietic arrangements networks give rise to components that through their interactions and transformations regenerate and, in turn, realize the network of processes that produced them (Armand, 2008). Such systems contrast with allopoietic systems that are characterized by systems producing something other than themselves – for example, car factories where the machines do not produce themselves and cars do not produce more cars. Guattari (1992) makes the distinction that such machines are haunted by death, and the potential for breakdown and catastrophe (and we may also add built-in obsolescence). In contrast autopoietic systems are characterized by being readied for eternity. They involve a modality of becoming and bringing-forth as a result of on-going relations between actors and parts. Autopoiesis found initial expression in biology during the late 1970s through the work of Maturana and Varela (1980) but spread, at times contentiously, to other fields of organizational study, much in the way that cybernetics did (Stacey, 2003). Despite autopoiesis being a biological expression, there is little reason why it cannot be applied to information systems, as Maturana and Varela (1980) themselves recognize. This has its antecedent in von Neumann (1963), who, in 1948, made the case for cellular automata arguing that computers and biological systems process data in similar ways, or at least to a 'certain segment of the [nervous] system's function' (1963, p. 290), also positing the potential for a relationship between neuronal transmitters whose 'impulse seems in the main to be an all-or-none affair, comparable to a binary digit' (ibid., p. 296). Mingers (1995) states that to qualify as an autopoietic system an arrangement should firstly be concerned with the production of the components that constitute the system. In contrast to allopoietic systems behavioural advertising reproduces itself over the networks through analysis of user's web history, presentation of advertising, user interaction with webpages and advertising, feedback delivered across the networks, processing through behavioural advertising systems and the distribution of more relevant advertising. Secondly, the entity should possess a boundary defining the entity as a unity: the network constitutes this. Thirdly, the organization should specify nothing beyond self-production: all that is specified here is relevant advertising. Autopoietic systems are not cut off from their environment, although they are separate. Like biological systems, the environment contributes to its ongoing process of autopoiesis and the original system as part of a suprasystem, that in the case of behavioural advertising incorporates the social, the political and the economic. Autopoietic systems are structurally coupled to other systems and are not formed through a pre-given environment but rather both co-create and are co-created with other entities and systems. Changes are however internally driven and should this identity forming process be lost, this will also involve the destruction of the system. Both organic systems and behavioural advertising systems are predicated on profiling. They relate to their environment by profiling and adapting in feedback-oriented and context-specific situations (Maturana and Varela, 1992). There are however tensions and contradictions within autopoietic

theory; on the one hand, we have observers projecting internal understanding, and on the other, we have the requirement of internal coher-
ence of any given autopoietic system. Thus, to what extent does the
system exist with structural integrity without the user observing it?
Hayles similarly asks: 'Is the claim that autopoietic closure is *intrinsically* a
feature of living systems, or is it how a human observer *perceives* living systems?' [italics original] (1999, p. 145)[5]. As Hayles also points out, this
contradiction is evident in Maturana and Varela's (1980) *Autopoiesis and
Cognition*. This is comprised of two main parts where the earlier essay,
'Biology of Cognition', argues that the system is distinguished by an
observer whereas the later essay, 'Autopoiesis: The Organization of the
Living', makes the case for a unity without an observer through strictly
self-realizing processes. For the purposes that autopoiesis is employed
here, the answer is yes to both in that the system is both self-organizing
and changes under observation. We know that the system is capable of
behaving differently because we know that other users have different
network-based experiences, although being coupled with the same behavioural advertising networks. This does not detract from the internal
structure of the system that remains self-referential and self-producing in
terms of how it is structured.

Likewise, we are left with another question in regards to profiling
systems: Is the user a coupled observer of the system or a component of
the system? My answer is that he or she must be both. Users are a necessary conduit through which circuits of behavioural advertising are relayed
as it generates more of itself, but also the observer that by dint of the act
of observing constructs the reality before them. Users as conduits are
eminently replaceable, but the individual is of course unique in terms of
how his or her interiority recursively generates an externalized metaphor. Moreover, where Lessig (2006) and Elmer (2004) are concerned
about feedback loops and the potential for behavioural advertisers to
dictate terms of engagement and preferences, wider life experience
and interests will circumvent this and also add sustenance to structurally
coupled relationships between users and systems. These include, for
example, new web experiences, life-stages, interests, activities, and both
the minutiae and the extraordinary of daily life that we may relay through
the web in some fashion. As biological organisms require nourishment,
behavioural advertising systems similarly require supplemental matter to
avoid atrophy caused by poor informational circulation. While we make
interpretations of the system in relation to changing modalities of advertising, privacy, regulation and political economy, in itself, behavioural

advertising specifies little. Of course, as with any conception of a system, it is tempting to keep scaling up. We could include an assemblage of wider social meta-systems and actors, for example regulators, innovation from technologists, wider economic activity that results in advertisers spending more on behavioural advertising, governments, lobbyists and privacy campaigners. However, such an account causes problems of boundary and is better thought of in terms of organizational closure where systems need not be isolated, nor closed (Varela, 1979, p. 54–59). Although allopoietic revenue generation through the mining of interiority is the aim for those who have created and manage the hardware and software components of behavioural advertising systems, the system itself functions autopoietically having inscribed within it the production of more of itself. My invocation of biological metaphors and information is far from unique, and as Thrift (2005) observes in relation to complexity and computer programming, descriptions of non-biological processes using biological models have circulated in society for some time. Biological analogies also turn up in relation to other forms of digital advertising, for example viral advertising and its mimetic properties (McStay, 2007a; Golan and Zaidner, 2008), drawing from Richard Dawkin's (1989[1976]) famous 'Selfish Gene'. Networks are also frequently discussed in relation to contagion (Parikka, 2005).

Guattari (2000) also took an interest in the theoretical biology of Bateson, Maturana and Varela, and the way in which people are inextricably involved within natural, societal and psychical eco-systems in which they are immersed. Heroux (2008) sums up Guattari's adopted conception of autopoiesis well, noting that living systems enact a necessary unity of life forms and mind. Mind in this view is comprehensible in even the most basic forms of life as we begin to see patterns of distinction and differentiation, for example, between light and dark, warm and cold, food and waste, me and not-me. This does not involve consciousness but rather embodied cognition predicated on feedback relationships, and regulation through relationships with an environment. The most basic forms of life from plant seedlings to people are defined through feedback. More complex feedback systems eventually invoke relations of information-about-information. As Bateson (1987) in discussion of 'orders of recursiveness' highlights, out of this arises the capacity to learn that invokes questions regarding the nature of intelligence. While this short summary cannot do justice to the ideas raised, it should highlight the immanent nature of ecology from which autopoietic arguments arise. Thrift (2005) sees autopoiesis as a nascent form of knowledge-producing actor networks to have come into existence. If this is correct, behavioural advertising as an autopoietic system sits within a wider meta-discourse of self-producing network systems. Outside of network-based conceptualizations, Luhmann (1995) sees autopoiesis as constituted by communications, society as manifested through communication, and whatever involves communication as a form of society. These systems are unities in constant self-renewal where components of social systems involve actions initiated by communication that in turn leads to more communicative action. Communication media are symbolic feats that ground the processing of communication and what can be achieved. Importantly it is through these techniques and mechanisms that social systems reproduce themselves and remain in motion. Similarly, in regards to technology itself, technology tends to beget technology as all technologies are sired from previous technologies and, as Arthur (2009) argues, technology may be seen in organic terms as it builds itself out of itself where new technologies emerge from existing ones. While larger fields such as technology, communication and society make autopoietic sense in their own right (technology produces more technology), internally these themes possess little in the way of equilibrium and instead continually undergo metamorphosis and new modes of organization. Rather, they exist at the 'edge of chaos' (Kauffman, 1995), between order and disorder involving high degrees of complexity and positive feedback.

The Hunt for Being

Stiegler (2009) argues that the media industry has created a malaise of disorientation and subsumed global memory. This affects the way that people both individually and collectively identify and differentiate events, happenings and phenomena in the world. Industrial memory in this regard is an unstable temporal product in which unique objects appear and later fall from consciousness. Accordingly, memory has been industrialized through both analogue and digital media technologies where a small coterie of producers decide what is event-izable, create the meter for how these should be relayed, and manufacture the present through a selective preservation of memory (for example in relation to news selection). The nature of this common temporality is characterized by what Stiegler calls 'fabricated facticality' and involves the 'industrial fabrication of time, which is due to the structure of temporal rapture induced by analogic and numeric syntheses as they operate "in light-time"' (2009, p. 116). However, as Hansen (2009) points out, digitally based media support a far broader set of potential temporalizations than preceding mediations of time, whether from the earliest sundials to the so-called real-time flux of global television. This affects time-consciousness 'itself'. In contrast to the media industries of old we see the introduction of heterogeneity, alterity and the potential for many multiple experiences of temporality. We do not have to choose between one or the more recent other, but rather recognize a fracturing or deepening in regards to the coupling of people with media and advertising systems. These temporalities do not arise by chance, but arise in relation to systems predicated on autopoiesis that depend on user co-optation. As advertising becomes less dependent on the macro-rhythms of the market economy (one message to rule them all) that seek to organize and impose a common sense of being and social arrangements, or even 'glocal' and regionalized variations where time and experience may be seen as tied to the social context of use (Odih, 2007), advertisers' endeavours require in-depth knowledge of our interests, preferences, ways of being, and as an end goal, the subjective quality of conscious experience.

A phenomenological approach to asynchronous temporality

As computer mediated communication continues to permeate our lifeworlds, behavioural advertising is informed by, feeds upon, and to some extent creates unique temporal experiences on the basis that we contribute to the system. Such occurrences require that we undergo increasing scrutiny so as to engender commercial experiences that tally with our wants, wishes and moods. Existential phenomenology eschews materialism and places much greater emphasis on experience and subjectivity. Traditionally phenomenology involves analyzing things 'in terms of themselves' rather than trying to re-interpret what is given. It is a primarily descriptive approach that pays close attention to evidence as it presents itself and is nearly always conceived of in relation to human analysis (Moran, 2002). Husserlian (1970 [1936]) phenomenology also typically stands opposed to any form of reductionism instead seeking essences of things. It endeavours to understand experiences that are graspable and understandable in their core form. It is in this we have our contradiction: how can a practice such as behavioural advertising based on reductionism pertain to understand or affect experience? What do behavioural advertising systems have to do with intuition or immediacy?

One approach is to address this through recognition of the role of consciousness and interiority as constituting the external world, and the means by which our media habits belie our selves. Such a proposition becomes more realizable when we shift away from Husserlian (1982 [1913]) perspectives based on transcendental subjectivity that sees absolute consciousness as removed from the natural world and eschews synthesized memory from consciousness' constitutive flux (Stiegler, 2009), to one based on routine practices, our environment, and a sense of the world conveyed through an orientation of mood or being (Heidegger, 1985 [1927]). This involves Heidegger's notion of 'Dasein' as a means of conceiving of Being, and being engaged in the world. This mood or temporality sets the terrain for engagement and does not arise from 'outside' or 'inside', but stems from being-in-the-world. These moods disclose and belie how we are and in autopoietic systems engender the mood of information, that is, the tone of interaction defined through our general orientation to the world and everyday life mediated through networked systems. This is then a style or melody and the 'mood is the "medium" which discloses things' (Zimmerman, 1990, p. 141). Behavioural advertising and the systems that underpin it may then offer a mirroring, a reflection and also anticipate in real-time. Stiegler (2009) makes a similar point in relation to how media integrate into ordinary life and to some extent produces it through narration and anticipation. Likewise, it is also useful to invoke Merleau-Ponty's notion of the phenomenal field (Merleau-Ponty, 1962; Priest, 2003). This is a useful phenomenological expression to better understand the lifeworlds that behavioural advertising interacts with, and becomes part of. This is the boundary of the field of experience, much like the visual field you see before and around you which Merleau-Ponty describes as 'an inside without an outside' (Priest, 2003, p. 234). Schutz (1967), borrowing from Bergson (2001 [1889]), similarly accounts for a person's phenomenal life as a 'stream of consciousness', or *durée*. As Schutz describes, 'experience in duration is not a being that is discrete and well-defined but a constant transition from a now-thus to a new now-thus' (1967, p. 45). The contents of this have no meaning, and meaning is only applied retrospectively. Both Schutz's streams and Merleau-Ponty's fields have no discernable end or beginning with the exception of death, but their contents do change over time. For Merleau-Ponty it is, however, characterized by a perpetual now. In fact, if asked what time is it, the time is always now. Perhaps a more figurative way of accounting for the phenomenal field is to understand it as a characteristic of soul, or what

Berardi (2009b) describes metaphorically as the breath that converts biological matter into an animated body. Although carrying overtones of traditional vitalism (the belief that to explain how living things work something more is needed than an understanding of physics and chemistry) [neo]vitalism is a useful means of conceiving the self when the soul is understood as comprising consciousness of one's field of immanence and where behavioural advertising taken as a model and potentiality seeks to put to work our immateriality, and what is perhaps most valuable.

Deleuze also offers a similar account describing that immanence does not *relate* to phenomena, but instead: 'We will say of pure immanence that it is A LIFE and nothing else' (2005, p. 27). This means there is no outside to the process or other dimension dictating relations and any conception of transcendence is always a product of immanence, as was demonstrated in 2010 when life was created from laboratory chemicals[6]. The essence of life is not Promethean or Frankenstein-like, but rather one born out of information itself: information is the essence of life. The phenomenal field is then a rendering of the cosmos, a means of orientation, or the singularization of a map from the infinite flux (Guattari, 1992). Reality is thus not stable nor perception representational – it is organizational. Hayles in discussion of Maturana similarly describes that the 'reality' 'comes into existence for us, and for all living creatures, only through the interaction processes determined solely by the organism's own organisation' (Hayles, 1999, p. 135). These singular temporalities and modes or moods of being that make orientation possible are the object of attention for information-hunters intent on coupling.

When we conceive of coupling, we are interested in the total state of relations between users and advertising systems. As behavioural advertising systems grow more complex and sophisticated they tend towards morphogenetic systems where forms and shapes are created out of transient and temporal events, such as human language, the emergence of biological structures, mass media, or indeed user-system behavioural advertising couplings. Whereas Poster (1990) insisted that we better understand the mode of information, in contrast to Marx's mode of production, what I present is the *Mood of Information*, as a means of conceiving of online behavioural advertising, negotiated temporality, and the information economies these experiences sit within. Such a notion sits within wider interest over what Thrift (2005) calls the 'experience economy' that has to do with consumers taking an active role in the creation of the commodity form. This, for Thrift, involves innovation in systems theory, new organizational techniques in market research (elaborated on in Chapter 6), database management, and new means of commercial representation. He describes that these produce 'a new field concerned with the management of impressions through the efficient use of expression' (2005, p. 8). Whereas Smythe in the 1970s observed that the audience is 'more a statistical abstraction than are, for example, the audience of the live or motion picture theatre because they have no possibility of simultaneously and totally interacting internally to create an audience mood or affect' (1981, p. 49), we may now observe and envisage that rather than existing only as a statistical abstraction, users of behavioural advertising generate a tone of dialogue with advertising systems. What we have is an economy and hunt of Being, or of the phenomenal self. In the recombining of subject and object, it is people and their relationships with environments that fuel autopoietic systems. This is a real-time operation where behavioural advertising systems compress autopoietic feedback loops into what is perceived as a continual present and all that exists is presentation where the only time that matters is now. Behavioural advertising is not something that 'captures' experiences, at least in the sense that phenomenologists mean. To capture means to be capable of reflection and it would at present be absurd to attribute lived streams of consciousness and reflection to behavioural advertising systems, although computers are highly effective simulators. The point is not that behavioural advertising (or other profiling systems) capture, but rather they predict. Despite commentators from Hegel to Baudrillard warning against formalism, reductionism, the imposition of grids on reality, and inept endeavours to render the complexity of the world (Taylor, 2001), in behaviourally coupled relations new potentialities emerge. Although a key function of autopoietic behavioural advertising systems is to give order and meaning to our online experiences in that it sorts, arranges, orders and categorizes, it also offers immediate feedback in the form of advertising that sits and flows appropriately with user's phenomenal lives. As a method of mediating ourselves, behavioural advertising operates near enough to real-time and both creates and is created autopoietically by user's *durée*, or absolute reality (Bergson, 1999 [1913]). To repeat, however, a machine cannot comprehend human experience, although it can notice evidence of prephenomenal life that a user has not reflected on, and remains undifferentiated. This implies a degree of co-existence although in contrast to human relationships characterized by growing older together there is little in the way of simultaneity where we understand one-another through appreciation of one's own consciousness, or of *durée* as the sum of absolute reality. It will however engage in explication of the user and the genuine because-motive, although limited by the inaccessible nature of true *durée* (this applies to both humans and machines). It is thus feasible to comprehend the field of expressions a person displays that have to do with a person's experiences. According to Schutz (1967), the important factor is simultaneity. In discussion of understanding another person he observes that two sets of flow durations may become interlocked and temporarily flow in parallel. This forms the essence of interpersonal relationships. There are two types of behaviour according to Schutz: the first that concerns us less is that which responds to pain and is instinctual; the second, however, involves attitudes and moods and has to do with response although of a prephenomenal nature. Attitude thus determines character and by extension profile and the types of choices a person makes, thus establishing the mood of information. Although lacking the critical reflection of consciousness (Ego), behavioural advertising offers relevant faculties. For example, it prides itself on sifting and sorting information so as to understand the context of a person's actions. Experiences are subject to accumulation, configuration, tiers or hierarchies of order, and experience is used as a reserve supply on which to orient and frame new experiences. Relevant experiences may be reactivated and brought to the fore as situations demand. This involves a form of judgement and categorization normally associated with mind but readily attributed to profiling systems. For example, Schutz states that

> our stock of knowledge (*Erfahrung*) does not by any means refer back directly to the inner time-form as its source and origin. Rather, the meaning-configuration of past experience is a higher-level configuration which has other configurations as its elements, and these in turn were constituted out of still lower-level complexes of meaning. (1967, p. 80)

The processing of knowledge in phenomenology may thus be highly systematized, perhaps more so than one would normally associate with a perspective that forms the base of much qualitative research. Schutz offers the example of a woodcutter: we may objectively analyze from a distance, or we may actually go and talk with the woodcutter so as to assess background, job and whether the man works for a lumber company. According to Schutz, genuine understanding has to do, not with the outward motion of an axe splicing both air and wood, but his in-order-to-motive and the meaning-contexts of what his actions stand for. Behavioural profiling works similarly thriving on maximum input and ideally a plenitude of information sources. It may offer *verisimilitude* of understanding, simulation and truth-effects whose effects can be judged by the extent to which advertising placed by behavioural advertising systems both inhabits online *durée* and redirects flow to an outcome desired by another agent. Although interpreting experience belonging to other people requires the capacity to frame in reference to our own lived experiences, behavioural advertising systems contain the potential in its form, array of resources and theoretical arrangement to offer a passing off of comprehension and insight. Introducing his understanding of metaphysics, Bergson (1999 [1913]) offers an account that does not easily tally with simple divisions between experiential approaches and scientific approaches. He argues that metaphysics, whose basis is *durée*, does not oppose sciences but rather complements them. To admit this however, he argues that scientific methods and objects of study require a change in priorities. For Bergson scientific analysis is the process of abstraction and expressing a thing in terms belonging to other objects. It is then a process of translation that does not deal with intuition or the object itself but rather a representation where we pick off as many resemblances to prior objects so to lock it within preordained schemata of knowledge. He argues that ready-made concepts are a net with which we attempt to capture something of the reality (or Deleuze's notion of pure immanence) that flows through it, and that positive science 'comes to believe that by putting together all these diagrams it can reconstitute the object itself' (1999 [1913], p. 35). Bergson (ibid., p. 43) offers a useful metaphor by stating that positive methodology has led us to seek the meaning of the poem in the form of the letters by which it is composed, which is underpinned by the opposition between semantics and syntax. Writing around one hundred years ago (quantum mechanics were only recently introduced to the world) he distinguishes between a view of science whose analysis is always of the immobile and intuition that places itself within mobility. Whereas much science then had to do with static conceptions of reality, Bergson argues that this is fruitless and misguided and we should instead turn to mobile and dynamic interpretations although as Leong et al. (2009) note, Bergson did not go as far as to defend the cause of coexistence of the multiplicity of lived times understood through relativity, relationships and multiple moving observers, or the social production of time (or space). Although somewhat scathing of scientific methodology, Bergson saw in mathematics contemporary of his time a tendency not to grasp motion from without, but rather from within. Although this requires the use of symbols, it departs from fixity and allows for change and mobility. This use of mathematics finds expression today in applications that capture in real-time representations of change, behaviour and mobility. For Bergson then, it is in mathematics that we may at least be in contact with the continuity and mobility of the real. Localized behavioural techniques as a means of audience research disturb (although do not overcome) the assertion that analysis is the freezing of a decontextualized moment. If intuition has to do with sharing of time as a means of approaching *durée*, then a re-evaluation of the boundaries of science and phenomenology is perhaps required. What is not implied is that behavioural advertising systems 'understand' or comprehend being but rather offer a passing off of understanding so as to be able to engage and immerse themselves into unique human lives. As highlighted in the discussion of cybernetics, information systems deal in syntax and formal symbols that are translatable across a range of knowledge-types. Computers do not understand, they may merely offer the appearance of understanding. As Searle points out, 'you cannot milk semantics out of syntactical processes alone' (1998, p. 12) although, as Bateson (1987) remarks, the difference between 'being right' and 'not being wrong' may not be entirely distinct. Although a non-being cannot 'understand' being, this does nor mean that an object or process cannot accurately reflect and pre-empt being, particularly through reflexive and adaptive learning. It is also possible that such externalization of identity, preferences and wishes may indicate that contents of informational flows and behavioural advertising couplings are better benchmarks of who we are, what our interests are and what motivates us then we could hope to judge ourselves.

Conclusion

This chapter has highlighted the role of user involvement in feedback systems, in particular those that involve autopoietic systems, and heterogeneous and constructivist experience. Although relationships of feedback between consumers, producers, image-makers and distributors exist throughout the history of advertising (after all, societies of simulation and spectacle are also feedback systems that reproduce themselves), the relationship is much more explicit in behavioural advertising, as are the modes of the commodification of experience and subjectivity on the plane of immanence. Such developments see duration as a stratum to be tapped. This understanding has been established through a wide-ranging exposition of technocultural practices of bureaucracy, cybernetics, information and feedback, and the co-optation and co-creation of unique temporal experiences. While at times this chapter has allowed itself to account for behavioural advertising as a potentiality if not yet a complete functioning actuality, the principle is correct in that self-managing or autonomic systems will inevitably play a role in advertising's future as message and delivery complexity increases through the mining of expressed interiority, tone of being or mood of information.

Chapter 6

Compiling Interiority

Chapter 5 presented an exposition of the relationship between behavioural advertising, control systems, autopoiesis, users' phenomenal experience and co-production and heterogeneity. This chapter examines more closely the nature of users' relationships within advertising systems in terms of bifurcation of subjects and objects, and biopolitical endeavour that has less to do with enclosure and exteriority, but rather a harnessing of neo-vitalist productivity. Paradoxically this situation is generated by abstract systems that utilize little in the way of real world signifiers yet may know our preferences better than we know ourselves.

Towards Consumer Aggregation

As Beniger (1986) notes, bureaucracy as a discursive practice traditionally tends towards trying to *decrease* the amount of information processed as a means of boiling down to what is valuable and relevant. While a reduction in information processing may seem slightly odd, this makes sense when one thinks about the objects of analysis. Early attempts to rationalize modern society and interpersonal relationships could only be done by objective, reliable and impersonal criteria. This led the influential utopian socialist and founder of French socialism, Claude Henri Comte de Saint-Simon, to observe in 1820 that such a practice saw a shift 'from the government of men to the administration of things' (Taylor, 1975, p. 3). Thus, although aggregation societies are avaricious for information and feedback, they also necessitate the ignoring of information, particularly given the finite nature of processing availability and power relative to each informational regime. Although the purposes and techniques of information management have developed in technological sophistication, the abstract nature of data has changed little. As Poster (1990) recognizes in his discussion of the malleability of data-selves, we are best understood through linguistics and as unstable entities reconfigurable for any given purpose (e.g. in assembling a target audience who may be interested in product X or service Y). Data and subsequently meta-data is, by definition, abstract and this leaves us with a paradox: data is stripped of individual referents yet advertising servers may potentially know us better than we care to admit.

Merchants of Data 1.0

Society may increasingly be thought of in terms of a reserve of consumption-power. This has been true for some time, and there has been little in the way of a cover-up of governmental and private sector needs for a consuming standing-reserve whose demand may be bent to the will of supply. The numerous consumption crises are testament to this with the first reflecting a milieu of over-production where, as the eighteenth century segued into the nineteenth, the exponential rise in capability of industrial production required a steady and predictable demand for products. This was the first time material flow outstripped in volume and speed the capacity to contain or consume them. This led to what Beniger describes as a 'control crisis in consumption' (1986, p. 264). A range of advertising and marketing techniques were concurrently innovated in the 1880s, for example, the use of national advertising (first by Quaker Mill Company which would become Quaker Oats), package design, packaging sizes, canning technologies (e.g. Heinz and Campbell), brand labels, trademarks, scientific endorsements, testimonials, prizes, arbitrary physical differentiation, box-top premiums, pre-prepared food mixes, on-site demonstrations of products, free samples, and even the invention of rituals such as the modern breakfast (ibid., p. 266). Here advertising emerged as a business that allowed companies and advertisers to access media (specifically newspapers) and expand beyond a company's local boundaries. This was vital as markets were shifting from local ones to systems that required higher levels of national organization. The issue was then one of integration, communication and information processing. Stemming from the demands of both governance and modern business, the 1800s saw a rise in bureaucratic processes, inventions and aggregating tools many of which are common in offices, drawers and stationary cupboards today. Hardware includes many unassuming items, for example blotting paper, the pencil with eraser and steel, envelopes, the desk telephone, pens, carbon paper, the QUERTY based modern typewriter keyboard, keyboard calculators, and as mentioned in the previous chapter, punch-card tabulators. Information storage and recording devices were also more highly organized and prized through the innovation and systematization of shorthand, office records, auditing, the dictation machine and the rise of business schools. Like the current informational regime, the private sector led improvements in classification and quantification of populations. Feedback to advertising was initially provided by responses to questionnaires posed by the early market researchers. Originating in the United States and subsequently adopted by media owners internationally, this also included the formation of the Audit Bureau of Circulation (ABC) in 1914, along with use of a range of other methods such as house-to-house calls, attitudinal and opinion surveys, retail sales, audience monitoring (AC Nielsen), statistical sample surveys, among a panoply of other approaches to identifying audiences and recording feedback. This brought a degree of predictability to potentially chaotic information flows. Developments in energy management, processing speed and population control led Beniger to posit that basic societal transformation from Industrial to Information Society had been essentially completed by the late 1930s. This stands in contrast to mainstream conceptions that place the emergence of these with the advent of television (McLuhan, 1964) or computers (Martin, 1978). Technologies for collecting audience data and market feedback appeared by the late 1910s and continued to develop through the 1930s, the period of transition that Beniger (1986) calls the Control Revolution. By 1935 a range of consumer feedback procedures had been instigated. These included the testing of advertisements (1906), systematic collection of retail statistics (1910s), questionnaire surveys (1911), coded mailings (1912), audits of publishers' circulations (1914), specialized market research, departments and house-to-house interviewing (1916), research text books (1919), saturation (1920), dry waste surveys (1926), a census of distribution (1929), sampling theory for large-scale surveys (c. 1930), field manuals (1931), retail sales indices (1933), national opinion surveys and audimeter monitoring of broadcast audiences (1935) (ibid., p. 378–80). Key figures in the history and practice of advertising such as Daniel Starch (1914) and Claude Hopkins (1998 [1923]) were insistent that advertising should be treated as a science through the use of feedback as a means of understanding and distinguishing between techniques which work and those that do not. In reference to coupon advertising, where discount or rebate may be obtained, Hopkins states that 'coupon returns are watched and recorded on hundreds of different lines. In a single line they are sometimes recorded on thousands of separate ads. Thus we test everything pertaining to advertising' (ibid., p. 216). Starch (1914) similarly sought to establish the scientific foundations of advertising and to ascertain its underlying principles by arguing that complete analysis of propositions and plans for execution may be assessed with certainty, at least as far as cause and effect are possible in human affairs. In tandem with advertisers, publishers of 'high grade' magazines similarly moved towards verification with clearer accounts of circulation and reach thus leading the way to 'cleaner and better advertising'. Such clinical and hygienic improvements allowed an advertiser to 'proceed far more intelligently in the selection and use of mediums than if he had merely vague assurances of enormous circulations to guide him' (1914, p. 96).

Constructing the user: the journey from mass society

Soft techniques of what Smythe (1981) calls the Consciousness Industry involve efficient applications of segmentation that began with the inception of audience market research companies. Stanley Resor who purchased the J. Walter Thompson agency[1] in 1916 was the first to support research into consumer behaviour, in addition to media and advertising effectiveness. He hired a number of behaviourist scientists to study advertising and audiences, their states of mind, feelings and modes of introspection in a systematic manner. This period saw the death and burial of the consumer conceived of as a unit of an unindividuated mass, and cognition that persuasion involves more than a simple account of the merits of a product or service. Moreover, advertisers and their agencies grew to recognize that as different approaches were reaching different segments of the population, message formats had to be tailored appropriately, and that effectiveness was connected to understanding of audiences in specific situations (Leiss et al., 2005). To trace the impetus to understanding populations as segments of one, we need a clearer understanding of how contemporary commercial audience researchers perceive people. Central here is innovation in segmentation strategy and statistics via tools such as conjoint analysis, regression analysis, cluster analysis, factor analysis and similar means of understanding consumer preferences through grouping (Hagerty, 1985). As Claycamp and Massy (1968) highlight, segmentation grew out of economic theory and pricing strategies. In an oft-cited paper from the *Journal of Marketing*, Wendell Smith describes that segmentation represents awareness of the heterogeneity of markets and that one-size does not fit all. He posits:

Market segmentation, on the other hand, consists of viewing a hetero-geneous market (one characterized by divergent demand) as a num-ber of smaller homogeneous markets in response to differing product preferences among important market segments. It is attributable to the desires of consumers or users for more precise satisfaction of their varying wants. (1956, p. 6)

Understanding that marketers and advertisers cannot cater for each individual in isolation, categories are required to cluster people. Clusters will be constructed according to the reason for the study being carried out and the market in question. Cluster analysis then, is the means by which groups or objects are analyzed according to statistical properties and is a method of finding out which particular cluster any given respon-dent is closest to (Funkhouser, 1983). Wedel and Kamakura (2003) unpack further, observing that early categories of segmentation involved cultural variables, geographic variables, neighbourhood, geographic mobility, demographic and socio-economic variables, postal code classi-fications, household life cycle, household and firm size and standard industrial classifications. Despite such an impressive list of information sources, Claycamp and Massy (1968) note that there were difficulties in the early application of segmentation, not least because of the lack of socioeconomic and demographic data publically available. Although it was recognized by analysts that segmentation at the level of individual consumer units would yield maximum profits, informational constraints and fewer data gathering opportunities than data miners are familiar with today proved a barrier. Further, the use of algorithms to analyze segmentation bases is far from unique to contemporary behavioural advertising with wide-ranging debates taking place in regards to the efficiency of respective computer-based algorithms in the 1970s (Wind, 1978; Funkhauser, 1983). However, data mining and warehousing came into greater prominence in the 1980s and the 1990s as a digital mode of classical statistical analysis that seeks to draw meaning from large data sets. Such approaches reflected the fact that by the 1980s, all major orga-nizations had built infrastructural databases about their clients, competi-tors, products and customers, and that computing power continued to fall in fiscal cost. The challenge was and remains to discover valuable knowledge in data, where there is now an over-profusion of information (Adriaans and Zantinge, 1996). Knowledge discovery in databases (KDD) tends to be associated with marketing although it is utilized in a variety of businesses and organizations ranging from maintenance issues in turbines to the correction of meteorological measuring data. In marketing it has found expression in the lexicon of 'customer relationship management', and the warehousing and processing of information at all points where a business interacts with a customer. Contemporary data mining then, is a type of intelligence that combs through the memory of a business and finds patterns useful for any given business objective or question on the basis of an increasingly richer understanding of customers and audiences. Key tasks include classification, estimation, prediction, affinity grouping and description and profiling (Berry and Linoff, 2004). As Baruh (2007) highlights, institutions may develop detailed profiles about individuals without even sharing personally identifiable information (PII), instead gathering information on physical, financial, emotional and intellectual prospects. Once such a profile is developed, decisions may be made on how to tailor advertising or other commercial messages without recourse to PII. Furthermore, as data-mining techniques often use market basket analysis (the process of analyzing customer shopping habits to find different associations between different elements of a basket) these enable institutions to make inferences about an individual based on analyses of how others who are similar to them behave (Baruh, 2007; also see Han and Kamber, 2001). In addition, such extraction may also lead to hitherto unthought-of advertising or marketing opportunities.

Manufacturing Audiences

The value of understanding customers and audiences then, has long been acknowledged.. Tracing media history from broadcasting to Google, Bermejo (2009) situates contemporary notions of manufactured audiences, where content acts as bait to deliver audiences to advertisers, in light of Smythe's (1977) now canonized Marxian proposal to focus on the economic dimensions of media industries in capitalism and to point to audiences as the main commodity manufactured by these industries. The audience-as-commodity argument stems from dissatisfaction with purely textual approaches to advertising as well as of critical approaches, such as accounts of base and superstructure, which do not fully account for the practice of advertising and the complexity of the construction and deconstruction of audiences. In the United Kingdom, Curran (1981) and McQuail (1997) have made similar observations about ratings discourses, the allocation of advertising, and how media competition for this allocation has influenced the character of the British mass media where media companies make revenue through selling audiences rather than content and programming. Seeing content as a means of baiting consumers, although admitting of a dialectical tension between audiences and producers, the audience-as-commodity argument has to do with a feedback process in which content entices consumers, advertising is served, data about audiences is generated, and advertising is again served on the basis of data generated. In such an account of events, 'You' are the commodity. This argument, tending to focus on television (rather than press, radio, cinema, outdoor or what has in the past been labelled above-the-line or mass advertising media), sees audience time as produced by television medium owners and audiences themselves, and measured and valorized by ratings organizations such as Broadcasters Audience Research Board (BARB) in the United Kingdom. In the traditional media sector this is based on less than perfect information. BARB for example, employs RSMB, Ipsos MORI, AGB Nielsen Media Research and TNS to carry out their surveys with samples of 5,100 households to represent over 25 million households with televisions across the United Kingdom (BARB, 2010). In this view the audience, or at least their potential attention-time, thus becomes a commodity to be sold to advertisers. In traditional media studies the audience as market represents the first, and often neglected, stage of the advertising process and circulation of commodity culture. This argument, as detailed by Jhally (1990), involves the conceptualization of viewing time as labour, arguing that as the working classes power capitalism, viewers also keep audience broadcasting in business too. Just as workers sell labour power, audiences sell watching power with wages equating to programming. Jhally (1990) also somewhat bluntly but accurately argues that both labour and watching commercials is mostly unpleasant and people attempt to stand outside the system and do what they can to avoid them (e.g. channel-hopping, talking with others, leaving the room, utilizing another media form, attending to others, mentally tuning out, the proverbial lavatory break, etc.). Jhally (1990), along with Neuman (1991), notes the rise of narrowcasting in the 1980s and describes increases in surplus value generated through refined categorization, pattern recognition and profiling. With behavioural advertising the value of the audience as commodity is increased, not only through precision of targeting but also through perception of relevance and the fact that behavioural advertising receives higher click-through rates and brand engagement with consumers than contextual and other forms of targeting. For example, a market report cited by Phorm utilizing a demographically diverse sample of online users who have made one online purchase within the year of being sampled highlights that 41 per cent of internet users pay more attention to personalized advertising (ChoiceStream, 2008). Mosco (2009) argues that new media amplify Smythe's (1977) arguments where the recursive nature of digital systems expands the commodification process in that companies may package users in a variety of bundles depending on the needs of prospective purchasers. For example, this may have to do with highly specific media preferences, purchasing habits, demographic or psychographic characteristics and social network habits, so that there is little waste generated in advertising to people who may be of an irrelevant category. As argued in Chapter 5, more important than the ideological positioning of content, at least for a critical understanding of contemporary behavioural advertising understood through the audience as commodity, is the symbiotic relationship between users and systems. Here information societies present themselves as the purest form of capitalism as its inhabitants more easily translate into capital and users' profiles represent malleable entities or assemblages recombinable for specific advertising needs. Users are immanent commodities in that they are constituted by, and aid in constituting, the cycle of feedback and commodity production. From the point of view of those who manage behavioural advertising systems, these audiences only exist in a simulational and cartographic sense, and even with advertising predicated on behaviour, aggregation processes must omit much detail and only include what is deemed necessary for the pre-determined goal (the serving of relevant advertising). Even this degree of representation is slightly misleading as it gives the impression of an indexical link, whereas in practice automated systems are either closed to people (as detailed in Chapter 2) or users are represented by an arbitrary code. A materialist argument is of more use, at least in regards to behavioural digital advertising, and perhaps more broadly, than one that oscillates between understanding audiences as somewhere on a continuum between being inert, active or co-producers (Ross and Nightingale, 2003). Although users play a key role in constituting the features of behavioural advertising, being based on their behaviour, ideological examination of texts is far less important than awareness of the means of segmentation, delivery systems and the power relations that exist beneath hybridized behavioural advertising-machines.

Aggregation, Biopower and Subjectivity

Without people to produce information there can be no phenomenal reality to mine and it is no coincidence that as advertising systems become more complex, they in turn require more from humans. With subjectivity in the frame it is clear that users are not merely passive termini but rather a productive force (Toscano, 2007). This applies not only to advertising but all sorts of technologies in that as machines simulate cognition and develop more lifelike characteristics, they demand more in the way of human vitality. Correspondingly, Guattari (1992) posits that it is impossible to deny the participation of human thought in the essence of machinism. In regards to behavioural advertising and user mobility, a kinetic or dynamo-like effect occurs where surplus information is skimmed without interfering with movement between sites too extensively. The mediation of mining techniques and intrusiveness thus needs to be kept to a minimum as users move from zone to zone, revealing more of themselves, particularly in their mobility. This is not novel as demographers and market researchers have for a number of years recognized that to understand behaviour and people's preferences, they have to comprehend the nature of their mobility, and more importantly what both mobility and behaviour represent. As Urry (2007) points out, interest in mobility-systems is wide-ranging encompassing the car-system, national telephone system, air power, high-speed trains, modern urban systems, budget air travel, mobile phones and central to our interests, networked computers. Underpinning this is recognition that it is not the objects in motion that are of primary importance, but rather the principles of circulation or the structures that facilitate movement. The production and mining of this activity or vitality bears a distinct similarity with Foucaultian conceptions of biopower (Foucault, 1990 [1979]) that has to do with the power of classification, strategic rationality and the history of subjectifying processes. This stems from a conceptualization of the body as a machine to be disciplined, optimized and integrated into systems of efficient control. Biopolitics then has to do with organizing populations so as to maximize their value as a resource. For Foucault, the regulation of people and their bodies was an indispensable element in the development of capitalism and the machinery of production; likewise, we may say that our digital selves play an indispensable role for the digital economy as it is traced, segmented, clustered, cross-checked and redistributed for given market purposes. Whereas traditional bureaucratic regimes were more interested in regulating the body, interiority was less of a priority, presuming workers arrived sober and able to behave in a machine-like fashion. More recently, however, it is interiority and mind that is to be mined. As Berardi (2009a; 2009b) highlights, contemporary capitalism seeks to put the soul to work. This involves the transformation of all areas of human activity so as to be under the aegis of capital. The souls or selves in question are not an aspect or portion but rather subjectivity itself mediated through the industry of information. Whereas modernity had to do with the celebration of machines as a means of mining and harnessing exterior environments and the planet's resources, more recent industrial and behavioural developments are part of a meta-suite of technologies that sees us as being both a productive component of the excavating technology, and that which is to be mined. Olma (2007, p. 130) phrases this as a 'fading of extensity' where the current phase of capitalism undergoes de-spatialization, at least as the defining principle of capitalist organization. Whereas capital in the past has sought to confine and control most obviously through the factory walls of modern capitalism, in addition to the mining of physical resources, what we now see is the appropriation of flows of production generated by interiority through digitally mediated solitary and social engagement, and the more prosaic traces we leave as we move around the network and delineate the web for those with fiscal interests. Rather than controlling and analyzing things in themselves, subjects and objects are best conceived through their relations, and as Fraser et al. (2005) also argue: the social and natural world should be understood in terms of constantly shifting relations between open-ended objects and processes of emergence, becoming and mobility. What is mooted is a neovitalist account of contemporary capitalism where power is much less seen through the dead labour of the commodity (Olma and Koukouzelis, 2007; Lash, 2007), but rather, defined in terms of the productive vitality of people and their informational mobility. As Greco (2005) delineates, despite vitalism being an oft-critiqued perspective, it remains an ongoing form of resistance to reductionism and is best conceived of as representative of what is between being and non-being, rather than a theory that explains being. Lazzarato similarly observes that contemporary biopolitics, informational capitalism and post-Fordism as represented by a plurality of temporalities has less to do with factory discipline and more to do with the organizing of 'affects, desires and technological dispositifs' for profit-based purposes (1999 cited in Toscano, 2007, p. 77 [original in Italian]). Such disciplinary perspectives also find expression in Stiegler (2009) who argues that the culture industries seek control over the mechanics of temporalization. In essence, what passes as reality and is knowable is potentially mineable. Such a conception has roots in Heidegger where power requires stability to be both enhanced and maintained. In this vision of calculation and objectification, the world is reduced to stock that is quantified, qualified and systematized (Rayner, 2001). Like other natural resources, 'every aspect of human culture is transformed into a stockpile' (Heidegger, 1991 [1939], p. 241). As Rabinow and Rose describe, biopower demands 'one or more truth discourses about the "vital" character of living human beings' (2006, p. 195). While this is true in most part, and behavioural advertising does offer a reserve to be mined, there is little that is static about such practices where the relations between people and systems are those characterized by flux. Biopower is therefore the governance and maintenance of life, and here in the case of behavioural advertising, the generation of online life so as to fuel behavioural advertising systems. Hardt and Negri (2000) similarly observe that in the passage from the modern to the postmodern there is less distinction between within and without, and life tends to be regulated from the inside rather than force being applied to the outside. Lash comments that this is not discipline, but power through control and non-linear communication systems where 'power is not just in the flows: it is in the emergent non-linear socio-technical systems that channel, block and connect the flows' (2007, p. 67). In the quest to understand behaviour, the administration of life itself becomes a primary goal for biopower. The management of such enterprises involves us being symbolically deconstructed and reconstructed, or aggregated and disaggregated, in databases as required so as to form categories, clusters and reference points by which advertisers will target users, and retailers may enjoy the dual opportunities of our custom and the ability to share data about our preferences. We are then caught in a paradoxical situation where informational assemblages have lost recognizable reference to the real world (Deleuze, 1992), data processing has long since taken on a life and language of its own (Poster, 1996), users exist in databases at most as data-doubles who appear as a potentiality as data intersects (Haggerty and Ericson, 2000), and what pertains to target us most intimately is precisely that which deals with us as a shifting and morphing abstraction.

Identity and the politics of algorithms

Data-selves, surveillant assemblages and capital flow share many similarities in that conceptions of control have to do with malleability and varying identities, not fixed ones (Haggerty and Ericson, 2000; Hier, 2003). In accounting for data-doubles and informational selves, Poster accounts for these entities as being linguistically constructed. He describes that 'the mode of information enacts a radical reconfiguration of language, one which constitutes subjects outside the pattern of the rational, autonomous individual' (1995, p. 57). In the collision between life and capital production, identity (understood as an assemblage) is articulated, re-articulated and de-articulated as required. Deleuze and Guattari describe assemblages as involving

> every constellation of singularities and traits deducted from the flow – selected, organized and naturally – in such a way as to converge (consistency) artificially and naturally; an assemblage, in this sense, is a veritable invention. (2003 [1987], p. 406)

In the online environment this plays out somewhat neatly given that behavioural advertising is predicated on web traces that form the basis of advertisement allocation.

Importantly however this is a dynamic environment and is constantly fluctuating. Digitally mediated life brings about a terrain of being represented by 'a set of equations and relationships that determine and combine variables and coefficients immediately and equally across the various terrains without reference to prior and fixed definitions' (Hardt and Negri, 2000, p. 326–27). Whereas audience research processes in the past have sought to reduce and capture so as to provide information for targeting decisions, behavioural advertising systems involve flows that can be followed and attended to in motion. Representations of audiences are characterized by instability, and multiple and modulating identities. These selves come together and are disbanded depending on the ends to which they are to be used. In this automated environment of programmed decision-making we see a-signifying systems in operation that involve not only social signs understood through the narrow frame of linguistics and signifiers/signifieds, but also the effects of the vehicles and systems through which they are delivered. In accounting for a-signifying processes, Guattari describes that 'these on one hand belong to a semiotic order and on the other intervene directly in a series of material machinic processes' (1992, p. 49). That is to say, the technologies that deliver content (such as advertising) are semiotically rich and meaningful in themselves and it is mistaken to give primacy to content over the form or means of expression. A-signifying systems need not be routed through the traditional mill of representation and may instead be approached by an understanding of the specific mechanics to trigger an action or reaction, a behaviour, or tone of interaction with a particular media system. This means that any conception of behavioural advertising should consider the mode of delivery and the reality effects these may institute through impact on qualia, and the co-creation of subjective experience. This invokes a conceptualization of machines that incorporate both technology and the incorporeal in the form of a-signifying semiotic machines that seek to couple directly with the body and mind along with its desires, emotions, perceptions and moods. In addition to subjective experience and a broader consideration of a-signifying semiotics, algorithmic technology and behavioural advertising reveals a reconfiguration of public space both in the form of sociality or search, and the means by which interiority is expressed. It also requires that we consider the politics of clustering and coding whose impetus is found outside of coupled autopoietic relations. This pushes autopoietic accounts of self-organization to admit to being informed by wider social systems of production and environment. We do not then entirely escape the terrain of enunciation and articulation as language and power is written DNA-like into the system so in part to guide its growth. Despite being self-learning, teleonomic and self-determining, there are environmental factors derived from the wider sphere of social relations that play a part. Although lacking agency, algorithms are not apolitical. They are codified politics and a formulation of social relations whose bureaucratic function is to allocate, divide, sort, designate and cluster. As Terranova (2004) argues, information processing has simultaneously attacked and reinforced macroscopic traditional identity categories (e.g. gender, race, class, nationality and sexuality). For her, the cultural politics of the network society have to do with dissection and modulation as people (their data-doubles) are segmented and distributed according to designated flows of potentiality having to do with the logic that underpins why you may be interested in one advertisement over another. What is the cultural logic that underpins this? 'You', or any given subject, are not seen as a stable entity but rather as an assemblage (a collection or set of relationships) who can be aggregated and disaggregated on the basis of advertising opportunities and the clustering of key user groups. Users then exist not as essences but potentialities and traces, and it is in these fleeting constructions we should direct our attention so as to better understand the structures that guide profiling systems. The notion of users as assemblages characterized by ephemerality and the transitory should not be seen as somehow less important, but rather we should better understand the construction of the informational and the manner in which it increasingly permeates the material conditions of daily life. As Turow (2003) highlights, the politics of code and algorithms are a concern due to the generalizations made about consumers through their click-stream data. Part of this is generational in that we are in the early stages of behavioural profiling that as a technique and means of soliciting users is only set to increase in use. Like other coding systems, algorithms are prone to faults and these have long been recognized as problematic in the marketing research literature due to trouble associated with choice of appropriate metrics, selection of variables, cross validation and external validation (Punj and Stewart, 1983). Moreover, stereotyping is inevitable where the nuances of complexity have not been accounted for. In addition, if heuristics are not granted enough experiential resources to allocate correctly, this will cause the system to assign profiles to the wrong clusters resulting in incorrect advertising and a fracturing of coupled relations. To this end, Leenes (2008) calls for transparency in regards to heuristics and automatic decision making about individuals on the basis of profiles. Further, as systems are created they have a priori formulation (and privacy brakes) that in part limits their scope for learning. While behavioural systems are teleonomic in that they rely on hindsight and history to determine their future, they are of course programmed with parameters. Importantly, there are a range of interests both inferential and overt that dictate these and although behavioural advertising systems are for the most part automated, social factors will play a role in regard to data miners' understanding of any given domain, the types of mining tools they will apply and what is deemed useful or interesting (Canhoto and BackHouse, 2008). Thus, although once in motion data-mining tools may be autonomic and autopoietic, social factors will certainly affect the profiling exercise. Economic factors and the trace of agency discourses also play a role. As Miles (2007) in discussion of cybernetic conceptions of advertising describes, the advertising message contains within it the eigenform, or indications of processes that give an object form. While there is much scope for autopoiesis and teleonomy in regard to the content as well as the delivery of advertising, current behavioural advertising texts represent a range of interests that converge on the advertisement itself. Miles highlights that eigenform artifacts represent the shared interests of the sponsor, agency, tested consumer and actual consumer held within the message production matrix at a particular time. The eigenform is an impression one has of another and by communicating, we are transmitting our construction of the observed (Kauffman, 2003). The eigenform of the consumer is then the construction an advertising system has of a particular user (or profiled set of users). Behavioural advertising has yet to offer any real personalization and the consumer's eigenform has yet to be found in the advertising text itself in any sophistication. This is presumably a matter of time and adequate heuristics, perhaps only realizable through truly co-opted revealing of personal information and data.

The Input of Cyborgs

If we accept autopoietic conceptions of behavioural advertising whereby users are coupled and part of a system that generates more of itself (involving more behavioural advertising), and that users are not configured as stable entities but are aggregated and disaggregated as required, we also need to account for how users fit within the ecology of the system. Technology may be thought of as an intersection, realization or manifestation of politics, technique and human creation, particularly if we accept that the boundary between subject and object is less than utterly distinct. As is becoming increasingly clear, the idea of a fixed dualism between our technologies and us is untenable and in many ways we are post-human (Hayles, 1999; Olma and Koukouzelis, 2007), or perhaps we have never been just-human, People not only learn how to use new machines and services, but also internalize aspects of them and concurrently externalize aspects of their own personality. We must then invoke an understanding of the cyborg that does not draw lineage from realms of science-fiction that too often has to do with subjugation or radical technologically enabled utopias, but rather, a more immanent and everyday approach to subject/object relations. Utopian/dystopian oppositions find themselves in understanding of cyborgs as a theoretical model for emancipation and empowerment. Here cybercultural theorization of cyborgs has to do with locative and mobile media, wearable optics, sousveillant and synoptic (bottom-up) forms of visuality characterized by watching those in power (Mann and Niedzviecki, 2001; Mann et al, 1998; Hier, 2003). On a less optimistic note are Baudrillard's (1987) post-humanist media musings that see the redundancy of the physical and the waning of community leaving only a vestige of human relations. Muri offers a range of definitions of cyborgs, but most appropriate here is the one she borrows from Harraway (1997) stating 'the cyborg is a cybernetic organism, a fusion of the organic and the technical forged in particular, historical, cultural practices' (Muri, 2007, p. 20). The presentation of cyborgs in popular culture and art history is a misleading one and poorly represents subject/object relations. Take for example Jacob Epstein's 'Rock Drill', a now mutilated and impotent man-machine that depicts a soulless future of man devoid of spirit, or uniquely identifying characteristics. Instead hybridized reality is much more pervasive and extreme in its scope. The technocultural history of the man-machine goes back much further than Vorticism and Futurism, perhaps drawing popular conception from La Mettrie who in the 1740s offered the metaphor of the human being as machine that stood in contrast to dominant Cartesian perspectives and insistence on the mind/body split (although Descartes was thoroughly engrossed in mechanistic views of the world positing that animals are automata devoid of mental states and that the human body is machine-like). La Mettrie also suggests that Descartes was perhaps a clandestine materialist who introduced the immaterial substance that excludes animals and automata arguably to stave off the interests of the Catholic Church, especially given Galileo's troubles over his heliocentric views (Franchi and Güzeldere, 2005). In 1695 Leibniz offered a similar split between soul and body arguing that these are automata programmed by the divine source and, although separate, work together in co-ordination like two clocks in harmony keeping time together (Mayr, 1986). Spinoza diverged from Descartes' two-substance view in preferring what has come to be called double-aspect theory that derives from the notion that the mental and the physical are simply different aspects of one and the same substance, which for Spinoza was God as the universal essence or nature of everything that exists (Leyden, 1968). In 1746 Diderot, in discussion of physicists such as Newton, stated that: 'Thanks to works of these great men, the world is no longer a god; it is a machine with cords, its pulleys, its springs, its weights' (Morley, 1905, p. 49). The materialist, La Mettrie goes further: 'But since all the soul's faculties depend so much on the specific organisation of the brain and the whole body that they are clearly nothing but that very organization, the machine is perfectly explained!' (1996 [1747], p. 26).

Following Latour (1993) along with those who recombine the mental and the physical the division between people, machines and subjects-objects need not be one of estrangement, certainly not for the clever animal as described by Heidegger who invented tools and extensions of its limbs (Zimmerman, 1990). By recombining body and soul, we admit for a much broader conception of the relationship between the organic and inorganic and the multitude of feedback relationships and associated autopoietic systems generated. It allows us to see that the distinction between technological systems and ourselves is merely one of convention and perception. Instead consciousness and what we regard as immaterial experiences are very much part of a world defined though immanence along with solidified technologies. Further, as Hayles (1999) points out, the premise of the cyborg need not have to do with augmentation or biological modification of the body, but rather the recognition that subjectivity itself may be altered through interaction with our technological systems. As behavioural advertising grows in complexity in terms of methods of interaction with us, autopoietic systems foster a deeper constructivism by which we navigate mediated environments predicated on the creation of more of itself. To this end, people and machines are much less distinct than we may think. Information machines whose parts are comprised of both people and objects (e.g. computers) thus insinuate themselves into culture and contribute to a reconfiguring of subject-object relations (Poster, 2006). A range of observers have recognized this dyadic breakdown: Thrift (2005), for example, argues that the digital environment has brought about a situation where traditional distinctions between human/non-human and organic/non-organic are less clear. For Latour (1993) the distinction between technology and people has long been an artificial one. In his exposition of the relationship between people and technology he describes that dualistic thinking and belief has caused the creation of quasi-objects and quasi-subjects as objects contain human elements and people behave more like reliable objects. These involve, but are not restricted to, a variety of control and feedback-oriented technologies including pumps, mills and engines as accounted for earlier, as well as more recent informational forms. Latour considers many of these technologies as 'hybrids' that escape subject-object relations. Both our technologies and ourselves carry out many similar functions in that we arrange, sort, profile, classify, measure, interpret and (as I write this book, and you subsequently read) process information. In behavioural advertising we are relied upon to play our role within autopoietic systems as algorithms pertain to higher levels of complexity and simulations of intelligence. What we have created, found, or more accurately – rediscovered, is a hybrid paradigm, or perhaps even a monstrous one, that Latour argues sits between the transcendent and the immanent. Thus, in recognizing ourselves as a behavioural assemblage within the system we may see an extension of ourselves constructed by our own traces and histories mediated through advertising. Behavioural advertising then is the utilization of media that externalize the human sensorium where users are fused with technology and subject/object relations are less than distinct. Arthur (2009) describes that technological structures consist of components that possess similarity to each other, or that they are recursive (that as a rule means it is defined in terms of itself). For humans to be part of behavioural advertising systems requires some training on our part so as to better relate to the system. This is manufactured through the mechanics of the human computer interface (HCI) whose purpose is to open up the system to the user. In this sense the user is the product of functionalist training from the HCI with such conceptions of labour deriving directly from Taylorism (Fuller, 2003). Computers, applications and online services are not only tools of users, but rather part of a symbiotic relationship in which the user/hybrid is the tool of the program and the program is the tool of the user. As machinic apparatus we are trained reading instruments where Stiegler's (2009) 'who' passes into the 'what' meaning that we cannot so easily distinguish between subject/object relations. If machines and technical systems train people, is it entirely certain who is the subject and what is the object?

Conclusion

To explore knowledge of selves and interaction with autopoietic systems employed for marketing and advertising we should extend our historical rear-view mirror to account for the inception of the market research industry and the associated discourses of control that feed into it. This is predicated on reliability, predictability and the need for empirical rather than hypothetical explanations of audience behaviour. Mapping began with exterior factors and geodemography although the market research industries quickly closed-in on demography, life stage, situational factors, and on to interiority. In addition to market research, the media industries also play a central role in constructing the user, particularly if one accepts the arguments of Smythe (1981) and the premise and value of the audience-as-commodity. Despite a flirtation with motivational and psychoanalytic approaches (the realm of unverifiable hypotheses), quantitative tools have re-emerged to generate biopolitical insight into interior qualities. This interiority has little to do with a mind/body Cartesian split but instead involves recognition of a hybrid universe where any notion of a transcendental self is jettisoned and we recognize the limitations, potential, but most importantly, responsibilities that come with a life lived immanently, autopoietically and co-creatively.

Chapter 7

Conclusions

Early chapters of this book sought to establish an understanding of the practice of behavioural advertising, particularly in regards to online techniques that employ DPI. Through an extended account of the Phorm case study that occurred between 2006 and 2010 it has offered a tangible account of the controversy unwittingly sparked by Phorm and BT, and the manner in which advertising based on DPI opened up a legal privacy schism between Europe and the United Kingdom. Although Phorm's practices eventually proved incommensurable with visions of Digital Britain, the willingness of the UK government to support such actors highlights the ongoing need for vigilance and the consciousness-raising role of pressure groups. Privacy rightly maintains centre stage of much digital discussion yet is undergoing redefinition with many digital businesses having few qualms about suggesting that yesterday's norms do not apply today. The position on privacy adopted here has less to do with repercussions of corporate use of personally identifiable information and more to do with the implications of aggregation and profiling, and processing and utilization of non-personally identifiable information. At the heart of this book has been an aspiration to better understand advertising predicated on the commodification of experience and subjectivity. With such interiority at play, mediated experiences tend towards a more constructivist nature and our environment becomes our own metaphor. Thus, what this book has keenly sought to explicate is the mining of individual temporality illustrated through the concepts of phenomenal fields. Rather than merely reflect a world, autopoietic systems instead bring forth a world. Behavioural advertising, as a recursive system and set of principles predicated on the creation of more of itself, does not represent a world, but rather enacts a world. It engenders a tone of being or a mood of information through processes of coupling and feedback. Although behavioural advertising is only one facet of the story – of on-demand technology, mediated sociality, time-shifting, co-creation, personalization and reconfigurable media experience – it is an important and under-recognized one, particularly for those companies who rely on advertising revenue for their survival. This leads us to recognize the lack of cognizance of the machinic in the past in regards to delivery systems and advertising imagery. Too often the literature on advertising foregrounds content and text so it is hoped that the approach to behavioural advertising presented here stimulates interest in underpinning mechanisms that contribute to the process of advertising. Following a-signifying approaches (Deleuze and Guattari, 2003 [1987]) we may recognize that any discussion of advertising should involve not only the surface execution of content but also the wider system of production and organization that informs it. In regards to advertising texts themselves, existing behavioural techniques and practices are highly syntactic and, although by definition well planned, are significantly lacking in semantic content instead often containing the most straightforward of reason-why sales pitches. In this regard behavioural advertising is trounced by traditional creative advertising concepts, the best of which fulfils advertisers' strategic objectives yet also adopts a place within the consensual hallucination of everyday life and lexicon. This is, of course, an unfair comparison given that behavioural advertising has more to do with direct response than branding, but it is in the field of content where there is much scope for development between technologists and creative advertising agencies. Whereas 'traditional' semiotic accounts of advertising rely on an uncomfortable and difficult relationship between constructivism, structuralism, brand ontology and ideology, we should instead conceive of relationships to advertising and information-machines in terms of autopoiesis and immanence. As Lash (2007) comments, in recent years the cultural logic of representation counts less than the means by which relationships are established between people and producers, as understood through economic, technological, social and political relations. Arguing for a shift in direction of cultural studies away from a discussion of symbolic power and domination through ideology or discourse, he argues that the issue is not representation but rather how power exercised is 'within' and not 'over' the means or modes of communication. He argues that: 'In the age of hegemony, power only appropriated your predicates: in the post-hegemonic present, it penetrates your very being. Power, previously extensive and operating from without, becomes intensive and now works from within' (2007, p. 59). This book has similarly argued that, at this current period of time, it is largely pointless to examine behavioural advertising from a textual perspective, or from 'without', as has been predominant within analyses of traditional advertising by media and cultural studies, and that a more robust appreciation of systems of production from within is required. Instead, at least in the case of nascent forms of advertising, we should turn to autopoietic functioning to better understand the role of feedback, circularity, self-organization, mediation and presentation, content generation, interactivity and user-system coupling as a dynamic and evolving relationship. Behavioural techniques represent well an ideal mode of traditional market and consumer research, along with a bureaucratic impulse possessing a longer history. This endeavour has at its core an aim for the elusive heart of human experience, that is, our lives experienced at a temporal or phenomenal level. This now manifests in a generalized Will to transparency and informational nakedness. Behavioural advertising is effective because overt representation and branding may be dialled down to low, allowing factors of constructivism and relevance to take charge. Operating optimally, mediation should be unnoticeable, with meta-systems in the background collecting and channelling, aggregating and disaggregating, and delivering information to users and associated businesses. It should not command attention or obstruct. If it hinders, then there is a problem; it should not jar, it should stimulate flow.

Being Naked

Technological innovation and pressure from marketization (the reduction of all to the commodity form) finds expression in Heidegger's conception of will. Zimmerman (1990) records that for Heidegger no human 'purpose', such as higher living standards or shared societal values, motivates the technological system. Instead, its impulse is of a positive feedback loop-like nature seeking to create greater power and more of itself. Allowing parts of systems to self-police and develop unchecked brings about growth that is not automatically commensurate with the broader aims of the meta-system and is potentially detrimental. In analyzing Nietzsche's doctrine of the Will to Power, Heidegger argues that 'Will does not will something it does not have, but instead the *Will wills itself*' (1991 [1939], p. 201 [italics in original]). Baudrillard (1987) similarly argues for an unfolding of processes that are no longer transcendent, or possessing a grand plan or even strategic. Instead we have a teleonomy where unlike rational or top-down conceptions of power, no one is at the wheel. Expressed through the accumulated output of a wide array of actors, no individual organization encompasses this impetus, although many embody it. The drive to interiority mining is more expansive than any clutch of organizations and it is this lack of a determinate loci of power and Will that makes the Phorm episode all the more interesting. There were distinctly novel features of this new media case study[1] in regards to their encroachment into ISP gateways, the cosy relationship with the UK government, the lack of will to implement legislation against Phorm and BT, subsequent UK/EU controversy and the manner that their enterprise was thwarted in the UK by civically motivated pressure groups. Although this book has been careful to limit itself to concerns over behavioural advertising and specific sub-technologies and principles that it informs and is informed by, there is much cross-applicability to other feedback-based information systems. The contemporary incarnation of this technological power conceived cybernetically involves the malleability of information, recursiveness and the manner in which autopoiesis engenders unique experiences of a given system or world. Like capital itself, its power stems from common currency, flexibility, translatability, mobility and fluidity. Contemporary information societies are thus those where interiority is effectively rendered into code. It is also here where we may reclaim the word *cyberculture* as one specifically having to do with cultures defined through feedback and the pliability of information. Whereas the expression has been conflated from its cybernetic origins with online communities, augmented bodies and dystopian panoramas of cyberpunk, it is best conceived in relation to control-oriented systems that make their presence felt daily as we navigate the web and the internet. With autopoietic, allopoietic and coupling arrangements increasing in prevalence, there is little need to reach out for metaphors or digital vistas. Such a proposition of immanence and informational equivalence led Heidegger (1993 [1964]) to critique market economy and argue that nothing in this organization is sacred and that everything has a price. Such observations tally well with later property-based conceptions of privacy and call for privacy to be redefined and marketized for a web and digital-based culture. Boltanski and Chiapello (2007) similarly maintain that capitalism is totally amoral and they are right in as far that, as a system, it is only interested in the production of more of itself. Guattari (1992) is also clear on this matter, noting that information of all varieties is eventually reduced to the capitalistic homogenesis of generalized equivalence. This cybernetic treatment requires that values be appraised by instruments of economic power in which existential riches, experiences and what has been discussed here in terms of the phenomenal self succumb to clutches of informational exchangeability as well as fiscal exchange value. Caution is then recommended as we work out what the long-term implications are of distributed cognition and that we better understand both the nature of autopoietic behavioural systems, and the financial and power-related allopoietic ends to which they may be put. Kent Ertugrul, founder and CEO of Phorm, is right then, when he says that concerns over behavioural advertising and privacy have to do with practice and not technology, as the real topic of discussion has to do with social organization, the ends to which such technologies are used, and whether informational practices are commensurate with our societal vision of who we would like to be. For Baudrillard, such a regime of informational visibility and transparency is tantamount to pornography and obscenity. Where nothing is hidden, where there are no secrets, where there is no illusion and all is exposed in the 'inexorable light of information and communication' (1987, p. 22), what is lived is the obscene through the pornography of information and cool de-sexualized coupling with behavioural advertising systems. We can develop this in regards to privacy arguments and the premise that privacy acts as a form of clothing, barrier or mediator. Privacy is then a guise we wear in digital environments and something that is quite normal to care about. Although most of us remove digital garments or barriers so as to reveal a little more of ourselves among friends in what are perceived as relaxed environments, generally, this is not for the benefit of watching third parties. To not recognize or respect these boundaries is intrusive and represents a high level of presumption, and, is perhaps, more than a little voyeuristic?

Inevitability

As an autopoietic system, online behavioural advertising is highly reliant on its environment and the wider legal, economic, political, cultural and creative suprasystem it operates within. It also hardly needs to be said that the economic sphere itself is also an autopoietic system. Like other dynamic systems, behavioural advertising is best thought of as a system where its parts are simultaneously affecting other parts. DPI-based advertising and Phorm in this view have potential for pathogenic qualities, although these were ultimately fought-off through privacy campaigning and regulation alike. As argued both in Chapters 2 and 3, there is little that is inevitable about capital conceived of as contagion, particularly given far-reaching crusades by privacy campaigners such as the ORG and NoDPI who have perhaps irrevocably affected the agenda of behavioural advertisers seeking to employ techniques of DPI in the United Kingdom. Such engagement with technological development is right in that we should not think of technology as something dished out by the market to consumers (Suarez-Villa, 2009), but rather as an ongoing process where society has a greater hand in shaping (or rejecting) the inclusion of any given technology into the social matrix. Where Will and the positive feedback it brings about manifests, a stronger regulatory hand is needed. Our technologies are then social and do not possess inevitability, nor a status outside of human relations. The false distinction between people and technology lies at the heart of this problem of the perceived autonomy of technology. Incorrect diagnosis of relations gives rise to regulatory and political systems that both praise and forgive technology and the consequences that their use may unleash. In discussion of technological determinism and the centrality of machines to the last few hundred years, Heilbroner observes it is '*a problem of a certain historical epoch* – specifically that of high capitalism and low socialism – *in which the forces of technical change have been unleashed, but when the agencies for the control or guidance of technology are still rudimentary*' (1994, p. 65, emphasis in original). Similarly, Winner indirectly offers a useful way of assessing the standing of behavioural advertising technologies and suggests that we should better understand the social contract implied by any given system and ask: 'How well do the proposed conditions match our best sense of who we are and what we want this society to be?' (1986, p. 55–56). The lure of techno-determinism and the division it creates from human relations stems from what was the technological sublime and what is better now described as the technological imaginary; that is, the repository of fixation, suspicion or elation that surround new media technologies, and the ends to which they are put. Historically, the application of new technologies has wrought enormous changes in the economy and the advertising business is no different. As Arthur (2009) describes, when new forms of technology spread through an economy, old structures fall apart and are replaced with new ones. Likewise, industries once taken for granted give way to new ones and prior ways of working begin to appear quaint. Relatively new companies to advertising, particularly Google, and the manner in which it has cast a veneer of simplicity over complexity, have pulled the rug from beneath traditional advertising and media-space buying agencies. Although for the advertising industry the winds of Schumpeter's (2003 [1942]) creative destruction do not blow strong, they are evident. Refinements of behavioural techniques have tipped us into what is currently a post-representational period and without doubt, behavioural advertising is not a technique ready to disappear any time soon. The logic of behavioural advertising derives from a vision and momentum that has gathered steam from the Enlightenment onwards that sought to rationalize, quantify and comprehend, but now updated seeks to engage mobility, dynamism, temporality and heterogeneity. As has become clear, it is difficult to tease out the objects and technological practices from the social arrangements that create and guide them although debates over technological determinism are not readily solved by recourse to social determinism whose corrective possesses its own shortcomings by suggesting that technical things do not matter at all. Although it is folly to ascribe essence or autonomy to technology, it is difficult to refute the effects of technology and the kinds of questions they force people to ask. As Winner (1986), in reference to Engels and his account of industrial production, argues: if technology possesses properties, and they impact on human arrangements and the way we live, they can be said to have politics. More specifically, where technology is based upon ongoing modelling and interaction with the social a political dimension is inevitable and on-going vigilance is required, particularly in regards to heuristics, biases of profiling, privacy, aggregation and disaggregation. At the very least, we should pay attention to their characteristics so to better understand their configuration within social relations.

Education, Media Literacy and Digital Citizenship

As we move towards increasingly intelligent environments dependent upon data and profiling we should do so in an informed and cautious fashion so as to better comprehend privacy trade-offs and arrive at more enlightened decisions about those exchanges potentially socially unacceptable. As Hirshleifer (1979) points out, a person who remains passive in the face of the invasion of his rights is unlikely to retain them. Decisions made regarding digital profiles increasingly relate to the corporeal and affect tailored offerings for real individuals via their preferences and modes of being online. Both critics and supporters believe that a more educated populus is favourable with both parties arguing that if people understood the nature of behavioural advertising, they would be more inclined to their point of view. In 2009, following BT's and Talk Talk's decision to step away from DPI-facilitated behavioural advertising, Nick Stringer, head of regulatory affairs at the IAB and former chair of the Behavioural Targeting Council[2], highlighted the importance of widespread consumer education (Bearne, 2009). Promoters see barriers to acceptance of behavioural advertising as a result of lack of awareness about data gathering techniques and that if consumers could only understand their practices, they would be more inclined to accept it, even on an opt-out basis (IAB, 2009c). Although less concerned about creating the ideal consumer for business' needs, this book agrees with the requirement for greater education over digital processes, particularly in regards to the nature of exchange for media content and services. Given the centrality of advertising and data to the digital economy, clarification is needed for both critique and informed choice. After all, a healthy democracy is an informed one. If we see behavioural advertising systems as having co-productive autopoietic qualities, then the nature of relationships with these systems needs to be more robustly and transparently established. Further, if we accept Norberg et al.'s (2009) premise that consumers are part of the marketing channel by dint of the information they provide and share, then consumers should be afforded channel member rights and privileges that protect their interests. Currently the opacity of the rules guiding behavioural advertising serves no one well, which only hinders and creates mistrust. As such, non-personal profiling apparatuses and applications need to be more transparent for both the benefit of businesses and potential customers so to build circuits and relationships of trust if they are to be properly accepted by the social corpus. This requires changes in legislation as well as practice, although it is appreciated that this is far easier said than done given the complexity of building privacy norms into technology. Profiling will only become more intense as the future unfolds so it is best that privacy and transparency are not only heeded and paid lip service to, but also handled with sincerity through transparency enhancing technologies (TETs) (Hildebrandt and Gutwirth, 2008). Although on the face of things, businesses have little incentive to build simpler and higher levels of privacy control into their systems (Koops and Leenes, 2005; Lessig, 2006), there are rich pickings for businesses that manage to win such trust. Rewards include the potential for users to customize profiles, and willingly offer richer and more detailed accounts of themselves. Following Hildebrandt (2008b), this book calls for intelligent interplay between technological design and legal regulation that allows individuals to aid in constructing their digital identities and better participate in increasingly semantic-based environments. This is tantamount to customization over personalization and such a premise is based on knowledge, education and participation. As we progress more slowly than expected, but all the more certainly, towards a commercial and media environment predicated on profiling and machinic-coupling, the role of informed choice is central. This serves both advertisers and consumers alike, particularly, if we admit of a dynamic conception of advertising as co-opted coupled relations. After all, the user as an unwilling component of a system is unlikely to be one that performs optimally. One effect of the opt-in model is that companies can charge higher fees to their clients as they will receive a higher quality user-base expressed in terms of rich and credible data about users who are genuinely interested in advertising and knowing more about useful or desired products and services. Furthermore, audiences may disclose more information than the minimum thus increasing audience-value potentially allowing data to be held for longer periods of time for the purposes of more refined advertising. Ultimately, in contrast to disingenuousness, there exists the potential for loyalty, based on choice, although advertisers would simply need to accept that large portions of their audience may prefer less rather than more profiling, no matter what the rewards. Widening the scope slightly, better education is needed regarding what happens to data relating to us and to what ends it is used. As Turow highlights in his comprehensive US study of citizens' awareness of privacy, the 'ignorance of data flow stands at the heart of the imbalance of power that currently exists when it comes to controlling personal information online' (2003, p. 33). This derives from the inability of users to protect their privacy online as well as offline (Turow et al., 2008). In combating informational myopia, what is required is wider education regarding the need to take care of oneself online, and the nature of disclosure and contractual obligations. While such a process sounds onerous, it is perhaps best to think of these in terms of life skills that one learns as a child, whether in the domestic or scholastic sphere. The understanding of one's data-self is a sub-section of the issue of citizenship, that is, how does a person fit into society, how are they constituted, what rights do they have, how do they exercise these, what organizations may seek to take advantage of the less aware and how can a person take a more active role in shaping the use of any given technologies within society? To put this into context, in a UK-based survey carried out by the ICO whose communications objectives and mandates are to 'maintain confidence in organisations' handling of personal information' and 'maintain awareness of rights amongst individuals', only 19 per cent of those interviewed had heard of the ICO (SMSR, 2009). This represents a 4 per cent decrease since 2008 and a 6 per cent decrease since 2007. Although all polls should be treated with a degree of caution and scepticism, the findings become more interesting when one considers that when the sample was asked which social issues they were concerned about, 'protecting people's personal information' came second at 94 per cent only to crime prevention (at 96%). This puts informational privacy concerns before unemployment (93%), the national health service (90%), national security (90%), environmental issues (90%), equal rights for everyone (89%), improving standards in education (89%), protection of freedom of speech (89%) and access to information held by public authorities (80%). Furthermore, over two-thirds (67%) of respondents believe that individuals have lost control over the way their personal details are collected and processed. Moreover, the most likely source of awareness of the UK's Data Protection Act 1998 is through media (35%), the work place (29%), other (16%), general knowledge (14%), word of mouth (9%) and the internet (6%). Formal education does not feature on this list. Although behavioural advertisers and their representatives at the IAB have developed self-regulation that in some parts goes further than legislation requires, the question remains as to whether self-regulation will provide the level of protection consumers really require, particularly in regards to choice. This book argues that a more robust and educational approach is needed to 'being digital', particularly given its centrality to sociality, culture, leisure, political processes, consumption and the economy. Leaving behavioural advertisers to educate us about protecting our data-selves is not enough. In the United States, Youn (2009) recommends that privacy education begin in early adolescent years due to the ending of protection from the Children's Online Privacy Protection Act of 1998 (COPPA) that addresses the online collection of personal information by persons or entities under US jurisdiction from children under 13 years of age. Similarly, education in earlier years will lead to user self-efficacy, and appreciation of importance and value regarding information about the self. It will also help in dispelling privacy phantoms that currently influence popular understanding and also contribute to tackling perceptions of toxicity in the digital ecology as broached in Chapter 4. Although, at the outset, much of the material may appear complicated, this has perhaps more to do with the novelty of such information-based lives. Milne et al. (2009) similarly highlight the importance of self-efficacy and that the emphasis should move beyond getting consumers and children to notice security symbols, but also understand cookie management, phishing scams, identity theft, privacy policies and online shopping terms. We may also add issues to do with management of one's self on social networks and self-broadcasting platforms, other online agora, and spaces and databases where data is retained, employed, shared and possibly sold. This takes on extra significance when we consider that many UK children's sites currently request personal information and on occasion encourage children to divulge information about their friends in exchange for free offers (Stanaland et al., 2009). There is also very little distinction between the data collection practices that take place for children and adults[3]. In addition to a stronger and clearer regulatory hand, it is desirable that management of one's informational self should be introduced at a school curricula level in relation to digital citizenship and care over one's image, as per developments initiated by the UK Council for Child Internet Safety (UKCCIS, 2009). With lessons in using the internet safely becoming a compulsory part of the curriculum for primary schoolchildren with the 'Click Clever Click Safe'[4] in operation in England from 2011, there is already a framework on which to build. What is recommended here is increasing awareness and understanding of the nature of profiling, data management, the value of information and consequences of the intimate relations we maintain with digital technologies in current and nascent semantic environments where both providers and third parties seek to understand behaviour through the mining of interiority that determines the tone of interaction or what has here been described as the mood of information. If McLuhan is right and future historians will see advertisements 'as the richest and most faithful daily reflections that any society ever made of its entire range of activities' (1965, p. 184), what then will be made of early behavioural advertising and the intensification of feedback processes via networked means in 100 years, and how will our choices about them be judged?

Notes

Chapter 1

[1] Launched in 1994 and closed in 1999, HotWired was a stablemate of Wired magazine, although carried separate and original content.

[2] For a longer list of behavioural advertising networks see the Network Advertising Initiative's list of participating networks: www.networkadvertising.org/participating/

[3] See www.Ghostery.com

Chapter 2

[1] See www.virginmedia.com/customers/webwise.php

[2] The UK government has initiated a switchover to digital television. Between 2008–2012, television services in the UK will go completely digital, TV region by TV region (The exception is Whitehaven in Cumbria which became the first place to switch in October 2007). The BBC earmarked £803 million from licence fees to ensure everybody could make the switch to digital television. However, the National Audit Office has worked out that up to £250 million of that might not be needed. The Government says it will be appropriated for forthcoming broadband commitments.

[3] For a more detailed account of this case, the involvement of the UK's Crown Prosecution Service (CPS) and decisions made by the Information Commissioner see Inphormationdesk (2009).

[4] Ports are endpoints for host-to-host communications. See Wikipedia (http://en.wikipedia.org/wiki/List_of_TCP_and_UDP_port_numbers) for a full account of all TCP and UDP numbers.

[5] Richard Clayton's fuller and more robust account can be found at www.cl.cam.ac.uk/~rnc1/080404phorm.pdf. This will be of particular interest to those with a computer science background.

[6] Netmums www.netmums.com/home/home/ is a network for parents offering information and advice on being a mum or dad.

[7] mySociety www.mysociety.org/ describes itself as a charity-funded project which builds websites that give people simple, tangible benefits in the civic and community aspects of their lives. It also teaching the public and voluntary sectors how to use the internet most efficiently to improve lives.

Chapter 3

[1] The FCC encapsulates the debate in a document issued October 22, 2009 headed by the title "Notice of Proposed Rulemaking". It is available from http://hraunfoss.fcc.gov/edocs_public/attachmatch/FCC-09-93A1.pdf

[2] Portrayed on Wikipedia as actor, writer, journalist, comedian, television presenter and film director, and self-described on Twitter as British Actor, Writer, Lord of Dance, Prince of Swimwear & Blogger.

[3] This is monitored by the Chief Surveillance Commissioner who leads the Office of Surveillance Commissioners (OSC), which provides supervision of the conduct of covert surveillance and the use of covert human intelligence sources (CHIS) under RIPA and the Police Act 1997 (House of Lords – Select Committee on the Constitution, 2009). Additionally, the Interception of Communications Commissioner keeps under review the issue and operation of warrants permitting interceptions and the acquisition of communications data under RIPA (ibid.). Other commissioners include the Intelligence Services Commissioner who handles the Intelligence Services Act 1994, and provides warrants and authorizations for surveillance and agents under RIPA. The National Identity Scheme Commissioner was charged with delivering the Identity Card Act 2006, although the ID card scheme along with the Office of the Identity Commissioner was confirmed for repeal and termination in 2010.

[4] In addition to criminalizing the interception of communications over public networks without consent or a warrant authorized by the secretary of state, it was also constructed with the intention that public authorities are able to carry out surveillance. UK public councils received much criticism between 2007–2008 for abusing these powers and using them to monitor petty offences such as dog fouling, littering, and to spy on families to ascertain whether they were actually living in a school catchment area. For full details of the Act see www.opsi.gov.uk/acts/acts2000/ukpga_20000023_en_1

[5] The IAB has publicly criticized a preliminary draft of the bill arguing that industry self-regulation is preferable to legislation due to the potential hampering of growth of the online advertising economy. Also, as reported by *ClickZ*, in April the IAB placed $1,000 each in the campaign coffers of key members of the House and Senate dealing with online privacy legislation (Kaye, 2010).

[6] In 2010 Advertising Age reported that the system, launched by called Better Advertising, is to place an icon in the upper right-hand corner of the ads that looks like a cross between an eye and power button called the 'power eye' (Learmonth, 2010).

[7] Available from www.networkadvertising.org/

Chapter 4

[1] Available from http://eur-lex.europa.eu/LexUriServ/site/en/oj/2006/ l_105/l_10520060413en00540063.pdf

[2] See video at www.oix.com/privacy/

[3] 'Lemon' is slang for a poor used car.

Chapter 5

[1] As Essinger (2004) highlights, IBM grew out of the Computing-Tabulating-Recording Company or C-T-R.

[2] Such an opposition between philosophy and information theory may be misleading as cyberneticists and artificial intelligence researchers' theorization was always, and continues to be, based on some philosophical background; for example, as Sharoff (2005) highlights: mental category determination, hermeneutic circle problems, the balance between empirical and a priori knowledge, the interrelations between abstract and specific knowledge, not to mention perspectives on consciousness itself.

[3] Daughter of Margaret Mead and Gregory Bateson.

[4] Typically expressed in terms of what a consumer should think, feel, or do as result of seeing an advertisement.

[5] Both as an example and as an admission, I, as author, have to admit to a long-standing interest in complexity that long precedes my interest in digital advertising.

[6] In 2010, Craig Venter, Hamilton Smith and their colleagues developed a creature without an ancestor that is capable of reproducing on its own. What it is, and how it lives, depends entirely on a design put together by scientists of the J. Craig Venter Institute and held on the institute's computers in Rockville, Maryland, and San Diego, California. *The Economist* has an account of this story at www.economist.com/displayStory.cfm?story_id=16163006

Chapter 6

[1] Now simply JWT owned by WPP, JWT lays claim to being the world's first full-service advertising agency.

Chapter 7

[1] This pattern replicates what has been seen in other industries seen as vital to the UK economy, for example oil and the Brent Spar controversy in the 1990s (Bakir, 2006).

[2] An industry organization designed to lobby government and promote behavioural advertising to brands and advertising agencies.

[3] UK law is unclear with the 1998 DPA stipulating that the data subject should give his/her consent to the processing, yet offering no clear guidance on the issue of obtaining consent from children.

[4] See http://clickclickclicksafe.direct.gov.uk/index.html for details.

List of Abbreviations

ABC:	Audit Bureau of Circulation
ALOHANET:	not an acronym. The name derives from being created at the University of Hawaii
ARPA:	Advanced Research Projects Agency
ASA:	Advertising Standards Authority
BARB:	Broadcasters Audience Research Board
BT:	British Telecom
CAP:	Codes of Advertising Practice
CCTV:	Closed Circuit Television
CEO:	Chief Executive Officer
CPS:	Crown Prosecution Service
DARPA:	Defense Advanced Research Projects Agency
DPA:	Data Protection Act
DPI:	Deep Packet Inspection
FIPR:	Foundation for Information Policy Research
FTP:	File Transfer Protocol
GDP:	Gross Domestic Product
HCI:	Human Computer Interface
HTTP:	Hypertext Transfer Protocol
IAB:	Internet Advertising Bureau
ICANN:	Internet Corporation for Assigned Names and Numbers
ICCB:	Internet Configuration Control Board
ICO:	Information Commissioner's Office
ICT:	Information and Communication Technologies
IP:	Internet Protocol
ISP:	Internet Service Provider
KDD:	Knowledge Discovery in Databases
MEP:	Member of the European Parliament
NAI:	Network Advertising Initiative

NPL:	National Physical Laboratory
NSF:	National Science Foundation
OBA:	Online Behavioural Advertising
OIX:	Open Internet Exchange
ORG:	Open Rights Group
OSC:	Office of Surveillance Commissioners
PECR:	Privacy and Electronic Communications Regulations
PII:	Personally Identifiable Information
PPP:	Public-Private Partnerships
RAND:	Research and Development
RIPA:	Regulation of Investigatory Powers Act
RSMB:	Research Services and Millward Brown
SATNET:	not an acronym. The name derives from being a satellite network
SMTP:	Simple Mail Transfer Protocol
SSH:	Secure Shell network protocol
TCP:	Transmission Control Protocol
TNS:	Taylor Nelson Sofres
WSIS:	World Summit on the Information Society

Bibliography

80/20 Thinking (2009) 'Privacy Impact Assessment', *Phorm*, http://privacy.phorm.com/Phorm_PIA_Final.pdf, date accessed 23 March 2009.

Acquisti, A. (2004) *Privacy in Electronic Commerce and the Economics of Immediate Gratification*, www.heinz.cmu.edu/~acquisti/papers/privacy-gratification.pdf, date accessed 04 June 2009.

Acquisti, A. and Grossklags, J. (2005) *Privacy and Rationality in Individual Decision Making*, www.dtc.umn.edu/weis2004/acquisti.pdf, date accessed 04 June 2009.

Acquisti, A. and Grossklags, J. (2007) 'What Can Behavioral Economics Teach Us About Privacy', *Digital Privacy: Theory, Technologies and Practices*, www.heinz.cmu.edu/~acquisti/papers/Acquisti-Grossklags-Chapter-Etrics.pdf, date accessed 04 June 2009.

Adam, B. (2003) 'Reflexive Modernization Temporalized', *Theory, Culture & Society*, 20 (2), 59–78.

Adriaans, P. and Zantinge, D. (1996) *Data Mining* (Harlow: Addison-Wesley).

Akerlof, G.A. (1970) 'The Market for "Lemons": Quality Uncertainty and the Market Mechanism', *The Quarterly Journal of Economics*, 84 (3), 488–500.

Albrechtslund, A. (2008) 'Online Social Networking as Participatory Surveillance', *First Monday*, 13 (3), http://firstmonday.org/htbin/cgiwrap/bin/ojs/index.php/fm/article/view/2142/1949, date accessed 09 February 2009.

Altman, I.; Vinsel, A. and Brown, B. (1981) 'Dialectic Conceptions in Social Psychology: An Application to Social Penetration and Privacy Regulation', *Advances in Experimental Social Psychology*, 14, 107–60.

Anderson, C. (2006) *The Long Tail: Why the Future of Business Is Selling Less of More* (New York: Hyperion).

Anderson, N. (2007) 'Deep packet inspection meets Net neutrality, CALEA', *Ars Technica*, http://arstechnica.com/hardware/news/2007/07/Deep-packet-inspection-meets-net-neutrality.ars, date accessed 23 August 2009.

Andrejevic, M. (2009) 'Control Over Personal Information in the Database Era', *Surveillance and Society*, 6 (3), 322–26.

Ang, P.H. (2001) 'The Role of Self-Regulation of Privacy and the Internet', *Journal of Interactive Advertising*, 1 (2), www.jiad.org/article8, date accessed 03 June 2009.

Aristotle (1965) 'The Rhetoric', in D. Bailey (ed.), *Essays on Rhetoric*, L. Cooper (trans.), (New York: Oxford University Press), pp. 55–83.

Armand, L. (2008) 'Language and the Cybernetic Mind', *Theory, Culture & Society,* 25 (2), 127–52.

Arvidsson, A. (2006) *Brands: Meaning and Value in Media Culture* (Abingdon, Oxon: Routledge).

Arthur, W. B. (2009) *The Nature of Technology: What It Is and How It Evolves* (London: Allen Lane/Penguin).

Ashby, W. R. (1940) 'Adaptiveness and Equilibrium', *Journal of Mental Science,* 86, 478–83.

Ashby, W. R. (1956) *An Introduction to Cybernetics* (London: Chapman and Hall).

AskCALEA (2009) *AskCALEA,* www.askcalea.net/, date accessed 12 November 2009.

AudienceScience (2010) *The Current State of Audience Targeting,* www.audiencescience.com/docs/MarketIntelligenceReport.pdf, date accessed 13 July 2010.

Aun, F. (2009) 'Internet Ad Spending Declined in Q1, Says IAB', *ClickZ,* www.clickz.com/3634009, date accessed 08 June 2009.

Bakir, V. (2006) 'Policy Agenda-Setting and Risk Communication: Greenpeace, Shell and Issues of Trust', *The Harvard International Journal of Press/Politics,* 11 (3), 67–88.

Bakir, V. (2007) 'Risk Communication, Television News and the Generation of Trust: The Utility of Ethos', in V. Bakir and D. Barlow (eds), *Communication in the Age of Suspicion: Trust and the Media* (Basingstoke: Palgrave-Macmillan), pp. 127–40.

Bakir, V. and Barlow, D. (eds) (2007) *Communication in the Age of Suspicion: Trust and the Media* (Basingstoke: Palgrave-Macmillan).

Ball, K.; Lyon, D.; Wood, D.M.; Norris, C. and Raab, C. (2006) 'A Report on the Surveillance Society', *The Surveillance Studies Network,* www.ico.gov.uk/upload/documents/library/data_protection/practical_application/surveillance_society_full_report_2006.pdf, date accessed 09 February 2009.

Baran, P. (1964) 'On Distributed Communications Series: I. Introduction to Distributed Communications Networks', *RAND Corporation,* www.rand.org/pubs/research_memoranda/2006/RM3420.pdf, date accessed 15 May 2009.

BARB (2010) *How Does the Audience Measurement Process Work?* www.barb.co.uk/about/faq?_s=4, date accessed 20 June 2010.

Barney, D. (2000) *Prometheus Wired: The Hope for Democracy in the Age of Network Technology* (Chicago: University of Chicago Press).

Barthes, R. (1972) *Mythologies* (London: Cape).

Baruh, L. (2007) 'Read at Your Own Risk: Shrinkage of Privacy and Interactive Media', *New Media and Society,* 9 (2), 187–221.

Bateson, G. (1979) *Mind and Nature: A Necessary Unity* (New York: Bantam Books).

Bateson, G. (1987) *Steps to an Ecology of Mind* (Northvale, NJ: Jason Aronson).

Bateson, M.C. (1972) *Our Own Metaphor: A Personal Account of a Conference on Conscious Purpose and Human Adaptation* (New York: Knopf).

Baudrillard, J. (1987) *The Ecstasy of Communication* (London: Sage).

Baudrillard, J. (1988) 'Simulacra and Simulations', in M. Poster (ed.), *Jean Baudrillard: Selected Writings* (Cambridge: Polity Press), pp. 166–84.

Baudrillard, J. (1998 [1970]) *The Consumer Society* (London: Sage).

Bauman, Z. (1989) *Modernity and the Holocaust* (Cambridge: Polity Press).

Bauman, Z. (2000) *Liquid Modernity* (Cambridge: Polity Press).

Bauman, Z. (2005) *Liquid Life* (Cambridge: Polity Press).

Bazalgette, P. (2008) 'Who Needs Digital Privacy?' *Prospect*, www.prospect-magazine.co.uk/article_details.php?id=10420, date accessed 10 June 2009.

BBC (2008) *Spy Law 'Used in Dog Fouling War'*, http://news.bbc.co.uk/1/hi/uk/7369543.stm, date accessed 20 March 2009.

BBC (2009a) *Google Serves up Behavioural Ads*, http://news.bbc.co.uk/1/hi/technology/7937201.stm, date accessed 24 March 2009.

BBC (2009b) *Home Office 'Colluded with Phorm'*, http://news.bbc.co.uk/1/hi/technology/8021661.stm, date accessed 22 May 2009.

BBC (2009c) *Phorm Shares Fall as BT Opts Out*, http://news.bbc.co.uk/1/hi/technology/8135850.stm, date accessed 6 July 2009.

BBC (2009d) *UK Broadband 'Not Fit' for Future*, http://news.bbc.co.uk/1/hi/technology/8282839.stm, date accessed 07 December 2009.

Beales, H. (2010) 'The Value of Behavioral Targeting', *Network Advertising Initiative*, www.networkadvertising.org/pdfs/NAI_Beales_Release.pdf, date accessed 12 April 2010.

Bearne, S. (2009) 'Cover Story: Industry Fails to Allay Consumer Fears over Behavioural Targeting', *New Media Age*, www.nma.co.uk/news/industry-fails-to-allay-consumer-fears-over-behavioural-targeting/3002134.article, date accessed 09 July 2009.

Beck, U. (1992) *Risk Society: Towards a New Modernity* (London: Sage).

Beck, U. (1996a) 'Risk Society and the Provident State', in S. Lash; B. Szerszynski and B. Wynne, *Risk, Environment & Modernity* (London: Sage), pp. 27–43.

Beck, U. (1996b) 'Subpolitics, Ecology and the Disintegration of Institutional Power', *Organisation and Environment*, 10 (1), 52–65.

Beck, U.; Giddens, A. and Lash, S. (eds) (1994), *Reflexive Modernization: Politics, Tradition and Aesthetics in the Modern Social Order* (Cambridge: Polity Press).

Beer, D. (2009) 'Power through the Algorithm? Participatory Web Cultures and the Technological Unconscious', *New Media and Society*, 11 (6), 985–1002.

Bell, D. (1973) *The Coming of the Postindustrial Society: A Venture in Social Forecasting* (New York: Basic Books).

Benedicktus, R. L. and Andrews, M. L. (2006) 'Building Trust with Consensus Information: The Effects of Valence and Sequence Direction', *Journal of Interactive Advertising*, 6 (2), www.jiad.org/article77, date accessed 03 June 2009.

Beniger, J. R. (1986) *The Control Revolution: Technological and Economic Origins of the Information Society* (Cambridge, MA: Harvard University Press).

Benoist, E. (2008) 'Collecting Data for the Profiling of Web Users', in M. Hildebrandt and S. Gutwirth (eds), *Profiling the European Citizen: Cross-Disciplinary Perspectives* (Dordrecht: Springer), pp. 169–84.

Berardi, F. (2009a) 'Futurism and the Reversal of the Future', *generation-online*, www.generation-online.org/p/fp_bifo8.htm, date accessed 10 March 2010.

Berardi, F. (2009b) *The Soul at Work: From Alienation to Autonomy* (Los Angeles, CA: Semiotext(e)).

Bergson, H. (2001 [1889]) *Time and Free Will: An Essay on the Immediate Data of Consciousness* (New York: Dover).

Bergson, H. (1999 [1913]) *An Introduction to Metaphysics* (Indianapolis, IN: Hackett).

Bermejo, F. (2009) 'Audience manufacture in historical perspective: from broadcasting to Google', *New Media and Society*, 11 (1&2), 133–54.

Berners-Lee, T. (2006) *Net Neutrality: This Is Serious*, http://dig.csail.mit.edu/breadcrumbs/node/144, date accessed 20 August 2009.

Berners-Lee, T. (2009) *No Snooping*, www.w3.org/DesignIssues/NoSnooping.html, date accessed 23 March 2009.

Berry, M. J. A. and Linoff, G. S. (2004) *Data Mining Techniques* (Indianapolis: Wiley).

Black, E. (2002) *IBM and the Holocaust* (London: Time Warner).

Blank, A.G. (2000) *TCP/IP Foundations* (Chichester: Wiley).

Bogard, W. (1996) *The Simulation of Surveillance* (Cambridge: Cambridge University Press).

Boltanski, L. and Chiapello, E. (2007) *The New Spirit of Capitalism* (London: Verso).

Booth, A. (2005) *A Subtle and Mysterious Machine: The Medical World of Walter Charleton 1619–1707 Studies in History and Philosophy of Science* (Dordrecht: Springer).

Bourdieu, P. (1984) *Distinction: A Social Critique of the Judgment of Taste* (Cambridge: Harvard University Press).

boyd, d. (2010) 'Facebook and "radical transparency" (a rant)', *apophenia*, www.zephoria.org/thoughts/archives/2010/05/14/facebook-and-radical-transparency-a-rant.html, date accessed 15 May 2010.

Brooks, M. (2009) 'Who Controls the Internet?' *New Scientist*, www.newscientist.com/article/mg20227062.000-who-controls-the-internet.html, date accessed, 30 April 2009.

Brown, G. (2009) 'The Internet Is as Vital as Water and Gas', *The Times*, www.timesonline.co.uk/tol/comment/columnists/guest_contributors/article6506136.ece, date accessed 18 June 2009.

BT Retail Technology (2007) 'British Telecom Phorm PageSense External Validation Report', *Wikileaks*, http://wikileaks.org.uk/leak/bt-phorm-report-2007.pdf, date accessed 21 March 2009.

Burnham, D. (1983) *The Rise of the Computer State* (New York: Random House).

Burrows, R. and Ellison, N. (2004) 'Sorting Places Out? Towards a Social Politics of Neighbourhood Informatisation', *Information, Communication and Society*, 7 (3), 321–36.

Burton, C. (2009) 'The Televised Revolution', *Wired*, July 2009.

Bush, V. (1945) 'As We May Think', *the Atlantic*, www.theatlantic.com/doc/194507/bush, date accessed 15 May 2009.

CableOne (2009) 'Letter, from Responses to August 1, 2008 Letters to Network Operators Regarding Data Collection Practices', *Committee on Energy and Commerce, U.S. House of Representatives*, http://energycommerce.house.gov/Press_110/Responses%20to%20080108%20TI%20Letter/110-ltr.080108responseCABLE001.pdf, date accessed 06 December 2009.

Canhoto, A. and BackHouse, J. (2008) 'General description of the Process of Behavioural Profiling', in M. Hildebrandt and S. Gutwirth (eds), *Profiling the European Citizen: Cross-Disciplinary Perspectives* (Dordrecht: Springer), pp. 47–63.

Cappo, J. (2003) *The Future of Advertising*. New York: McGraw-Hill.

Capra, F. (2005) 'Complexity and Life', *Theory, Culture & Society*, 22 (5), 33–44.

Carruthers, P. (2000) *Phenomenal Consciousness: A Naturalistic Theory* (Cambridge: Cambridge University Press).

Castells, M. (1977) *The Urban Question* (London: Edward Arnold).

Castells, M. (2001) *The Rise of the Network Society* (Oxford: Blackwell).

Castells, M. (2003) *The Power of Identity* (Oxford: Blackwell).

Castells, M. (2009) *Communication Power* (Oxford: Oxford University Press).

Cate, F.H. (2007) 'The Autonomy Trap', *The Privacy Symposium*, Cambridge, MA, paper delivered 24 August 2007, www.fredhcate.com/Publications/The%20 Autonomy%20Trap.revised.pdf, date accessed 17 December 2009.

Cellan-Jones, R. (2009) 'Britons Say Broadband "Essential"', *BBC*, http://news. bbc.co.uk/1/hi/technology/8079637.stm, date accessed 10 June 2009.

Cerf, V. (2006) 'Prepared Statement of Vinton G. Cerf Vice President and Chief Internet Evangelist Google Inc', *Google*, http://commerce.senate.gov/pdf/ cerf-020706.pdf, date accessed 20 August 2009.

Chandler A. D. Jr. (1977) *The Visible Hand* (Cambridge, MA: The Belknap Press of Harvard University Press

Charlesworth, A. (2006) 'The Future of UK Data Protection Regulation', *Information Security Technical Report*, 11, 46–54.

ChoiceStream (2008) *ChoiceStream Personalization Survey*, www.choicestream. com/surveyresults/, date accessed 30 October 2009.

Clarke, R. (2000) *Beyond the OECD Guidelines: Privacy Protection for the 21st Century*, www.rogerclarke.com/DV/PP21C.html#OECD, date accessed 11 December 2009.

Claycamp, H. J. and Massy, W. F. (1968) 'A Theory of Marketing Segmentation', *Journal of Marketing Research*, 5 (4), 388–94.

Clayton, R. (2008a) *The Phorm 'Webwise' System*, www.cl.cam.ac.uk/~rnc1/080404phorm. pdf, date accessed 23 March 2009.

Clayton, R. (2008b) *The Phorm 'Webwise' System*, www.lightbluetouchpaper. org/2008/04/04/the-phorm-webwise-system/#comments, date accessed 23 March 2009.

Clifford, S. (2009) 'The Online Ad That Knows Where Your Friends Shop', *The New York Times*, www.nytimes.com/2009/06/26/business/media/26adco. html?_r=1&partner=rss&emc=rss, date accessed 26 June 2009.

ConsumersUnion.org (2008) *Consumer Reports Poll: Americans Extremely Concerned About Internet Privacy*, www.consumersunion.org/pub/core_telecom_and_ utilities/006189.html, date accessed 12 December 2009.

Crogan, P. (2008) 'Targeting, Television and Networking', *Convergence: The International Journal of Research into New Media Technologies*, 14 (4), 375–85.

Cryptome (2009) *Home Office Note on Phorm Spyware TXT*, http://cryptome.org/ ho-phorm.htm, date accessed 11 June 2009.

Curran, J. (1981) 'The Impact of Advertising on the British Mass Media', *Media, Culture & Society*, 3 (1), 43–69.

Dahlberg, L. (1998) 'Cyberspace and the Public Sphere', *Convergence: The International Journal of Research into New Media Technologies*, 4 (1), 70–84.

Dahlgren, P. (2001) 'The Public Sphere as Historical Narrative', in D. McQuail (ed.), *McQuail's Reader in Mass Communication Theory* (London: Sage), pp. 194–200.

Darby, I. (1998) 'Diary: Robertson Reveals a History of Notorious Clients', *PR Week*, www.prweek.com/uk/news/search/93428//, date accessed 18 January 2010.

Davies, D. W. (1972) 'The Control of Congestion in Packet-Switching Networks', *IEEE Transactions on Communications*, 20 (3), 546–50.

Davies, S. (1998) 'Biometrics – A Civil Liberties and Privacy Perspective', *Information Security Technical Report*, 3 (1), 90–94.

Davis, W. (2009) 'AT&T In Bed With BT Company', *MediaPost*, www.mediapost. com/publications/?fa=Articles.showArticle&art_aid=104740, date accessed 07 December 2009.

Dawkins, R. (1989 [1976]) *The Selfish Gene* (Oxford: Oxford University Press).

Debord, G. (1992 [1967]) *Society of the Spectacle* (London: Rebel Press).

De Certeau, M. (1988) *The Practice of Everyday Life* (Berkeley, CA: University of California Press).

De Landa, M. (1997) *A Thousand Years of Nonlinear History* (New York: Zone).

Deleuze, G. (1992) 'Postscript on the Societies of Control', *October*, 59 (4), 3–7 .

Deleuze, G. (2005) *Pure Immanence: Essays on a Life* (Cambridge, MA: MIT Press).

Deleuze, G. and Guattari, F. (2003 [1987]) *A Thousand Plateaus: Capitalism and Schizophrenia* (London: Continuum).

Department for Culture, Media and Sport, and Department for Business and Enterprise and Regulatory Reform (2009a) *Digital Britain: Final Report*, www.culture.gov.uk/images/publications/digitalbritain-finalreport-jun09. pdf, date accessed 16 June 2009.

Department for Culture, Media and Sport, and Department for Business and Enterprise and Regulatory Reform (2009b) *Digital Britain: Interim Report*, www. culture.gov.uk/images/publications/digitalbritain-finalreport-jun09.pdf, date accessed 16 June 2009.

Dodd, A. B. (1887) *The Republic of the Future, or Socialism a Reality*, www.archive. org/stream/republicofthefut00doddrich#page/n0/mode/2up, date accessed 10 May 2010.

Dorf, R. C. and Bishop, R. H. (2008) *Modern Control Systems* (New Jersey: Pearson Prentice Hall).

Du Gay, P. (2000) *In Praise of Bureaucracy* (London: Sage).

Durkheim, E. (1964) *The Division of Labour in Society*, G. Simpson (trans.), (New York: Free Press).

The Economist (2008a) *Know-alls*, www.economist.com/world/international/ displaystory.cfm?story_id=12295455, date accessed 04 April 2009.

The Economist (2008b) *Watching While You Surf*, www.economist.com/science/ tq/displaystory.cfm?story_id=11482452, date accessed 09 March 2009.

The Economist (2009) *Tossed by a Gale*, www.economist.com/displaystory. cfm?story_id=13642689, date accessed 22 May 2009.

Elliot, C. and Quinn, F. (2005) *Tort Law* (London: Longman).

Ellul, J. (1964) *The Technological Society* (New York: Vintage Books).

Elmer, G. (2004) *Profiling Machines: Mapping the Personal Information Economy* (Cambridge, MA: MIT Press).

Erickson, J. (2003) *Hacking: The Art of Exploitation* (San Francisco: No Starch Press).

Espiner, T. (2009) 'GCHQ Supplier Pans Government File-sharing Plans', *ZDNet UK*, http://news.zdnet.co.uk/security/0,1000000189,39906065,00.htm, date accessed 04 December 2009.

Essinger, J. (2004) *Jacquard's Web* (Oxford: Oxford University Press).

EuroDIG (2009) *European Dialogue on Internet Governance*, http://eurodig.org/, date accessed 30 October 2009.

EUROPA (2009a) *Telecoms: Commission Launches Case Against UK over Privacy and Personal Data Protection* http://europa.eu/rapid/pressReleasesAction.do?refe rence=IP/09/570&format=HTML&aged=0&language=EN&guiLanguage=e n, date accessed 03 May 2009.

EUROPA (2009b) *Telecoms: Commission Steps up UK Legal Action over Privacy and Personal Data Protection* http://europa.eu/rapid/pressReleasesAction.do?refe rence=IP/09/1626&format=HTML&aged=0&language=EN&guiLanguage=e n, date accessed 30 November 2009.

European Convention on Human Rights (1963) *Convention for the Protection of Human Rights and Fundamental Freedoms as Amended by Protocol No. 11 with Protocol Nos. 1, 4, 6, 7, 12 and 13*, www.echr.coe.int/NR/rdonlyres/D5CC24A7-DC13–4318-B457–5C9014916D7A/0/EnglishAnglais.pdf, date accessed 03 June 2009.

European Commission (2009) *EU Telecoms Reform – One Market for Consumers*, http://ec.europa.eu/news/science/071113_1_en.htm, date accessed 09 November 2009.

Fernback, J. and Papacharissi, Z. (2007) 'Online Privacy as Legal Safeguard: The Relationship among Consumer, Online Portal, and Privacy Policies', *New Media and Society*, 9 (5), 715–34.

Flash Eurobarometer – The Gallup Organization (2008) *Data Protection in the European Union: Citizens' Perceptions Analytical Report*, ec.europa.eu/public_opinion/flash/fl_225_sum_en.pdf, date accessed 19 January 2010.

Forceville, C. (1996) *Pictorial Metaphor in Advertising* (London: Routledge).

Forster, E. M. (1909) *The Machine Stops*, http://manybooks.net/titles/forstereother07machine_stops.html, date accessed 09 May 2010.

Foucault, M. (1972) *The Archaeology of Knowledge* (London: Routledge).

Foucault, M. (1977) *Discipline and Punish* (London: Penguin).

Foucault, M. (1990 [1979]) *The History of Sexuality Vol.1* (London: Penguin).

Foundation for Information Policy Research (2008) *Continuing Concerns about Phorm*, www.fipr.org/press/080406phorm.html, date accessed 11 June 2009.

Franchi, S. and Güzeldere, G. (2005) 'Machinations of the Mind: Cybernetics and Artificial Intelligence from Automata to Cyborgs', in S. Franchi and G. Güzeldere (eds), *Mechanical Bodies, Computational Minds: Artificial Intelligence from Automata to Cyborgs* (Cambridge, MA: MIT Press).

Fraser, F.; Kember, S. and Lury, C. (2005) 'Inventive Life: Approaches to the New Vitalism', *Theory, Culture & Society*, 22 (1), 1–14.

Fry, S. (2009) http://twitter.com/stephenfry, 2:07 am, 22 November 2009 posted from web.

F-Secure (2009) *PeopleOnPage*, www.f-secure.com/sw-desc/peopleonpage.shtml, date accessed 02 December 2009.

Fukuyama, F. (1995) *Trust: The Social Virtues and the Creation of Prosperity* (New York: Simon and Schuster).

Fuller, M. (2003) *Essays on the Software Culture: Behind the Blip* (New York: Autonomedia).

Funkhouser, G. R. (1983) 'A Note on the Reliability of Certain Clustering Algorithms', *Journal of Marketing Research* 20 (1), 99–102.

Galbraith, J. K. (1958 [1991]) *The Affluent Society* (London: Penguin).

Gambetta, D. (ed.) (1988) *Trust: Making and Breaking Cooperative Relations* (Oxford: Blackwell).

Garbarino, E. C. and Edell, J. A. (1997) 'Cognitive Effort, Affect, and Choice', *Journal of Consumer Research*, 24 (2), 147–58.

Gefen, D. (2000) 'E-Commerce: The Role of Familiarity and Trust', *International Journal of Management Science*, 28 (6), 725–37.

Genachowski, J. (2009) 'Preserving a Free and Open Internet: A Platform for Innovation, Opportunity, and Prosperity', *Openinternet.gov*, http://openinternet.gov/read-speech.html, date accessed 10 December 2009.

Gere, C. (2002) *Digital Culture* (London: Reaktion Books).

Geyskens, I.; Steenkamp, J-B.; Scheer, L.K. and Kumar, N. (1996) 'The Effects of Trust and Interdependence on Relationship Commitment: A Transatlantic Study', *International Journal of Research in Marketing*, 13 (4), 303–17.

Giddens, A. (1990) *The Consequences of Modernity* (Cambridge: Polity Press).

Giddens, A. (1991) *Modernity and Self Identity: Self and Society in the Late Modern Age* (Cambridge: Polity Press).

Giddens, A. (2000) *The Third Way and Its Critics* (Cambridge: Polity Press).

Godin, S. (1999) *Permission Marketing: Turning Strangers into Friends, and Friends into Customers* (New York: Simon & Schuster).

Golan, G. J. and Zaidner, L. (2008) 'Creative Strategies in Viral Advertising: An Application of Taylor's Six-Segment Message Strategy Wheel', *Journal of Computer-Mediated Communication*, (13), 959–72.

Gomez, J.; Pinnick, T. and Soltani, A. (2009) 'KnowPrivacy', *UC Berkeley School of Information*, www.knowprivacy.org/report/KnowPrivacy_Final_Report.pdf, date accessed 04 June 2009.

Goodwin, C. (1991) 'Privacy: Recognition of a Consumer Right', *Journal of Public Policy and Marketing*, 10, 149–66.

Graham, S. and Marvin, S. (1996) *Telecommunications and the City: Electronic Spaces, Urban Places* (London: Routledge).

Greco, M. (2005) 'On the Vitality of Vitalism', *Theory, Culture & Society*, 22 (1), 1–14.

The Guardian (2009) *Digital Economy Bill: A Punishing Future*, www.guardian.co.uk/commentisfree/2009/nov/23/editorial-digital-economy-bill, date accessed 23 November 2009.

Guardian.co.uk (2009a) *Phorm Loses $15m in Six Months But Stays Confident?* www.guardian.co.uk/technology/blog/2009/sep/21/phorm-results-losing-money, date accessed 07 December 2009.

Guardian.co.uk (2009b) *Poor Phorm*, http://image.guardian.co.uk/sys-files/Business/documents/2009/07/07/Phorm_Shares_0707.pdf, date accessed 07 December 2009.

Guattari, F. (1992) *Chaosmosis: An Ethico-aesthetic Paradigm* (Bloomington, IN: Indiana University Press).

Guattari, F. (2000) *The Three Ecologies* (London: Athlone Press).

Gutwirth, A. and Hert, P. D. (2008) 'Regulating Profiling in a Democratic Constitutional State', in M. Hildebrandt and S. Gutwirth (eds), *Profiling the European Citizen: Cross-Disciplinary Perspectives* (Dordrecht: Springer), pp. 271–302.

Ha, V.; Inkpen, K.; Al Shaar, F. and Hdeib, L. (2006) 'An Examination of User Perception and Misconception of Internet Cookies', Conference on Human Factors in Computing Systems, Montréal, Québec, Canada, *Association for Computing Machinery*, http://portal.acm.org/ft_gateway.cfm?id=1125615&typ e=pdf&coll=GUIDE&dl=GUIDE&CFID=77713567&CFTOKEN=56134692, date accessed 10 December 2009.

Hagerty, M. R. (1985) 'Improving the Predictive Power of Conjoint Analysis: The Use of Factor Analysis and Cluster Analysis', *Journal of Marketing Research*, 22 (2), 168–84.

Haggerty, J. and Ericson, R. (2000) 'The Surveillant Assemblage', *British Journal of Sociology*, 51 (4), 605–22.

Hahn, R. and Wallsten, S. (2006) *The Economics of Net Neutrality*, Washington, D.C.: AEI Brookings Joint Center for Regulatory Studies, www.aeibrookings. org/publications/abstract.php?pid=1067, date accessed 14 January 2010.

Han, J. and Kamber, M. (2001) *Data Mining: Concepts and Techniques* (San Francisco, CA: Morgan Kaufmann).

Hanff, A. (2008) *A Critical Evaluation of the 2006/2007 Trials of Phorm Inc. Technology by BT PLC*, https://nodpi.org/documents/phorm_paper.pdf, date accessed 10 December 2009.

Hansen, M.B.N. (2009) 'Living (with) Technical Time: From Media Surrogacy to Distributed Cognition', *Theory, Culture & Society*, 26 (2–3), 294–315.

Haraway, D. (1991) 'A Cyborg Manifesto: Science, Technology, and Socialist-Feminism in the Late Twentieth Century,' in *Simians, Cyborgs and Women: The Reinvention of Nature* (New York: Routledge).

Haraway, D. (1997) *Modest Witness@Second Millenium. FemaleMan Meets OncoMouse: Feminism and Technoscience* (New York: Routledge).

Hardt, M. and Negri, A. (2000) *Empire* (Cambridge, MA: Harvard University Press).

Harvey, D. (1985) *The Urbanization of Capital* (Oxford: Blackwell).

Harvey, D. (1990) *The Condition of Postmodernity* (Massachusetts: Blackwell).

Hayles, K. (1999) *How We Became Posthuman* (Chicago: University of Chicago Press).

Haythornthwaite, C. and Wellman, B. (2001) 'The Internet in Everyday Life', in B. Wellman and C. Haythornthwaite (eds), *The Internet in Everyday Life* (Malden, MA: Blackwell).

Hegel, G. W. F. (1969 [1812]) *Science of Logic*, A.V. Miller (trans.), (London: G. Allen & Unwin).

Heidegger, M. (1985 [1927]) *Being and Time*, J. Macquarrie and E. Robinson (trans), (Oxford: Basil Blackwell).

Heidegger, M. (1991 [1939]) *Nietzsche: Vol. IV: Nihilism*, J. Stambaugh; D. F. Krell and F. A. Capuzzi (trans), (San Francisco: Harper and Row).

Heidegger, M. (1993 [1954]) 'The Question Concerning Technology', in M. Heidegger, *Basic Writings*, D. F. Krell (ed.), (New York: Harper Collins).

Heidegger, M. (1993 [1964]) 'The End of Philosophy and the Task of Thinking', in M. Heidegger, *Basic Writings*, D. F. Krell (ed.), (New York: Harper Collins).

Heilbroner, R.L. (1994) 'Do Machines Make History', in, M. L. Smith and L. Marx (eds), *Does Technology Drive History: The Dilemma of Technological Determinism* (Cambridge, MA: MIT Press), pp. 53–66.

Heroux, E. (2008) 'Guattari's Triple Discourses of Ecology', in B. Herzogenrath (ed.), *An [Un]Likely Alliance: Thinking Environment[s] with Deleuze/Guattari* (Newcastle: Cambridge Scholars Publishing).

Heylighen, F. and Joslyn, C. (2001) 'Cybernetics and Second-Order Cybernetics', in R. A. Meyers (ed.), *Encyclopedia of Physical Science & Technology* (3rd ed.), (New York: Academic Press).

Hier, S. (2003) 'Probing the Surveillant Assemblage: On the Dialectics of Surveillance Practices as Processes of Social Control', *Surveillance and Society*, 1 (3), 399–411.

Hildebrandt, M. (2008a) 'Defining Profiling: A New Type of Knowledge', in M. Hildebrandt and S. Gutwirth (eds), *Profiling the European Citizen: Cross-Disciplinary Perspectives* (Dordrecht: Springer), pp. 17–45.

Hildebrandt, M. (2008b) 'Profiling and the Identity of the European Citizen', in M. Hildebrandt and S. Gutwirth (eds), *Profiling the European Citizen: Cross-Disciplinary Perspectives* (Dordrecht: Springer), pp. 303–43.

Hildebrandt, M. and Gutwirth, S. (2008) 'Concise Conclusions: Citizens out of Control', in M. Hildebrandt and S. Gutwirth (eds), *Profiling the European Citizen: Cross-Disciplinary Perspectives* (Dordrecht: Springer), pp. 365–68.

Hill, S.; Provost, F. and Volinky, C. (2006) 'Network-BasedMarketing: Identifying Likely Adopters via Consumer Networks', *Statistical Science*, 21 (2), 256–76.

Hirshleifer, J. (1979) 'Privacy: It's Origin, Function and Future', *The Economics and the Law of Privacy*, University of Chicago, November 30–December 01, www.econ.ucla.edu/workingpapers/wp166.pdf, date accessed 20 January 2009.

HM Treasury (2009) *Budget 2009: Building Britain's Future, Economic and Fiscal Strategy Report and Financial Statement and Budget Report April 2009*, www.hm-treasury.gov.uk/d/Budget2009/bud09_completereport_2520.pdf, date accessed 10 June 2009.

Holm, N. (2009) 'Conspiracy Theorizing Surveillance: Considering Modalities of Paranoia and Conspiracy in Surveillance Studies', *Surveillance and Society*, 7 (1), 36–48.

Home Office (2003) *The Legal Framework Common Law*, www.crimereduction.homeoffice.gov.uk/infosharing22-1.htm, date accessed 20 January 2010.

Home Office (2009) *Protecting the Public in a Changing Communications Environment*, www.official-documents.gov.uk/document/cm75/7586/7586.pdf, date accessed 16 December 2010.

Hood, K. and Schumann, D. W. (2007) 'The Process and Consequences of Cognitive Filtering of Internet Content: Handling the Glut of Internet Advertising', in D. W. Schumann and E. Thorson (eds), *Internet Advertising: Theory and Research* (New Jersey: Lawrence Erlbaum), pp. 185–202.

Hopkins, C. (1998 [1923]) *My Life in Advertising & Scientific Advertising* (Chicago: NTC Business Books).

House of Commons (2009) *Communications Data Bill*, www.commonsleader.gov. uk/output/Page2461.asp, date accessed 06 March 2009.

House of Commons – Home Affairs Committee (2008) *A Surveillance Society?*, HC 58-I, Fifth Report of Session 2007–08 – Volume I: Report, Together with Formal Minutes (London: TSO)

House of Lords (2009) *Digital Economy Bill [HL] 2009–2010*, http://services.parliament.uk/bills/2009–10/digitaleconomy.html, date accessed 24 December 2009.

House of Lords – Select Committee on the Constitution (2009) *Surveillance: Citizens and the State*, HL Paper 18–I, Volume I: Report, www.publications. parliament.uk/pa/ld200809/ldselect/ldconst/18/18.pdf, date accessed 29 May 2009.

Husserl, E. (1970 [1936]) *The Crisis of European Sciences and Transcendental Philosophy*, Carr, D. (trans.), (Evanston, IL: Northwestern University Press).

Husserl, E. (1982 [1913]) *Ideas Pertaining to a Pure Phenomenology and to a Phenomenological Philosophy – First Book: General Introduction to a Pure Phenomenology*, F. Kersten (trans.), (The Hague: Nijhoff).

Huxley, A. (1994 [1932]) *Brave New World* (London: Flamingo).

Inphormationdesk (2009) *BT, Webwise and Phorm*, www.inphormationdesk.org/, date accessed 06 April 2009.

InternetAdvertisingBureau (2009a) *BehaviouralAdvertising*,www.youronlinechoices. co.uk/en/1/aboutbehaviouraladvertising.html, date accessed 17 March 2009.

Internet Advertising Bureau (2009b) *Good Practice Principles for Online Behavioural Advertising*, www.iabuk.net/media/images/IABGoodPracticePrinciplesforOn lineBehaviouralAdvertising_4180.pdf, date accessed 17 March 2009.

Internet Advertising Bureau (2009c) *A Guide to Online Behavioural Advertising*, www.iabuk.net/media/images/OnlineBehaviouralAdvertisingHandbook_ 5455.pdf, date accessed 06 December 2009.

Internet Advertising Bureau (2009d) *Internet Advertising Targeting*, www.iabuk. net/en/1/internetadvertisingtargeting.html, date accessed 28 October 2009.

Internet Advertising Bureau (2010) *IAB Online Adspend Study – Full Year 2009*, www.iabuk.net/en/1/researchadspendiabadspendstudy2009.mxs, date accessed 15 May 2010.

Internet Services Providers' Association (2010) *ISPA Outraged by Amendment on Network Level Blocking to Digital Economy Bill*, www.ispa.org.uk/press_office/ page_767_a39a1f17a5a4b823db3ba7b947f11834.html, date accessed 03 April 2010.

Internet Society (2010) *About the Internet*, www.isoc.org/internet/history/brief. shtml, date accessed 14 April 2010.

Investors Chronicle (2009) *Phorm (PHRM)*, www.investorschronicle.co.uk/Tips/ Sell/TipsOfTheWeek/article/20080515/6e7d0bb2–20d4–11dd-b4c9– 0015171400aa/Phorm-PHRM.jsp, date accessed 22 May 2009.

IPA (2008) *Q2 Bellwether Reveals Marketing Budgets Cut at Fastest Rate since 9/11*, www.ipa.co.uk/Content/Q2-Bellwether-reveals-marketing-budgets-cut-at-fastest-rate-since-911-, date accessed 04 April 2009.

Jameson, F. (1996) *Seeds of Time* (New York: Columbia University Press).
Jhally, S. (1990) *The Codes of Advertising: Fetishism and the Political Economy of Meaning in the Consumer Society* (New York: Routledge).
Joinson, A.; Rieps, U-D.; Buchanan, T. and Schofield, C. B. P. (2008) *Privacy, Trust and Self-Disclosure Online*, http://people.bath.ac.uk/aj266/pubs_pdf/joinson_et_al_HCI_final.pdf, date accessed 10 December 2009.
Judge, E. (2009) 'Phorm Stranded as BT and Carphone Pull Plug on Online 'Spying' Technology', *The Times*, http://business.timesonline.co.uk/tol/business/industry_sectors/technology/article6652692.ece, date accessed 30 October 2009.
Kafka, F. (1994 [1925]) *The Trial* (London: Penguin).
Kant, I. (2008 [1790]) 'The Critique of Judgement', J. C. Meredith (trans.), http://ebooks.adelaide.edu.au/k/kant/immanuel/k16j/, date accessed 08 June 2010.
Katz, E. and Lazarsfeld, P. F. (1955) *Personal Influence: The Part Played by People in the Flow of Mass Communications* (New York: Free Press).
Kauffman, L. H. (2003) 'Eigenforms – Objects as Tokens for EigenBehaviors', *Cybernetics and Human Knowing*, 10 (3–4), 73–89.
Kauffman, S. (1995) *At Home in the Universe: The Search for Laws of Self-Organization and Complexity* (New York: Oxford University Press).
Kavada, A. (2010) 'Activism Transforms Digital: The Social Movement Perspective', in M. Joyce (ed.), *Digital Activism Decoded: The New Mechanics of Change* (New York: Idebate), pp. 101–18.
Kaye, K. (2010) 'IAB Gives to Re-Election Campaign of Privacy Bill Lawmaker', *ClickZ*, www.clickz.com/3640662?utm_source=feedburner&utm_medium=feed&utm_campaign=Feed%3A+clickz+%28ClickZ+News%29, date accessed 21 June 2010.
Kent-Uritam, E. (2009) 'T's and C's – What's the Fuss?' *Advertising Age*, http://adage.com/digitalnext/post.php?article_id=135363, date accessed 20 March 2009.
Klang, M. and Murray, A. (2005) *Human Rights in the Digital Age* (London: Glasshouse Press).
Kleinrock, L. (1961) 'Information Flow in Large Communication Nets, RLE Quarterly Progress Report', *UCLA*, www.cs.ucla.edu/~lk/REPORT/RLEreport-1961.html, date accessed 14 August 2009.
Kobie, N. (2009) 'Virgin Media Not Planning Phorm Rollout', *ITPro*, www.itpro.co.uk/612553/virgin-media-not-planning-phorm-rollout, date accessed 11 July 2009.
Koops, B-J. (2008) 'Reply: Some Reflections of Profiling, Power Shifts and Protection Paradigms', in M. Hildebrandt, M. and S. Gutwirth (eds), *Profiling the European Citizen: Cross-Disciplinary Perspectives* (Dordrecht: Springer), pp. 326–37.
Koops, B-J. and Leenes, R. (2005) ' "Code" and the Slow Erosion of Privacy', *Michigan Telecommunications & Technology Law Review*, 12 (1), 115–88, www.mttlr.org/voltwelve/koops&leenes.pdf, date accessed 04 January 2009.
Kumar, S. (2009) 'BBC Online and Behavioural Targeting', *BBC Internet Blog*, www.bbc.co.uk/blogs/bbcinternet/2009/05/bbc_online_and_behavioral_targ.html, date accessed 23 May 2009.

La Mettrie, J. O. de (1996 [1747]) *Machine Man and Other Writings*, A. Thomson (ed.), (Cambridge: Cambridge University Press).

Lanier, C. D, Jr. and Saini, A. (2008) 'Understanding Consumer Privacy: A Review and Future Directions', *Academy of Marketing Science Review*, www.amsreview. org/articles/lanier02–2008.pdf, date accessed 09 February 2009.

LaRose, R. and Rifon, N. (2006) 'Your Privacy is Assured – of Being Disturbed: Websites with and without Privacy Seals', *New Media and Society*, 8 (6), 1009–29.

LaRose, R. and Rifon, N. (2007) 'Promoting i-Safety: Effects of Privacy Warnings and Privacy Seals on Risk Assessment and Online Privacy Behavior', *Journal of Consumer Affairs*, 41 (1), 127–69.

Lash, S. (2002) *Critique of Information* (London: Sage).

Lash, S. (2007) 'Power after Hegemony: Cultural Studies in Mutation', *Theory, Culture & Society*, 24 (3), 55–78.

Latour, B. (1993) *We Have Never Been Modern* (Harlow: Harvester Wheatsheaf).

Latour, B. (1997a) 'On Actor-Network Theory: A Few Clarifications – Bruno Latour', *Nettime*, www.nettime.org/Lists-Archives/nettime-l-9801/msg00019. html, date accessed 18 August 2009.

Latour, B. (1997b) 'Trains of Thought: Piaget, Formalism and the Fifth Dimension', *Common Knowledge*, 6 (3), 170–91.

Latour, B. (2003) 'Is Re-modernization Occurring – and If So, How to Prove It?: A Commentary on Ulrich Beck', *Theory, Culture & Society*, 20 (2), 35–48.

Lauer, T. W. and Deng, X. (2007) 'Building Online Trust through Privacy Practices', *International Journal on Information Security*, 6, 323–31.

Learmonth, M. (2010) '"Power Eye" Lets Consumers Know Why That Web Ad Was Sent to Them', *Advertising Age*, http://adage.com/digital/article?article_id=144557, date accessed 03 July 2010.

Lee, E-J. (2007) 'Computer Agents as Sources of Trust in Internet Advertising', in D. W. Schumann and E. Thorson (eds), *Internet Advertising: Theory and Research* (New Jersey: Lawrence Erlbaum), pp. 121–47.

Leenes, R. (2008) 'Reply: Addressing the Obscurity of Data Clouds', in M. Hildebrandt and S. Gutwirth (eds), *Profiling the European Citizen: Cross-Disciplinary Perspectives* (Dordrecht: Springer), pp. 293–301.

Lefebvre, H. (1971) *Everyday Life in the Modern World* (New York: Harper Torchbook).

Lefebvre, H. (1991 [1974]) *The Production of Space* (Oxford: Blackwell).

Lefebvre, H. (2003) *Key Writings* (London: Continuum).

Leibniz, G. W. (2005 [1686]) *Discourse on Metaphysics and The Monadology* (New York: Dover Philosophical Classics).

Leiner, B. M.; Cerf, V. G.; Clark, D. D.; Kahn, R. E.; Kleinrock, L.; Lynch, D. C.; Postel, J.; Roberts, L. G. and Wolff, S. (2003) 'A Brief History of the Internet', *Internet Society*, www.isoc.org/internet/history/brief.shtml#cerf, date accessed 16 August 2009.

Leiss, W.; Kline, S.; Jhally, S. and Botterill, J. (2005) *Social Communication in Advertising: Consumption in the Mediated Marketplace* (New York: Routledge).

Leong, S.; Mitew, T; Celletti, M. and Pearson, E. (2009) 'The Question Concerning Internet Time', *New Media and Society*, 11 (8), 1267–85.

Lessig, L. (2006) *Code Version 2.0* (New York: Basic Books).

Leyden, W. (1968) *Seventeenth-century Metaphysics: An Examination of Some Main Concepts and Theories* (London: Duckworth).

Lister, M.; Dovey, J.; Giddings, S.; Grant, I. and Kelly, K. (2003) *New Media: A Critical Introduction* (London: Routledge).

Lovink, G. and Zehle, S. (2005) 'Incommunicado Glossary', in G. Lovink and S. Zehle (eds), *The Incommunicado Reader* (Amsterdam: Institute of Network Cultures), pp. 3–10.

Luhmann, N. (1979) *Trust and Power: Two Works by Niklas Luhmann*, H. Davis; J. Raffan and K. Rooney (trans), (Chichester: John Wiley and Sons).

Luhmann, N. (1988) 'Familiarity, Confidence, Trust: Problems and Alternatives', in D. Gambetta (ed.), *Trust: Making and Breaking Cooperative Relations* (Oxford: Basil Blackwell), pp. 94–107.

Luhmann, N. (1995) *Social Systems* (Stanford, CA: Stanford University Press).

Lyon, D. (1988) *The Information Society: Issues and Illusions* (Cambridge: Polity Press).

Lyon, D. (2001) *Surveillance Society: Monitoring Everyday Life* (Buckingham: Open University Press).

Lyotard, J. (1979) *The Postmodern Condition* (Manchester: Manchester University Press).

Machlup, F. (1962) *The Production and Distribution of Knowledge in the United States.* (New Jersey: Princeton University Press).

MacRury, I. (2009) *Advertising* (Abingdon, Oxon: Routledge).

Mann, S. and Niedzviecki, H. (2001) *Cyborg: Digital Destiny and Human Possibility in the Age of the Wearable Computer* (Toronto: Random House Doubleday).

Mann, S.; Nolan, J. and Wellman, B. (1998) 'Sousveillance: Inventing and Using Wearable Computing Devices for Data Collection in Surveillance Environments', *Surveillance & Society*, 1 (3), 331–55.

Marcuse, H. (1964) *One-Dimensional Man*, www.marxists.org/reference/archive/marcuse/works/one-dimensional-man/index.htm, date accessed 07 April 2009.

Marks, P. (2009) 'Berners-Lee: We No Longer Fully Understand the Web', *New Scientist*, www.newscientist.com/article/mg20227111.400, date accessed 05 June 2009.

Marsden, C. (2010) *Net Neutrality: Towards a Co-Regulatory Solution* (London: Bloomsbury).

Marshall, J. (2009a) 'Behavioral Targeting Gains Ground in Europe', *ClickZ*, www.clickz.com/3633336, date accessed 30 November 2009.

Marshall, J. (2009b) 'European Commission Takes Legal Action over Phorm Trials', *ClickZ*, www.clickz.com/3633398, date accessed 10 June 2009.

Marshall, J. (2010) 'Limited Data and Privacy Concerns Restrain Behavioral in Europe', *ClickZ*, www.clickz.com/3639780, date accessed 16 March 2010.

Marshall, N.J. (1974) 'Dimensions of Privacy Preferences', *Multivariate Behavior Research*, 9 (3), 255–72.

Martin, J. (1978) *The Wired Society* (Englewood Cliffs, NJ: Prentice Hall).

Marx, G.T. (2003) 'A Tack in the Shoe: Neutralizing and Resisting the New Surveillance', *Journal of Social Issues*, 59 (2), 369–90.

Marx, K. (1976 [1848]) *Collected Works, Vol. 5* (New York: International Publishers).

Marx, K. (1973 [1939]) *The Grundrisse: Foundations of the Critique of Political Economy* (New York: Vintage Books).

Marx, L. (1994) 'The Idea of "Technology" and Postmodern Pessimism', in M. R. Smith and L. Marx (eds), *Does Technology Drive History: The Dilemma of Technological Determinism* (Cambridge, MA: MIT Press), pp. 237–58.

Masani, P.R. (2000) 'Mind and Matter: The Question of Primacy', *Current Science*, 79 (3), 290–302.

Maslow, A. H. (1943) 'A Theory of Human Motivation', *Psychological Review*, 50 (4), 370–96.

Masuda, Y. (1980) *The Information Society as Post-Industrial Society* (Bethesda, MD: World New York: Unipub. Future Society).

Maturana, H. R. and Varela, F. J. (1980) *Autopoiesis and Cognition: The Realization of the Living* (Dordrecht: Kluwer Academic Publishers).

Maturana, H. R. and Varela, F. J. (1992) *The Tree of Knowledge: The Biological Roots of Human Understanding* (Boston: Shambhala).

Mayer, R. C.; Davis, J. H. and Schoorman, F. D. (1995) 'An Integration Model of Organizational Trust', *Academy of Management Review*, 20 (3), 709–34.

Mayr, O. (1986) *Authority, Liberty and Automatic Machinery in Early Modern Europe* (Baltimore, MD: Johns Hopkins University Press).

McLuhan, M. (1965) *Understanding Media: The Extensions of Man* (New York: McGraw-Hill).

McQuail, D. (1997) *Audience Analysis* (London: Sage).

McStay, A. (2007a) 'Regulating the Suicide Bomber: A Critical Examination of Viral Advertising and Simulations of Self-Broadcasting', *Ethical Space: Journal of Communication*, 4 (1/2), 40–48.

McStay, A. (2007b) 'Trust, Data-mining and Instantaneity: The Creation of the Online Accountable Consumer', in V. Bakir and D. Barlow (eds), *Communication in the Age of Suspicion: Trust and the Media* (London: Palgrave-Macmillan), pp. 114–24.

McStay, A. (2009a) *Digital Advertising* (Basingstoke: Palgrave-Macmillan).

McStay, A. (2009b) *Phorm Town Hall Meeting*, http://advertising-communications-culture.blogspot.com/2009/04/phorm-town-hall-meeting.html, date accessed 18 November 2009.

McStay, A. (2010) 'A Qualitative Approach to Understanding Audience's Perceptions of Creativity in Online Advertising', *The Qualitative Report*, 15 (1), 37–58, www.nova.edu/ssss/QR/QR15-1/mcstay.pdf, date accessed 25 January 2010.

McStay, A. (2011) '*Profiling Phorm: An Autopoietic Approach to the Audience-as-commodity*', *Surveillance and Society*, forthcoming paper.

McStay, A. and Bakir, V. (2006) 'Privacy, Online Advertising and Marketing Techniques: The Paradoxical Disappearance of the User', *Ethical Space: Journal of Communication*, 3 (1), 24–31.

Melucci, A. (1996) *Challenging Codes: Collective Action in the Information Age* (Cambridge: Cambridge University Press).

Merleau-Ponty, M. (1962) *Phenomenology of Perception* (London: RKP).

Messaris, P. (1997) *Visual Persuasion: The Role of Images in Advertising* (London: Sage).

Metro (2009) : '60 Second Interview', 29 April 2009.

Miles, C. (2007) 'A Cybernetic Communication Model for Advertising', *Marketing Theory*, 7 (4), 307–34.

Mill, J. S. (2009 [1868]) 'State of Ireland', *Hansard*, http://hansard. millbanksystems.com/commons/1868/mar/12/adjourned-debate, date accessed 19 July 2010.

Miller, J. G. (1978) *Living Systems* (New York: McGraw-Hill).

Milne, G. R.; Labrecque, L. I. and Cromer, C. (2009) 'Toward an Understanding of the Online Consumer's Risky Behavior and Protection Practices', *Journal of Consumer Affairs*, 43 (3), 449–73.

Mingers, J. (1995) *Self-Producing Systems: Implications and Applications of Autopoiesis* (New York: Plenum).

Misztal, B. A. (1996) *Trust in Modern Societies* (Cambridge: Polity Press).

Miyazaki, A. D. (2008) 'Online Privacy and the Disclosure of Cookie Use: Effects on Consumer Trust and Anticipated Patronage', *Journal of Public Policy and Marketing*, 27 (1), 19–33.

Miyazaki, A. D. and Krishnamurthy, S. (2002) 'Internet Seals of Approval: Effects on Online Privacy Policies and Consumer Perceptions', *Journal of Consumer Affairs*, 36 (1), 28–49.

Mokyr, J. (2001) *The Gifts of Athena: Historical Origins of the Knowledge Economy* (Princeton, NJ: Princeton University Press).

Möllering, G. (2001) 'The Nature of Trust: From Georg Simmel to a Theory of Expectation, Interpretation and Suspension', *Sociology*, 35 (2), 403–20.

Moran, D. (2000) *Introduction to Phenomenology* (London: Routledge).

Moran, D. (2002) 'Editor's Introduction', in D. Moran and T. Mooney (eds), *The Phenomenology Reader* (Abingdon, Oxon: Routledge), pp. 1–26.

Morley, J. (1905) *Diderot* (New York: Macmillan).

Mosco, V. (2009) *The Political Economy of Communication* (London: Sage).

Munro, I. (2001) 'Informated Identities and The Spread of the Word Virus', *Ephemera*, 1 (2), 149–62.

Muri, A. (2007) *The Enlightenment Cyborg: A History of Communications and Control in the Human Machine 1660–1830* (Toronto: University of Toronto Press).

Narus (2009) *Intercept Solution*, www.narus.com/index.php/solutions/intercept, date accessed 12 November 2009.

Neate, R. (2009) 'Phorm Loses Technology Chief', *Telegraph.co.uk*, www.telegraph. co.uk/finance/newsbysector/mediatechnologyandtelecoms/media/ 6209787/Phorm-loses-technology-chief.html, date accessed 07 December 2009.

Nehf, J. P. (2007) 'Shopping for Privacy on the Internet', *Journal of Consumer Affairs*, 41 (2), 351–65.

Nelson, M. G. (2007) 'Users Request More Targeted Ads, Study Says', *ClickZ*, www.clickz.com/showPage.html?page=3627288, date accessed 09 February 2009.

Network Advertising Initiative (2009) *What Is the NAI Doing to Help You Protect Your Privacy?*, www.networkadvertising.org/managing/, date accessed 20 March 2009.

Network Advertising Initiative (2010) *Study Finds Behaviorally-Targeted Ads More Than Twice as Valuable, Twice as Effective as Non-Targeted Online Ads*, www.networkadvertising.org/pdfs/NAI_Beales_Release.pdf, date accessed 15 December 2010.

Neuman, W. R. (1991) *The Future of the Mass Audience* (Cambridge: Cambridge University Press).

NoDPI (2008) *ICO Admit BT 2007 Trials Breached PECR 2003 But Refuse to Act!*, https://nodpi.org/tag/privacy-and-electronic-communications-ec-directive-re/, date accessed 17 January 2010.

NoDPI (2009a) *BBC on Phorm – FOI Response*, https://nodpi.org/2009/05/22/bbc-on-phorm-foi-response/, date accessed 10 December 2009.

NoDPI (2009b) *Lessons to Be Learned?* https://nodpi.org/2009/04/29/lessons-to-be-learned, date accessed 29 June 2009.

NoDPI (2009c) *Meeting at the EU Commission in Brussels – 27th May 2009*, https://nodpi.org/2009/05/28/meeting-at-the-eu-commission-in-brussels-27th-may-2009/, date accessed 29 May 2009.

NoDPI (2009d) *Meeting at Millbank*, https://nodpi.org/2009/05/11/muffins-at-millbank/, date accessed 11 June 2009.

NoDPI (2009e) *Off to Brussels*, https://nodpi.org/2009/05/26/off-to-brussels/, date accessed 27 May 2009.

Nora, S. and Mine, A. (1978) *The Computerization of Society: A Report to the President of France* (Cambridge, MA: MIT Press).

Norberg, P. A.; Horne, D. A. and Horne, D. (2009) 'Standing in the Footprint: Including the Self in the Privacy Debate and Policy Development', *Journal of Consumer Affairs*, 43 (3), 495–515.

NORDICOM (2009) *European Media Policy: European Union Council of Europe*, www.nordicom.gu.se/mt/letter.php#Much%20Concern%20about%20Privacy%20Issues, date accessed 01 November 2009.

Norris, C. and Armstrong, G. (1999) *The Maximum Surveillance Society: The Rise of CCTV* (New York: Oxford University Press).

Norris, C. and Wilson, D. (2006) *Surveillance, Crime and Social Control* (Aldershot: Ashgate).

O'Connor, C. (2008) 'Web Tool Firm in PR Fightback', *PR Week*, www.prweek.com/uk/news/794618/, date accessed 02 December 2009.

Odih, P. (2007) *Advertising in Modern and Postmodern Times* (London: Sage).

Office of Public Sector Information (2008) *Regulation of Investigatory Powers Act 2000 (c. 23)*, www.opsi.gov.uk/acts/acts2000/ukpga_20000023_en_1, date accessed 09 August 2009.

Olma, S. (2007) 'Physical Bergsonism and the Worldliness of Time', *Theory, Culture & Society*, 24 (6), 123–37.

Olma, S. and Koukouzelis, K. (2007) 'Introduction: Life's (Re-)Emergences', *Theory, Culture & Society*, 24 (6), 1–17.

O'Neil, D. (2001) 'Analysis of Internet Users' Level of Online Privacy Concerns', *Social Science Computer Review*, 19 (1), 17–31.

Open Rights Group (2009a) *Data Retention Endangers Democracy*, www.openrightsgroup.org/2009/04/06/data-retention-endangers-democracy/#comments, date accessed 06 April 2009.

Open Rights Group (2009b) *Digital Britain: Closing Down the Open Internet*, www.openrightsgroup.org/blog/2009/digital-britain-closing-down-the-open-internet, date accessed 12 September 2009.

Organisation for Economic Co-operation and Development (2008) *OECD Guidelines on the Protection of Privacy and Transborder Flows of Personal Data*, www. oecd.org/document/18/0,3343,en_2649_34255_1815186_1_1_1_1,00.html, date accessed 11 December 2009.

Orwell, G. (2004 [1949]) *Nineteen Eighty-Four* (London: Penguin).

Packard, V. (1959) *The Status Seekers* (London: Longmans).

paidContent:UK (2009) *Updated: Phorm Bags Korea ISP Trial, Carphone Mulls Bid For Tiscali*, http://paidcontent.co.uk/article/419-phorm-launches-korean-isp-trial-carphone-warehouse-considers-tiscali-bi/, date accessed 04 July 2009.

Paley, W. (1986 [1802]) *Natural Theology, or Evidences of the Existence and Attributes of the Deity Collected from the Appearances of Nature* (Charlottesville, VA: Lincoln-Rembrandt).

Parikka, J. (2005) 'Contagion and Repetition: On the Viral Logic of Network Culture Ephemera', *Fibreculture*, http://journal.fibreculture.org/issue4/issue4_parikka.html, date accessed 09 February 2009.

Pedersen, D. M. (1997) 'Psychological Functions of Privacy', *Journal of Environmental Psychology*, 17 (2), 147–56.

Perez, C. (2002) *Technological Revolutions and Financial Capital: The Dynamics of Bubbles and Golden Ages* (Cheltenham: Edward Elgar).

Petronio, S. (2000) 'The Boundaries of Privacy: Praxis of Everyday Life', in S. Petronio (ed.), *Balancing the Secrets of Private Disclosures* (Hillsdale, NJ: Lawrence Erlbaum), pp. 37–49.

Phelps, E. S. (1985) *Political Economy* (New York: Norton).

Phelps, J.; Nowak, G. and Ferrell, E. (2000) 'Privacy Concerns and Consumer Willingness to Provide Personal Information', *Journal of Public Policy and Marketing*, 19 (1), 27–41.

Phorm (2008a) www.phorm.com/, date accessed 23 March 2009.

Phorm (2008b) *User Privacy and Choice Guaranteed by Phorm*, www.phorm.com/reports/FIPR_Response_7-Apr-2008.pdf, date accessed 11 June 2009.

Phorm (2008c) *Report and Financial Statements*, www.phorm.com/reports/2008_Financial_Statements.pdf, date accessed 18 June 2009.

Phorm (2009a) 'This Is How They Work', *Stop Phoul Play*, www.stopphoulplay.com/this-is-how-they-work/, date accessed 01 May 2009.

Phorm (2009b) 'This Is Who They Are', *Stop Phoul Play*, www.stopphoulplay.com/this-is-how-they-work/, date accessed 22 May 2009.

Posner, R.A. (1990) *The Problems of Jurisprudence* (Cambridge, MA: Harvard University Press).

Poster, M. (1990) *The Mode of Information: Poststructuralism and Social Context* (Chicago: University Of Chicago Press).

Poster, M. (1995) *The Second Media Age* (Cambridge, MA: Polity Press).

Poster, M. (1996) 'Databases as Discourse, or Electronic Interpellations', in P. Heelas; S. Lash and P. Morris (eds), *Detraditionalization* (Oxford: Blackwell), pp. 277–93.

Poster, M. (2004) 'Consumption and Digital Commodities in the Everyday', *Cultural Studies*, 18 (2–3), 409–23.

Poster, M. (2006), *Information Please: Culture and Politics in the Age of Digital Machines* (Durham, NC: Duke University Press).

Postman, N. (1993) *Technopoly* (New York: Vintage Books).

Poulakos, J, (2002) 'Kairos in Gorgias' Rhetorical Compositions', in P. Sipiora and J. S. Baumlin (eds), *Rhetoric and Kairos: Essays in History, Theory, and Praxis* (Albany, NY: State University of New York Press), pp. 89–96.

Presbrey, F. (1929) *The History and Development of Advertising* (Garden City, NY: Doubleday, Doran).

Priest, S. (2003) *Merleau-Ponty* (London: Routledge).

Prigogine, I. and Stengers, I. (1984) *Order Out of Chaos: Man's New Dialogue with Nature* (New York: Bantam Books).

Procera (2008a) *Data Sheet: Packetlogic Software Modules,* www.proceranetworks.com/images/datasheets-2008–10-31/ds-plsoftwareoverview_10–31-08_a4.pdf, date accessed 12 November 2009.

Procera (2008b) *A Quick Introduction to DRDL,* www.proceranetworks.com/documents/a4/WP-DRDL-10–3-08-A4.pdf, date accessed 12 November 2009.

Punj, G. and Stewart, D. W. (1983) 'Cluster Analysis in Marketing Research: Review and Suggestions for Application', *Journal of Marketing Research,* 20 (2), 134–48.

Putnam, R. D. (1993) *Making Democracy Work: Civic Traditions in Modern Italy* (Princeton, NJ: Princeton University Press)

Quenqua, D. (2009) 'Some NAI Members Don't Fully Comply With Behavioral Targeting Standards', *ClickZ,* www.clickz.com/3635994?utm_source=feedburner&utm_medium=feed&utm_campaign=Feed%3A+clickz+(ClickZ+News), date accessed 18 January 2010.

Rabinow, P. and Rose, N. (2006) 'Biopower Today', *Biosocieties,* 1 (2), 195–217.

Rayner, T. (2001) 'Biopower and Technology: Foucault and Heidegger's Way of Thinking', *Contretemps,* (2), 142–56, www.usyd.edu.au/contretemps/2may2001/rayner.pdf, date accessed 20 January 2010.

Reidenberg, J.R. (2000) 'Resolving Conflicting International Data Privacy Rules in Cyberspace', *Stanford Law Review,* 52, 1315–76

Roberts, M (1972) *A Portrait of Europe 1789–1914: Machines and Liberty* (Oxford: Oxford University Press).

Roberts, M. S. and Ko, H. (2001) 'Global Interactive Advertising: Defining What We Mean and Using What We Have Learned', *Journal of Interactive Advertising,* 1 (2), www.jiad.org/article10, date accessed 03 June 2009.

Robertshaw, G. S. and Marr, N. E. (2006) 'The Implications of Incomplete and Spurious Personal Information Disclosures for Direct Marketing Practice', *Journal of Database Marketing and Customer Strategy Management,* 13 (3), 186–97.

Rodgers, Z. (2009a) 'Few Google Users Are Opting Out of Behavioral Targeting', *ClickZ,* www.clickz.com/3635881?utm_source=feedburner&utm_medium=feed&utm_campaign=Feed%3A+clickz+(ClickZ+News), date accessed 26 December 2009.

Rodgers, Z. (2009b) 'IAB Tackles Privacy Worries with Big Display Ad Campaign', *ClickZ,* www.clickz.com/3635817?utm_source=feedburner&utm_medium=feed&utm_campaign=Feed%3A+clickz+(ClickZ+News), date accessed 11 December 2009.

Rojas, R. (2002) *The First Computers: History and Architectures* (Cambridge, MA: MIT Press).

Ross, K. and Nightingale, V. (2003) *Media and Audiences* (London: Open University Press).

Rossiter, N. (2006) *Organized Networks: Media Theory, Creative Labour, New Institutions* (Rotterdam: NAi Publishers).

Rotzoll, K. B.; Haefner, J. E. and Hall, S. R. (1996) *Advertising in Contemporary Society* (Urbana, IL: University of Illinois Press).

Rowan, D. (2009) 'Free Choice? Don't be Naïve', *Wired*, July 2009.

Rushkoff, D. (1994) *Media Virus* (New York: Ballantine Books).

Schön, D. A. and Rein, M. (1994) *Frame Reflection: Toward the Resolution of Intractable Policy Controversies* (New York: Basic Books).

Schroeder, J. E. and Salzer-Mörling, M. (2006) *Brand Culture* (London: Routledge).

Schumann, D. W. and Thorson, E. (eds) (2007) *Internet Advertising: Theory and Research* (New Jersey: Lawrence Erlbaum).

Schumann, D. W.; Artis, A. and Rivera, R. (2001) 'The Future of Interactive Advertising Viewed Through an IMC Lens', *Journal of Interactive Advertising*, 1 (2), www.jiad.org/article12, date accessed 03 June 2009.

Schumpeter, J. (2003 [1942]) *Capitalism, Socialism and Democracy* (New York: Harper and Brothers).

Schutz, A. (1967) *Phenomenology of the Social World* (Evanston, IL: Northwestern University Press).

Schwiderski-Grosche, S. (2006) 'Security: An End User Perspective', *Information Security Technical Report*, 11, 109–10.

Searle, J. (1980) 'Minds, Brains and Programs', *Behavioral and Brain Sciences*, 3 (3), 417–57.

Searle, J. R. (1998) *The Mystery of Consciousness* (London: Granta Publications).

Shannon, C. E. (1976 [1938]) 'A Symbolic Analysis of Relay and Switching Circuits', in E. E. Swartzlander, Jr. (ed.), *Computer Design Development: Principal Papers*, (New Jersey: Hayden).

Shapiro, J. (2009a) 'Back from Web 3.0 – with Some Problems to Solve', *Advertising Age*, http://adage.com/digitalnext/post.php?article_id=136875, date accessed 28 May 2009.

Shapiro, J. (2009b) 'The Tyranny of Technology in Testing Marketing Effectiveness', *Advertising Age*, http://adage.com/digitalnext/post.php?article_id=137011, date accessed 03 June 2009.

Shapiro, S. P. (1987) 'The Social Control of Impersonal Trust', *American Journal of Sociology*, 93 (3), 623–58.

Sharoff, S. (2005) 'Phenomenology and Cognitive Science', in S. Franchi, S. and G. Güzeldere (eds), *Mechanical Bodies, Computational Minds: Artificial Intelligence from Automata to Cyborgs* (Cambridge, MA: MIT Press), pp. 471–87.

Sheehan, K. B. and Hoy, M. G. (1999) 'Flaming, Complaining, Abstaining: How Online Users Respond to Privacy Concerns', *Journal of Advertising*, 28 (3), 37–51.

Sismondo, S (2004) *Science and Technology Studies* (Oxford: Blackwell).

Simmel, G. (1990 [1900]) *The Philosophy of Money* (London: Routledge),

Sipiora, P. (2002) 'Introduction: The Ancient Concept of Kairos', in P. Sipiora and J. S. Baumlin (eds), *Rhetoric and Kairos: Essays in History, Theory, and Praxis* (Albany, NY: State University of New York Press), pp. 1–22.

Smith, A. (1993 [1776]) *An Inquiry into the Nature and Causes of the Wealth of Nations* [Abridged] (Indianapolis, IN: Hackett).

Smith. M. L (1994) 'Recourse of Empire', in M. L. Smith and L. Marx (eds), *Does Technology Drive History: The Dilemma of Technological Determinism* (Cambridge, MA: MIT Press), pp. 37–52.

Smith, M. L. and Marx, L. (eds) (1994) *Does Technology Drive History: The Dilemma of Technological Determinism* (Cambridge, MA: MIT Press).

Smith, W. (1956) 'Product Differentiation and Market Segmentation as Alternative Marketing Strategies', *Journal of Marketing*, 21 (1), 3–8.

SMSR (2009) *Report on Information Commissioner's Office – Annual Track*, www.ico. gov.uk/ . . . reports/ico_annual_tracking_individuals_final_report2009.pdf, date accessed 01 March 2010.

Smythe, D. W. (1977) 'Communications: Blindspot of Western Marxism', *Canadian Journal of Political and Social Theory*, 1 (3), 1–27.

Smythe, D. W. (1981) *Dependency Road: Communications, Capitalism, Consciousness, and Canada* (New Jersey: ABLEX).

Soenens, E. (2008) 'Web Usage Mining for Web Personalisation in Customer Relations Management', in M. Hildebrandt and S. Gutwirth (eds), *Profiling the European Citizen: Cross-Disciplinary Perspectives* (Dordrecht: Springer), pp. 175–84.

Soja, E. W. (1989) *Postmodern Geographies: The Reassertion of Space in Critical Social Theory* (London: Verso).

Speta, J. B. (2002) 'A Common Carrier Approach to Internet Interconnection', *Federal Communications Law Journal*, 54 (2), 225–80.

Spurgeon, C. (2008) *Advertising and New Media* (Abingdon, Oxon: Routledge).

Stacey, R.D. (2003) *Strategic Management and Organisational Dynamics: The Challenge of Complexity* (Harlow, UK: FT Prentice Hall).

Stafford, M. R. and Faber, R. J. (eds) (2005) *Advertising, Promotion and New Media* (New York: M.E. Sharpe).

Stafford, T. F. and Urbaczewski, A. (2004) 'Spyware: The Ghost in the Machine', *Communications of the Association for Information Systems*, 14, 291–306

Stanaland, A. J. S.; Lwin, M. O. and Leong, S. (2009) 'Providing Parents with Online Privacy Information: Approaches in the US and the UK', *Journal of Consumer Affairs*, 43 (3), 474–94.

Starch, D. (1914) 'Advertising: Its Principles, Practice, and Technique', *Internet Archive*, www.archive.org/download/advertisingitspr00stariala/advertisingitspr00stariala.pdf, date accessed 20 April 2010.

Stiegler, B. (2009) *Technics and Time, v. 2 Disorientation* (Stanford, CA: Stanford University Press).

Stewart, C. M.; Gil-Egui, G.; Tian, Y. and Pileggi, M. I. (2006) 'Framing the Digital Divide: A Comparison of US and EU Policy Approaches', *New Media and Society*, 8 (5), 731–51.

Suarez-Villa, L. (2009) *Technocapitalism* (Philadelphia, PA Temple University Press).

Sujon, Z. (2007) 'New Citizenships? New Technologies, Rights and Discourses', in N. Carpentier; P. Pruulmann-Vengerfeldt; K. Nordenstreng; M. Hartmann; P. Vihalemm; B. Cammaerts and H. Nieminen (eds), *Media Technologies and Democracy in an Enlarged Europe* (Tartu: Tartu University Press), pp. 201–17.

Sweney, M. (2009a) 'Decline in UK Advertising Spend Slowing, Says IPA's Bellwether Report', *The Guardian*, www.guardian.co.uk/media/2009/apr/06/advertising-spend-bellwether-report, date accessed 6 March 2009.

Sweney, M. (2009b) 'Internet Overtakes Television to Become Biggest Advertising Sector in the UK', *The Guardian*, www.guardian.co.uk/media/2009/sep/30/internet-biggest-uk-advertising-sector, date accessed 30 September 2009.

Symantec (2009) *Spyware.Apropos*, www.symantec.com/security_response/writeup.jsp?docid=2004–113018-3823–99&tabid=2, date accessed 02 December 2009.

Sztompka, P. (1999) *Trust: A Sociological Theory* (Cambridge: Cambridge University Press).

Taylor, K. (ed.) (1975) *Henri Saint-Simon (1760–1825): Selected Writings on Science, Industry, and Social Organization* (New York: Holmes and Meier).

Taylor, M. C. (2001) *The Moment of Complexity: Emerging Network Culture* (Chicago: University of Chicago Press).

Terranova, T. (2004) *Network Culture: Politics for the Information Age* (London: Pluto Press).

Thomas, R. and Walport, M. (2008) 'Data Sharing Review', *Ministry of Justice*, www.justice.gov.uk/reviews/docs/data-sharing-review-report.pdf, date accessed 10 December 2009.

Thompson, C. (2008) 'Brave New World of Digital Intimacy', *The New York Times*, www.nytimes.com/2008/09/07/magazine/07awareness-t.html?_r=3&pagewanted=1&partner=rssnyt&emc=rss&oref=slogin&oref=slogin, date accessed 09 February 2009.

Thompson, E. (2004) 'Life and Mind: From Autopoiesis to Neurophenomenology. A Tribute to Francisco Varela', *Phenomenology and the Cognitive Sciences*, 3, 381–398.

Thompson, E. P. (1967) 'Time, Work-Discipline and Industrial Capitalism', *Past and Present*, 38, 56–97

Thrift, N. (2005) *Knowing Capitalism* (London: Sage).

Tilly, C. (2007) *Democracy* (New York: Cambridge University Press).

Toscano, A. (2007) 'Vital Strategies: Maurizio Lazzarato and the Metaphysics of Contemporary Capitalism', *Theory, Culture & Society*, 24 (6), 71–91.

Toth, E. L. and Heath, R. L (1992) 'Preface', in, E. L.Toth and R. L.Heath (eds), *Rhetorical and Critical Approaches to Public Relations* (London: Lawrence Erlbaum), pp. xi–xvi.

Toynbee, A. (1884 [1920]) *Lectures on the Industrial Revolution of the Eighteenth Century in England* (London: Longmans, Green).

Trahair, R. C. S. (1999) *Utopias and Utopians: An Historical Dictionary* (Westport, CT: Greenwood Press).

Traynor, I. (2009) 'Online Advertisers Face Tighter EU Privacy Laws', *The Guardian*, www.guardian.co.uk/world/2009/mar/31/online-adverts-eu-privacy-law, date accessed 10 June 2009.

Turow, J. (2003) 'Americans and Online Privacy: The System is Broken', *Annenberg Public Policy Center*, University of Pennsylvania, www.asc.upenn.edu/usr/jturow/Internet-privacy-report/36-page-turow-version-9.pdf, date accessed 22 May 2009.

Turow, J.; Hennessy, M. and Bleakley, A. (2008) 'Consumers' Understanding of Privacy Rules in the Marketplace', *Journal of Consumer Affairs*, 42 (3), 411–24.

UKCCIS (2009) *Click Clever Click Safe*, www.dcsf.gov.uk/ukccis/download.cfm?ca tstr=research&downloadurl=UKCCIS%20Strategy%20Report-WEB1.pdf, date accessed 20 January 2010.

United Nations (2001) *Trade Facilitation and E-commerce in the ESCWA Region, United Nations, Economic and Social Commission for Western Asia*, E/ESCWA/ED/2001/2, 17 January, www.escwa.org.lb/information/publications/division/docs/ed-01–2-e.pdf, date accessed April 2006.

Urban, G. L.; Sultan, F. and Qualls, W. J. (2000) 'Placing Trust at the Center of Your Internet Strategy', *MIT Sloan Management Review*, 42 (1), 39–48.

Urry, J. (2005a) 'The Complexities of the Global', *Theory, Culture & Society*, 22 (5), 235–54.

Urry, J. (2005b) 'The Complexity Turn', *Theory, Culture & Society*, 22 (5), 1–14.

Urry, J. (2007) *Mobilities* (Cambridge, MA: Polity Press).

Van der Hof, S. and Prins, C. (2008) 'Personalisation and Its Influence on Identities, Behaviour and Social Values', in M. Hildebrandt, M. and S. Gutwirth (eds), *Profiling the European Citizen: Cross-Disciplinary Perspectives* (Dordrecht: Springer), pp. 111–27.

Van Dijk, J. (2006) *The Network Society* (London: Sage).

Varela, C. F. (2006) 'The Ethogenics of Agency', in J. Lopez and G. Potter (eds), *After Postmodernism: An Introduction to Critical Realism* (London: Continuum), pp. 63–71.

Varela, F. (1979) *Principles of Biological Autonomy* (New York: Elsevier).

Venkatraman, V. (2009) 'You'll Buy More from Web Ads that Know How You Think', *New Scientist*, www.newscientist.com/article/dn18245-youll-buy-more-from-web-ads-that-know-how-you-think.html?DCMP=OTC-rss&nsref=online-news, date accessed 26 December 2009.

Vila, T.; Greenstadt, R. and Molnar, D. (2003) *Why We Can't Be Bothered to Read Privacy Policies: Models of Privacy Economics as a Lemons Market*, www.eecs.harvard.edu/~greenie/econprivacy.pdf, date accessed 10 December 2009.

Virilio, P. (1986 [1977]) *Speed and Politics: An Essay on Dromology* (New York: Semiotext(e)).

Virilio, P. (1994) *The Vision Machine* (London: BFI).

Virilio, P. (1997) *Open Sky* (London: Verso).

von Foerster, H. (1974) *Cybernetics of Cybernetics* (Urbana, IL: University of Illinois).

von Foerster, H. (1981) *Observing Systems* (Seaside, CA: Intersystems Publications).

von Neumann, J. (1963) *John von Neumann: Collected Works Vol 5*, A. H. Taub (ed.) (Pergamon Press).

Wakefield, J. (2009) 'Internet Service Providers Urge Changes to Digital Bill', *BBC*, http://news.bbc.co.uk/1/hi/technology/8390793.stm, date accessed 10 December 2009.

Weaver, W. (1949) *Recent Contributions to The Mathematical Theory of Communication*, http://grace.evergreen.edu/~arunc/texts/cybernetics/weaver.pdf, date accessed 17 May 2009.

Weber, M. (1922) *Gesammelte Politische Schriften* (Tübingen : Mohr).

Webwise (2008) *Webwise Chat Transcript*, www.webwise.com/how-it-works/transcript_080320.html, date accessed 12 June 2009.

Wedel, M. and Kamakura, W. A. (2003) *Market Segmentation: Conceptual and Methodological Foundations* (Dordrecht: Kluwer).

Wernick, A. (1991) *Promotional Culture: Advertising, Ideology and Symbolic Expression* (London: Sage).

Westin, A. F. (1967) *Privacy and Freedom* (New York: Atheneum).

Wiener, B. (2009) 'Rethinking the Way We Buy and Sell Display Ads', *Advertising Age*, http://adage.com/digitalnext/post.php?article_id=135813, date accessed 07 April 2009.

Wiener, N. (1948) *Cybernetics, or Control and Communication in the Animal and the Machine* (Cambridge, MA: MIT Press).

Wikimedia (2009) *Wikimedia Foundation Opting out of Phorm*, http://techblog.wikimedia.org/2009/04/wikimedia-opting-out-of-phorm/, date accessed 22 May 2009.

Wikipedia (2009) *Network Neutrality*, http://en.wikipedia.org/wiki/Network_neutrality, date accessed 24 April 2009.

Williams, C. (2008) 'BT's "illegal" 2007 Phorm Trial Profiled Tens of Thousands', *The Register*, www.theregister.co.uk/2008/04/14/bt_phorm_2007/, date accessed 23 March 2009.

Williams, C. (2008a) 'Police Drop BT-Phorm Probe', *The Register*, www.theregister.co.uk/2008/09/22/bt_phorm_police_drop/, date accessed 23 March 2009.

Williams, C. (2009a) 'Phorm CEO Clashes with Berners-Lee at Parliament', *The Register* www.theregister.co.uk/2009/03/11/phorm_berners_lee_westminster/, date accessed 27 March 2009.

Williams, C. (2009b) 'Phorm Director Advises UK Gov Broadband Minister', *The Register*, www.theregister.co.uk/2009/04/15/kip_meek_berr/print.html/, date accessed 27 March 2010.

Williams, R. (1975) *Marxism and Literature* (Oxford: Oxford University Press).

Williams, R. (2005 [1980]) *Culture and Materialism* (London: Verso).

Williamson, J. (1978) *Decoding Advertisements: Ideology and Meaning in Advertising* (London: Boyars).

Wind, Y. (1978) 'Issues and Advances in Segmentation Research', *Journal of Marketing Research*, 15 (3), 317–37.

Winner, L. (1986) *The Whale and the Reactor: A Search for Limits in an Age of High Technology* (Chicago: University of Chicago Press).

Winston, B. (1998) *Media Technology and Society. A History: From the Telegraph to the Internet* (London: Routledge).

Wittgenstein, L. (1961) *Tractatus Logico-philosophicus*, B. F. McGuiness and D. F. Pears (trans), (London: Routledge).

World Privacy Forum (2009) *Behavioral Advertising and Privacy*, www.worldprivacyforum.org/behavioral_advertising.html, date accessed 18 March 2009.

World Summit on the Information Society (2003) *Declaration of Principles*, www. itu.int/dms_pub/itu-s/md/03/wsis/doc/S03-WSIS-DOC-0004!!PDF-E.pdf, date accessed 16 May 2009.

Wray, R. (2009) 'Amazon pts out of Phorm's Targeted Internet Advertising System after Privacy Fears', *The Guardian*, www.guardian.co.uk/technology/2009/apr/16/amazon-phorm-targeted-advertising, date accessed 22 March 2009.

Wurster, C. (2002) *Computers* (Cologne: Taschen).

Youn, S. (2009) 'Determinants of Online Privacy Concern and Its Influence on Privacy Protection Behaviors Among Young Adolescents', *The Journal of Consumer Affairs*, 43 (3), 389–418.

Zimmerman, M. E. (1990) *Heidegger's Confrontation with Modernity: Technology, Politics, Art* (Bloomington, IN: Indiana University Press).

Zuboff, S. and Maxmin, J. (2002) *The Support Economy* (New York: Penguin Books).

Index

	DATE DUE		
NOV 1 8 2010			